ISAAC NEWTON: PHILOSOPHICAL WRITINGS

CAMBRIDGE TEXTS IN THE
HISTORY OF PHILOSOPHY

Series editors
KARL AMERIKS
Professor of Philosophy, University of Notre Dame

DESMOND M. CLARKE
Emeritus Professor of Philosophy, University College Cork

The main objective of Cambridge Texts in the History of Philosophy is to expand the range, variety, and quality of texts in the history of philosophy which are available in English. The series includes texts by familiar names (such as Descartes and Kant) and also by less well-known authors. Wherever possible, texts are published in complete and unabridged form, and translations are specially commissioned for the series. Each volume contains a critical introduction together with a guide to further reading and any necessary glossaries and textual apparatus. The volumes are designed for student use at undergraduate and postgraduate level, and will be of interest not only to students of philosophy but also to a wider audience of readers in the history of science, the history of theology, and the history of ideas.

For a list of titles published in the series, please see end of book.

ISAAC NEWTON

Philosophical Writings

EDITED BY

ANDREW JANIAK

Duke University

Revised Edition

CAMBRIDGE
UNIVERSITY PRESS

University Printing House, Cambridge CB2 8BS, United Kingdom

One Liberty Plaza, 20th Floor, New York, NY 10006, USA

477 Williamstown Road, Port Melbourne, VIC 3207, Australia

4843/24, 2nd Floor, Ansari Road, Daryaganj, Delhi - 110002, India

79 Anson Road, #06-04/06, Singapore 079906

Cambridge University Press is part of the University of Cambridge.

It furthers the University's mission by disseminating knowledge in the pursuit of education, learning and research at the highest international levels of excellence.

www.cambridge.org
Information on this title: www.cambridge.org/9781107615939

© Andrew Janiak, 2014

First published 2004 and reprinted once.
Revised edition first published 2014.

A catalogue record for this publication is available from the British Library

Library of Congress Cataloging in Publication data
Newton, Isaac, 1642–1727.
[Works. Selections. English. 2014]
Isaac Newton, philosophical writings / edited by Andrew Janiak,
Duke University. – Revised Edition.
pages   cm. – (Cambridge texts in the history of philosophy)
Includes index.
ISBN 978-1-107-04238-4 (Hardback) – ISBN 978-1-107-61593-9 (Paperback)
1. Philosophy.   I. Janiak, Andrew, editor of compilation.   II. Title.
B1299.N32E5 2014
192–dc23   2013045310

ISBN 978-1-107-04238-4 Hardback
ISBN 978-1-107-61593-9 Paperback

Contents

Acknowledgments

The archival work that enabled me to read and transcribe some of the original versions of the texts published here was made possible by a generous grant from the American Philosophical Society in Philadelphia.

For their extremely helpful comments on the earlier version of the Introduction, I would like to thank several colleagues and friends, especially Nico Bertoloni Meli, Des Clarke, Mary Domski, Christian Johnson, Tad Schmaltz, and Richard Stein. I learned most of what I know about Newton first from Nico Bertoloni Meli and Michael Friedman, and later from George Smith; I am grateful for all their guidance over the years. For discussions that influenced the second version of the Introduction, I thank Lisa Downing, Niccolo Guicciardini, Gary Hatfield, Rob Iliffe, Scott Mandelbrote, Christia Mercer, and Steve Snobelen. Christian Johnson produced an amended version of the A. R. and Marie Boas Hall translation of *De Gravitatione* with my assistance; I am grateful for his expert work on that difficult text. Since the time the volume was first proposed, through its final production, my editors at Cambridge, Des Clarke and Hilary Gaskin, have shown great patience and much wisdom; they did so once again with the proposal and production of a second edition.

One couldn't find a more supportive partner or a better interlocutor than Rebecca Stein, who always finds time amidst her myriad publishing projects to talk with me about mine. I'd like to dedicate this volume to my wonderful mom, Joan Saperstan, and to the memory of my dad, Chester Janiak (1944–96); I only wish he were here to see it.

Introduction

In the preceding books I have presented principles of philosophy that are not, however, philosophical but strictly mathematical - that is, those on which the study of philosophy can be based. These principles are the laws and conditions of motions and of forces, which especially relate to philosophy. But in order to prevent these principles from becoming sterile, I have illustrated them with some philosophical scholia, treating topics that are general and that seem to be the most fundamental for philosophy, such as the density and resistance of bodies, spaces void of bodies, and the motion of light and sounds. It still remains for us to exhibit the system of the world from these same principles.

. . . to treat of God from phenomena is certainly a part of natural philosophy.

– Isaac Newton[1]

Newton as natural philosopher

Isaac Newton's influence is ubiquitous 300 years after his death. We employ Newtonian mechanics in a wide range of cases, students world-wide learn the calculus that he co-discovered with Leibniz, and the law of universal gravitation characterizes what is still considered a fundamental force. Indeed, the idea that a force can be "fundamental," irreducible to any other force or phenomenon in nature, is largely due to Newton, and

---

[1] The first passage is from the preface to Book III of the *Principia*, and the second is from its General Scholium, which was added to the second edition of the text in 1713 (793 and 943 of *Principia*, respectively).

still has currency in the twenty-first century. Remarkably, Newton's status as a theorist of motion and of forces, and his work as a mathematician, is equaled by his status as an unparalleled experimentalist. His experiments in optics, for instance, would be enough to guarantee his place in the early modern canon. Because of these achievements, Newton is regularly mentioned along with figures like Copernicus and Galileo as a founder of modern science. One might even contend that Newton helped to shape the very idea of the modern "scientist."

Despite these important facts, we should resist the temptation to think of Newton as a scientist in any straightforward sense. At a meeting of the British Association for the Advancement of Science in June of 1833, the Cambridge philosopher William Whewell coined the word "scientist." At the meeting, Whewell said that, just as the practitioners of art are called "artists," the practitioners of science ought to be called "scientists," indicating that they should no longer be called philosophers.[2] Indeed, before the early nineteenth century, people like Newton were called "philosophers," or, more specifically, "natural philosophers." This is not mere semantics. This fact of linguistic history reflects a deeper conceptual point: during the seventeenth century, and well into the eighteenth, figures like Newton worked within the centuries-old tradition of natural philosophy.[3]

---

[2] Whewell was responding to Samuel Taylor Coleridge's plea that the members of the British Association stop calling themselves "natural philosophers," for the scope of their research had narrowed considerably in recent years. For details, see Laura Snyder, *The Philosophical Breakfast Club* (New York: Broadway, 2011), 1–7. The first time that "scientist" was used in print was a year later, when Whewell – in an anonymous review – discussed the outcome of the British Association meeting in his review of Mary Somerville's book, *On the Connexion of the Physical Sciences* (*The Quarterly Review* 51 [1834], 59). The word "science," which derives from the Latin term "scientia" (meaning, roughly, knowledge), has been in continuous use in numerous contexts since the fourteenth century, but it did not obtain its modern meaning until the mid-to-late nineteenth century. Thus the new meaning of "science," referring to the natural sciences specifically, arose roughly at the time that the word "scientist" was coined (the OED has the new meaning of "science" first appearing in 1867).

[3] Two recent studies of the discipline of natural philosophy are Roger French and Andrew Cunningham, *Before Science: The Invention of the Friars' Natural Philosophy* (Brookfield: Scholar's Press, 1996), and Edward Grant, *A History of Natural Philosophy* (Cambridge University Press, 2007). For interpretations of Newton's work in natural philosophy, see Howard Stein, "Newton's Metaphysics," in *The Cambridge Companion to Newton*, ed. I. Bernard Cohen and George Smith (Cambridge University Press, 2002), ch. 8, and, more recently, Andrew Janiak, *Newton as Philosopher* (Cambridge University Press, 2008), Mary Domski, "Newton's Empiricism and Metaphysics," *Philosophy Compass* 5 (2010), 525–34, and Steffen Ducheyne, *The Main Business of Natural Philosophy* (Dordrecht: Springer, 2012). For a different perspective on Newton's status as a natural philosopher or a scientist, see Cohen and Smith's introduction to the *Cambridge Companion*, 1–4.

The modern disciplines of physics, chemistry, biology and so on had not yet been formed. Philosophers who studied nature investigated such things as planetary motions and the possibility of a vacuum, but they also discussed many aspects of human beings, including the psyche, and how nature reflects its divine creator. As the title of Newton's magnum opus, *Mathematical Principles of Natural Philosophy*, suggests, he intended his work to be in dialogue with Descartes's *Principles of Philosophy* (1644), a complex text that includes discussions of everything from the laws of nature to the nature of God's causal influence on the world. Just as Descartes had sought to replace Aristotelian or "Scholastic" methods and doctrines in natural philosophy, Newton intended his work to replace Descartes's. It is therefore illuminating to interpret Newton within the historical stream of natural philosophy.

Natural philosophy in the Aristotelian traditions of the thirteenth through the sixteenth centuries involved an analysis of Aristotle's ideas about causation within the natural world, especially within the Christianized context of the medieval period. Philosophers studying nature were often actually studying texts – such as commentaries on Aristotle – rather than conducting experiments or engaging in observations, and they rarely employed mathematical techniques. In the seventeenth century, natural philosophers like Galileo, Boyle, Descartes, and Newton began to reject not only the doctrines of the Aristotelians, but their techniques as well, developing a number of new mathematical, conceptual and experimental methods. Newton respected Descartes's rejection of Aristotelian ideas, but argued that Cartesians did not employ enough of the mathematical techniques of Galileo, or of the experimental methods of Boyle, in trying to understand nature. Of course, these developments have often been regarded as central to the so-called Scientific Revolution. Despite the centrality of these changes during the seventeenth century, however, the *scope* of natural philosophy had not changed. Natural philosophers like Newton expended considerable energy trying to understand, e.g., the nature of motion, but they regarded that endeavor as a component of an overarching enterprise that also included an analysis of the divine being.

Newton was a natural philosopher – unlike Descartes, he was not a founder of modern philosophy, for he never wrote a treatise of the order of the *Meditations*. Nonetheless, his *influence* on philosophy in the eighteenth century was profound, extending well beyond the bounds of philosophers studying nature, encompassing numerous figures and traditions in Britain, on the Continent, and even in the new world.[4] Newton's influence has at least two salient aspects. First, Newton's achievement in the *Opticks* and in the *Principia* was understood to be of such philosophical import that few philosophers in the eighteenth century ignored it. Most of the canonical philosophers in this period sought to interpret various of Newton's epistemic claims within the terms of their own systems, and many saw the coherence of their own views with those of Newton as a criterion of philosophical excellence. Early in the century, Berkeley grappled with Newton's work on the calculus in *The Analyst* and with his dynamics in *De Motu*, and he even discussed gravity, the paradigmatic Newtonian force, in his popular work *Three Dialogues between Hylas and Philonous* (1713). When Berkeley lists what philosophers take to be the so-called primary qualities of material bodies in the *Dialogues*, he remarkably adds "gravity" to the more familiar list of size, shape, motion, and solidity, thereby suggesting that the received view of material bodies had already changed before the second edition of the *Principia* had circulated widely. Hume interpreted Newtonian natural philosophy in an empiricist vein and noted some of its broader implications in his *Treatise of Human Nature* (1739) and *Enquiry Concerning Human Understanding* (1750). On the Continent, Kant attempted to forge a philosophically robust mediation between Leibnizian metaphysics and Newtonian natural philosophy, discussing Newtonian science at length in his *Metaphysical Foundations of Natural Science* (1786).[5]

Newton's work also served as the impetus for the extremely influential correspondence between Leibniz and the Newtonian Samuel Clarke

---

[4] See "Newton and Newtonianism," a special issue of *The Southern Journal of Philosophy* 50 (September 2012), edited by Mary Domski, which contains details of Newton's connections to figures such as Descartes, Spinoza, Wolff, and Kant. For a broader perspective on Newton's influence on the eighteenth century, see "Isaac Newton and the Eighteenth Century," *Enlightenment and Dissent* 25 (2009), ed. Stephen Snobelen.

[5] See the detailed account of Kant's reflections on Newtonian science in Michael Friedman, *Kant's Construction of Nature: A Reading of the Metaphysical Foundations of Natural Science* (Cambridge University Press, 2012).

early in the century, a correspondence that proved significant even for thinkers writing toward the century's end. Unlike the *vis viva* controversy and other disputes between the Cartesians and the Leibnizians, which died out by the middle of the century, the debate between the Leibnizians and the Newtonians remained philosophically salient for decades, serving as the impetus for Emilie Du Châtelet's influential work during the French Enlightenment, *Foundations of Physics* (1740), and also as one of the driving forces behind Kant's development of the "critical" philosophy during the 1770s, culminating in the *Critique of Pure Reason* (1781). Newton's work also spawned an immense commentarial literature in English, French, and Latin, including John Keill's *Introduction to Natural Philosophy* (1726), Henry Pemberton's *A View of Sir Isaac Newton's Philosophy* (1728), Voltaire's *Elements of the Philosophy of Newton* (1738), Willem 's Gravesande's *Mathematical Elements of Natural Philosophy* (1747), Colin MacLaurin's *An Account of Sir Isaac Newton's Philosophical Discoveries* (1748), which probably influenced Hume, and Du Châtelet's and Clairaut's commentary on Newton's *Principia* (1759). These and other commentaries were printed in various editions, were translated into various languages, and were often influential.

A second aspect of Newton's influence involves thinkers who attempted in one way or another to articulate, follow, or extend, the Newtonian "method" in natural philosophy when treating issues and questions that Newton ignored. Euclidean geometry and its methods were seen as a fundamental epistemic model for much of seventeenth-century philosophy – Descartes's *Meditations* attempts to achieve a type of certainty he likens to that found in geometry, and Spinoza wrote his *Ethics* according to the "geometrical method." Propositions deduced from axioms in Euclidean geometry were seen as paradigm cases of knowledge. We might see Newton's work as providing eighteenth-century philosophy with one of its primary models, and with a series of epistemic exemplars as well. David Hume is perhaps clearest about this aspect of Newton's influence. His *Treatise* of 1739 has the subtitle "An Attempt to Introduce the Experimental Method of Reasoning Into Moral Subjects," and there can be little doubt that he meant the method of the *Opticks* and the *Principia*. Indeed, as Hume's text makes abundantly clear, various eighteenth-century philosophers, including not only Hume in Scotland but Jean-Jacques Rousseau on the Continent, were taken to be, or attempted to become, "the Newton of the mind."[6] For Hume, this meant following what he took to be Newton's empirical method by providing the proper description of the relevant natural phenomena and then finding the most general principles that account for them. This method would allow us to achieve the highest level of knowledge attainable in the realm of what Hume calls "matters of fact."[7]

Despite the influence of Newton's "method" on eighteenth-century philosophy, it is obvious that the *Principia*'s greater impact on the eighteenth century is to have effected a branching within natural philosophy that led to the development of mathematical physics on the one hand, and philosophy on the other. And yet to achieve an understanding of how Newton himself approached natural philosophy, we must carefully bracket such historical developments. Indeed, if we resist the temptation to understand Newton as working within a well-established discipline called mathematical physics, if we see him instead as a philosopher studying nature, his achievement is much more impressive, for instead of contributing to a well-founded field of physics, he had to begin a process that would eventually lead natural philosophy to be transformed into a new field of study. This transformation took many decades, and involved a series of methodological and foundational debates about the proper means for obtaining knowledge about nature and its processes. Not only did Newton himself engage in these debates from his very first publication in optics in 1672, his work in both optics and in the *Principia* generated some of the most significant discussions and controversies in the late seventeenth and early eighteenth centuries. These debates concerned such topics as the proper use of hypotheses, the nature of space and time, and the appropriate rules for conducting research in natural philosophy. Newton's achievement was in part to have vanquished both Cartesian and Leibnizian approaches to natural

---

[6] Surprisingly, Kant declared that Rousseau was "the Newton of the mind" – for discussion, see Susan Neiman, "Metaphysics, Philosophy: Rousseau on the Problem of Evil," in *Reclaiming the History of Ethics: Essays for John Rawls*, ed. Andrews Reath, Barbara Herman and Christine Korsgaard (Cambridge University Press, 1997).

[7] A proposition expressing a matter of fact cannot be known to be true without appeal to experience because, unlike in the case of "relations of ideas," the negation of the proposition is not contradictory. For discussion of Hume's relation to Newton, with citations to the voluminous literature on that topic, see Graciela De Pierris, "Newton, Locke and Hume," in *Interpreting Newton: Critical Essays*, ed. Andrew Janiak and Eric Schliesser (Cambridge University Press, 2012).

philosophy; in the eighteenth century, and indeed much of the nine-teenth, physics was largely a Newtonian enterprise. But this achieve-ment, from Newton's own perspective, involved an extensive, lifelong series of philosophical debates. I discuss several of them in what follows.

Newton's career and correspondence

Isaac Newton was born into a rural family in Woolsthorpe, Lincolnshire on Christmas Day of 1642, the year of Galileo's death.[8] Newton's philosophical training and work began early in his intellectual career, while he was an undergraduate at Trinity College, Cambridge in the early 1660s. The notebooks that survive from that period[9] indicate his wide-ranging interests in topics philosophical, along with a reasonably serious acquaintance with the great "moderns" of the day, including Boyle, Hobbes, Gassendi, and especially Descartes. Later in his life, Newton corresponded directly with a number of significant figures in natural philosophy, including Boyle, Huygens, and Leibniz, and he developed personal relations with many others, including Henry More and John Locke. Newton's primary works, of course, are *Philosophiae Naturalis Principia Mathematica* – or *Mathematical Principles of Natural Philosophy* – and the *Opticks*. Each went through three successive edi-tions during Newton's lifetime, which he oversaw under the editorship of various colleagues, especially Richard Bentley, Samuel Clarke, and Roger Cotes, two of whom became important Newtonians in their own right.[10]

---

[8] By the old calendar; other dates throughout this volume are given according to the new calendar.

[9] See J. E. McGuire and Martin Tamny (eds.), *Certain Philosophical Questions: Newton's Trinity Notebook* (Cambridge University Press, 1983).

[10] The *Principia* first appeared in 1687, ran into its third edition in 1726, just before Newton's death, and was translated into English by Andrew Motte in 1729; the Motte translation – as modified by Florian Cajori in a 1934 edition – remained the standard until I. Bernard Cohen and Anne Whitman published their entirely new version in 1999 (selections in this volume are from this edition; see the Note on texts and translations below). It also appeared in 1759 in an influential French translation by Emilie du Châtelet, the famous French Newtonian; remarkably, her translation remains the standard in French to this day. The *Opticks* first appeared in 1704, ran into its third edition in 1721, and was translated into Latin in 1706 by Samuel Clarke, Newton's famous defender in the correspondence with Leibniz; the Clarke translation ensured the text's accessibility on the Continent. There are many salient differences between Newton's two great works despite the tremendous influence each had on subsequent research in their respective fields in the eighteenth century and beyond. As I. Bernard Cohen has argued, Newton's choice of the vernacular rather than Latin for the presentation of his optical views

In addition to his published works and unpublished manuscripts, Newton's correspondence was extensive. It is important to remember that in Newton's day, intellectual correspondence was not seen solely, or perhaps even primarily, as a private affair between two individuals. It was viewed in much less constrained terms as a type of text that had an important public dimension, not least because it served as the primary vehicle of communication for writers separated by what were then considered to be great distances. As the thousands of letters sent to and from the Royal Society in Newton's day testify, science and philosophy would have ceased without this means of communicating ideas, results, and questions. It was therefore not at all unusual for letters between famous writers to be published essentially unedited. The Leibniz–Clarke correspondence was published almost immediately after Leibniz's death in 1716, Newton's correspondence with Richard Bentley was published in the mid-eighteenth century, and several of the letters reprinted in this volume were published in various journals and academic forums – including the Royal Society's *Philosophical Transactions* – in the late seventeenth and early eighteenth century.[11]

Early work in optics

In three significant respects, Newton's earliest work in optics – published in the *Philosophical Transactions* of the Royal Society beginning in 1672 – set the stage for important themes of his lifelong career in natural philosophy. Firstly, Newton's letter to the Society's secretary, Henry Oldenburg, often called the "New theory about light and colours," generated an immediate, extensive, and protracted debate that eventually involved important philosophers such as Robert Hooke in Britain and Christiaan Huygens, G. W. Leibniz and Ignatius Pardies on the Continent. Newton consistently regarded these figures not merely

---

may reflect his opinion that English was more appropriate for a field like optics, which had not yet achieved the same status as the science of the *Principia*, in part because it had not yet been sufficiently mathematized.

[11] Of course, there were exceptions: most prominently, perhaps, is Newton's private correspondence with John Locke concerning "two notable corruptions of Scripture" that concerned the underpinnings of Newton's belief that the standard doctrine of the Trinity was a corruption of the original version of Christianity. See Newton's extremely long letter of November 14, 1690 in *The Correspondence of Isaac Newton*, ed. Herbert Turnbull, John Scott, A. R. Hall, and Laura Tilling (Cambridge University Press, 1959–77), vol. III, 83–129.

as disagreeing with his views, but as misinterpreting them. This experience helped to shape Newton's famous and lifelong aversion to intellectual controversy, a feature of his personality that he often mentioned in letters, and one that he would never outgrow. Secondly, because Newton regarded himself as misinterpreted by his critics, he had recourse to meta-level or methodological discussions of the practice of optics and of the kinds of knowledge that philosophers can obtain when engaging in experiments with light. The novelty and power of Newton's work in the *Principia* years later would eventually generate similar controversies that led Newton to analogous kinds of methodological discussions of his experimental practice within natural philosophy and of the kinds of knowledge that one can obtain in that field using either experimental or mathematical techniques. From *our* point of view, Newton's science was unusually philosophical for these reasons. Thirdly and finally, in his earliest optical work Newton began to formulate a distinction that would remain salient throughout his long intellectual career, contending that a philosopher must distinguish between a conclusion or claim about some feature of nature that is derived from experimental or observational evidence, and a conclusion or claim that is a mere "hypothesis," a kind of speculation about nature that is not, or not yet anyway, so derived. Newton's much later proclamation in the second edition of the *Principia* (1713), "*Hypotheses non fingo*," or "I feign no hypotheses," would infuriate his critics just as much as it would prod his followers into making the pronouncement a central component of a newly emerging Newtonian method.

The field of optics has its origins in the Ancient Greek period, when figures like Euclid and Ptolemy wrote works on the subject, but they focused less on light than on the science of vision, analyzing (e.g.) the visual rays that were sometimes thought to extrude from the eye, enabling it to perceive distant physical objects. In the early modern period, Kepler and Descartes each made fundamental contributions to the field, including the discovery of the inversion of the retinal image (in the former case) and an explanation of refraction (in the latter case). Newton's work helped to shift the focus of optics from an analysis of vision to an investigation of light. In "New Theory about Light and Colours," published in the *Philosophical Transactions* in 1672, Newton presented a number of experiments in which sunlight was allowed to pass through one or two prisms in order to probe some of its basic features. But what counts as a *feature* of light? Numerous philosophers during the seventeenth century, including Hooke and Huygens, developed doctrines concerning the fundamental physical nature of light in answer to the question: is light a stream of particles (or "corpuscles"), or is it a wave? This question obviously continued to have relevance into the twentieth century, when wave-particle duality was discovered. In his experiments with the prism, however, Newton sought to investigate something else, viz. what he calls "the celebrated *Phenomena of Colours.*" Newton's various prism experiments, which he describes in considerable depth, suggested to him a "Doctrine" that he expresses in thirteen consecutive numbered propositions. Included in these propositions are the following claims about features of rays of light: first, the rays of light that emerge when sunlight passes through a prism exhibit various colors; second, these colors differ in their "degrees of Refrangibility," which means that they exhibit and retain an index of refraction, even when they are passed through a second prism; third, these colors – or colorful rays – are not modifications of sunlight itself, but rather are "*Original* and *connate properties*" of it; and, fourth, this means that although ordinary sunlight appears white, or perhaps colorless, to our perception, it actually contains numerous colors within it, which can be experimentally revealed.

Newton's paper exhibits what a contemporary reader would regard as an intriguing blend of experimental evidence and philosophical argumentation. The latter hinges on Newton's interpretation of the concept of a property or a quality, as the following passage, which follows the "Doctrine" expressed in thirteen propositions, tellingly reveals:

> These things being so, it can be no longer disputed, whether there be colours in the dark, nor whether they be the qualities of the objects we see, no nor perhaps, whether Light be a Body. For, since Colours are the *qualities* of Light, having its Rays for their entire and immediate subject, how can we think those Rays *qualities* also, unless one quality may be the subject of and sustain another; which in effect is to call it *substance*. We should not know Bodies for substances, were it not for their sensible qualities, and the Principal of those being now found due to something else, we have as good reason to believe that to be a substance also. (This volume, p. 11)

Newton argues as follows here: since rays of light have colors as basic features, we should regard these colors as qualities or properties of the rays; but doing so requires us to think of the rays as bearers of qualities, which is to say, as substances in their own right. And if rays of light are substances, this means that we cannot also think of them as qualities or properties of anything else – a point that follows from a widely accepted notion of a substance at the time, one easily found in Descartes, among others.[12] And if we cannot think of rays of light as properties or qualities, then they are not waves, for waves are features of some medium (think of waves on the surface of a lake). Light must be a stream of particles.

This line of argument became one of the centerpieces of the debate that Newton's paper generated. In some parts of his paper, when Newton wrote of the "rays" of light, he had evidently intended to remain neutral on whether the rays are particles or waves (this is reminiscent of the ancient Greek practice of avoiding physical discussions of visual rays). But then toward the paper's end, Newton added his new line of argument, which employed some philosophical analysis together with some experimental evidence to support the conclusion that rays of light cannot be waves after all. Newton's critics pounced. This led to the first problem he encountered in response to his paper: what he calls his "theory" of light and colors was not merely rejected, but rather immediately misunderstood, at least from his own perspective. Just days after Newton's paper was read at the Royal Society, Robert Hooke responded with a detailed letter to Oldenburg. In the first few sentences, Hooke indicates that, from his point of view, Newton's "Hypothesis of saving the phenomenon of colours" essentially involves the contention that rays of light are particulate, rather than wavelike.[13] Hooke argues, in contrast, that light "is nothing but a pulse or motion propagated through an homogeneous, uniform and transparent medium;" that is, he argues that light is indeed wavelike. He makes it perfectly clear, moreover, that his hypothesis can save the phenomena of colours just as well as Newton's, which is to say, that his hypothesis is compatible with the experimental evidence Newton gathers. Evidently, the line of argument in the passage quoted above caught Hooke's eye. Among philosophers,

---

[12] Newton would have been familiar with the discussion of substances in Descartes, *Principles of Philosophy*, part I: §§51–53.

[13] See Hooke to Oldenburg, February 15, 1671/2, in *Correspondence of Isaac Newton*, vol. I, 113. In recounting Newton's theory, Hooke does mention the points about refrangibility and heterogeneity, but he thinks that Newton's "first proposition" is "that light is a body" and that differently colored rays of light are in fact "several sorts of bodies." I take this to represent Hooke's interpretation of how Newton can account for the data with the theory that light consists of particles.

he was not alone. In a letter to Huygens explaining Newton's theory of light, Leibniz writes that Newton takes light to be a "body" propelled from the sun to the earth which, according to Leibniz, Newton takes to explain both the differential refrangibility of rays of light and the phenomena of colors.[14]

After the extensive correspondence, and controversy, generated in response to Newton's early optical views and experiments, he often threatened to avoid engaging in mathematical and philosophical disputes altogether. He insisted to friends and colleagues that he found intellectual controversy unbearable. Fortunately for us, he never followed through with his threat to disengage from discussions in natural philosophy, and sent many important letters in his later years. One of his more important pieces of correspondence after the optics controversy was with the natural philosopher Robert Boyle in 1679 (Newton's letter was published for the first time in the mid-eighteenth century).[15] In his lengthy letter to Boyle, Newton presents his speculations concerning various types of what we would now call chemical interactions; many of these speculations bear similarities to passages that appeared years later in the queries to the *Opticks*. The letter is also famous for presenting one of Newton's early speculations concerning how gravity might be physically explained; it presents, among other things, a picture of what Newton would countenance as a viable explanation of gravity in physical terms. This issue became of paramount importance once the *Principia* appeared.

Newton's relation to Descartes

Like many philosophers who worked in the wake of Galileo and of Descartes, Newton never seriously analyzed Aristotelian ideas about

[14] In *Oeuvres complètes de Christiaan Huygens*, ed. Johan Adriaan Vollgraff (The Hague: Nijhoff, 1888–1950), vol. x, 602. Ignatius Pardies, another of Newton's interlocutors, similarly found it difficult to differentiate the claim about the corporeal nature of light from Newton's ideas concerning refrangibility and heterogeneity. See his two letters to the Royal Society concerning Newton's work, both of which are reprinted in *Isaac Newton's Papers and Letters on Natural Philosophy*, ed. I. Bernard Cohen and Robert Schofield, revised edn (Cambridge, MA: Harvard University Press, 1978,); cf. the discussion of Pardies in A. I. Sabra, *Theories of Light from Descartes to Newton*, 2nd edn (Cambridge University Press, 1981), 264–7.
[15] The letter to Boyle first appeared in *The Works of the Honourable Robert Boyle*, ed. Thomas Birch (London, 1744), vol. I, 70–4.

nature. As is especially clear from the unpublished anti-Cartesian tract, *De Gravitatione* (see below), Newton expended considerable energy engaging with Cartesian ideas,[16] and when he published the first edition of the *Principia* in 1687, Cartesianism remained the reigning view in natural philosophy and served as the backdrop for much important research.[17] This feature of the intellectual landscape persisted for many years: Cotes's famous and influential preface to the second edition of the *Principia* – see chapter IV below – indicates that Cartesianism remained a primary competitor to Newton's natural philosophy in 1713. Despite the astonishing impact that Newton's work had on various fields, including of course what we would call philosophy proper, it would be anachronistic to conclude that Newtonianism had replaced its primary competitor, for Cartesianism's influence did not dissipate until some time after Newton's death in 1727.

As *De Gravitatione* shows, Newton not only read Descartes's *Principles of Philosophy* carefully, he attempted to refute some of the central notions in that text. *De Gravitatione* raises a number of controversial interpretive issues, including first and foremost the provenance of the text itself. No consensus has emerged as to the dating of the manuscript – which remained unpublished until 1962 – and there is insufficient evidence for that question to be answered as of now,[18] but two things remain clear:

---

[16] In his library, Newton had a 1656 Amsterdam edition of Descartes's *Principles*, along with a 1664 London edition of the *Meditations*. On Newton's relation to Descartes and to Cartesianism, see the classic treatments in the chapter "Newton and Descartes" in Alexandre Koyré, *Newtonian Studies* (Cambridge, MA: Harvard University Press, 1965), and in Stein, "Newton's Metaphysics."

[17] See John Heilbron, *Elements of Early Modern Physics* (Berkeley: University of California Press, 1982), 30. Even in Newton's home university, Cambridge, and alma mater, Trinity College, his works and ideas did not displace those of the Cartesians within the standard curriculum until roughly 1700; indeed, Cartesianism was so popular that the Vice-Chancellor of Cambridge University, Edmund Boldero, decreed in November 1688 that undergraduates could no longer base their disputations on Descartes, but had to use Aristotle instead (see John Gascoigne, *Cambridge in the Age of the Enlightenment* (Cambridge University Press, 1985), 54–5 and 143–5). Part of the shift toward Newtonian ideas reflected the growing influence of Richard Bentley, who became Master of Trinity in 1700, a post he retained for decades. Roger Cotes, whom Bentley chose to be the editor of the second edition of the *Principia* in 1709, entered Trinity in 1699 and became a fellow in 1705.

[18] The text first appeared, in a transcription of the original Latin and an English translation, in *Unpublished Scientific Writings of Isaac Newton*, ed. A. R. Hall and Marie Boas Hall (Cambridge University Press, 1962). In the Halls' judgment, the text is juvenile and probably originates in the period from 1664 to 1668. In an influential interpretation, Betty Jo Teeter Dobbs contends, in contrast, that the work is mature and was written in late 1684 or early 1685, while Newton was preparing the first edition of the *Principia*. See Dobbs, *The Janus Faces of Genius: The Role of*

first, the text is an extended series of criticisms of Cartesian natural philosophy; and, second, it is significant for understanding Newton's thought, not least because it represents a sustained philosophical discussion. *De Gravitatione* helps to dispel the easily informed impression that Newton sought, in the *Principia*, to undermine a Leibnizian conception of space and time, as his defender, Samuel Clarke, would attempt to do years later in the correspondence of 1715–16. Although Leibniz did eventually express what became the canonical early modern formulation of relationalism concerning space and time – the view, roughly, that space is nothing but the order of relations among physical objects, and time nothing over and above the succession of events involving those objects – and although Newton and Clarke were highly skeptical of such a view, it is misleading to read the *Principia* through the lens provided by the later controversy with the Leibnizians. Newton's extensive attempt in *De Gravitatione* to refute Descartes's conception of space and time in particular indicates that the Scholium should be read as providing a replacement for the Cartesian conception.[19] Newton had a Cartesian, and not a Leibnizian, opponent primarily in mind when he wrote his famous articulation of "absolutism" concerning space and time. It may be thought a measure of Newton's success against his Cartesian predecessors that history records a debate between the Leibnizians and the Newtonians as influencing every subsequent discussion of space and time in the eighteenth century and beyond.

Mathematical Principles of Natural Philosophy

As is the stuff of legend, in August of 1684, Edmond Halley – for whom the comet is named – came to visit Newton in Cambridge in order to discover his opinion about a subject of much dispute in celestial mechanics. At this time, many in the Royal Society and elsewhere were at work on a cluster of problems that might be described as follows: how

Alchemy in Newton's Thought (Cambridge University Press, 1991), 141–6, where she also reviews various alternative opinions on the matter. In a recent essay, Jim Ruffner raises important doubts concerning earlier interpretations, concluding that the text must have been written before Halley's famous visit to Newton in 1684 – see "Newton's *De gravitatione*: A Review and Reassessment," *Archive for the History of the Exact Sciences* 66 (2012).

[19] Stein presents this interpretation of Newton's *Principia* in his classic essay, "Newtonian Space-Time," in *The Annus Mirabilis of Sir Isaac Newton 1666–1966*, ed. Robert Palter (Cambridge, MA: MIT Press, 1970).

can one take Kepler's Laws, which were then considered among the very best descriptions of the planetary orbits, and understand them in the context of dynamical or causal principles? What kind of cause – for some, what kind of *force* – would lead to planetary orbits of the kind described by Kepler? In particular, Halley asked Newton the following question: what kind of curve would a planet describe in its orbit around the sun if it were acted upon by an attractive force that was inversely proportional to the square of its distance from the sun? Newton immediately replied that the curve would be an ellipse (rather than, say, a circle).[20] Halley was amazed that Newton had the answer at the ready. But Newton also said that he had mislaid the paper on which the relevant calculations had been made, so Halley left empty handed. He would not be disappointed for long. In November of that year, Newton sent Halley a nine-page paper, entitled *De Motu* (on motion), that presented the sought-after demonstration, along with several other advances in celestial mechanics. Halley was delighted, and immediately returned to Cambridge for further discussion. It was these events that precipitated the many drafts of *De Motu* that eventually became *Principia mathematica* by 1686. Several aspects of the *Principia* have been central to philosophical discussions since its first publication, including Newton's novel methodology in the book, his conception of space and time, and his attitude toward the dominant orientation within natural philosophy in his day, the so-called mechanical philosophy.

Methodology

When Newton wrote the *Principia* between 1684 and 1686, he was not contributing to a preexisting field of study called mathematical physics; he was attempting to show how philosophers could employ various mathematical and experimental methods in order to reach conclusions about nature, especially about the motions of material bodies. In his

---

[20] Although astronomers for centuries had thought that the planetary orbits must be circular, for various important reasons, in the seventeenth century Kepler had argued that they are in fact elliptical (although this is consistent with the idea, which became important in later contexts, that the orbits are nearly circular). This innovation proved to be crucial for later work in celestial mechanics. Ellipses are figures in which a straight line from the center to any arbitrary point on the surface does not describe a single radius that is equal in length to all other radii. So they are more difficult to deal with geometrically than circles.

lectures presented as the Lucasian Professor, Newton had been arguing since at least 1670 that natural philosophers had to employ geometrical methods in order to understand various phenomena in nature.[21] The *Principia* represented his attempt to reorient natural philosophy, taking it in a direction that neither his Aristotelian predecessors, nor his Cartesian contemporaries, had envisioned. He did not immediately convince many of them of the benefits of his approach. Just as his first publication in optics in 1672 had sparked an intense debate about the proper methods for investigating the nature of light – and much else besides – his *Principia* sparked an even longer-lasting discussion about the methodology that philosophers should adopt when studying the natural world. This discussion began immediately with the publication of the *Principia*, and intensified considerably with the publication of its second edition in 1713, since many of Newton's alterations in that edition involved changes in his presentation of his methods. Discussions of methodology would eventually involve nearly all of the leading philosophers in England and on the Continent during Newton's lifetime.

Unlike Descartes, Newton placed the concept of a force at the very center of his thinking about motion and its causes within nature. In that regard, his reactions to the shortcomings of Cartesian natural philosophy parallel Leibniz's, who coined the term "dynamics." But Newton's attitude toward understanding the forces of nature involved an especially intricate method that generated intense scrutiny and debate amongst many philosophers and mathematicians, including Leibniz.[22] Newton's canonical notion of a force, which he calls a *vis impressa* or "impressed force," is the notion of an "action exerted on a body" that changes its state of motion. This was a confusing notion at the time. If you throw me a ball and I catch it, I have impressed a force on the ball, since I have changed its state of motion. We have a good idea of what I am, and of what the ball is, but what exactly is this "force" that I impressed on it? Is the force some physical item? Is it not physical? It does not seem likely that a force is itself a physical thing, or a substance, to use a philosophical notion popular in Newton's day (as we saw above in his first optics

---

[21] See the "Lectiones opticae" of 1670 in *The Optical Papers of Isaac Newton*, ed. Alan Shapiro (Cambridge University Press, 1984), vol. I, 86–7.

[22] See Daniel Garber, "Leibniz, Newton and Force," in *Interpreting Newton*, ed. Janiak and Schliesser, ch. 2.

paper). In Definition Four in the *Principia*, which defines an impressed force for the first time, Newton remarks: "This force consists solely in the action and does not remain in a body after the action has ceased." So when I caught the ball, the force I impressed on it was the action of catching the ball, or an action associated with catching the ball, and not a property of me or of the ball after the action ceased. This idea confused many of Newton's readers. By the mid-eighteenth century, the time of Hume's analysis of causation in the *Treatise* and the *Enquiry*, many philosophers had started to think that actions and other kinds of event are important items to have in one's ontology, and they often contended that causal relations hold between events. But in Newton's day, philosophers typically regarded objects or substances as the causal relata. So actions were difficult to analyze or often left out of analyses.

Newton did try to clarify his method of characterizing forces. If one brackets the question of how to understand forces as ephemeral actions that do not persist after causal interactions have ceased, one can make progress by conceiving of forces as *quantities*. In particular, since Newton's eight definitions and three laws indicate that forces are proportional to mass and acceleration, and since mass – or the quantity of matter – and acceleration are both quantities that can be measured, Newton gives us a means of measuring forces. This is crucial to his method. If one thinks of forces as measurable quantities, moreover, then one can attempt to identify two seemingly disparate forces as in fact the same force through thinking about measuring them. Newton does this in Book III of the *Principia*, when he argues in proposition 5 and its Scholium that the centripetal force maintaining the planetary orbits is in fact gravity, viz., the force that causes the free fall of objects on earth. This culminates in the claim in proposition 7 that all bodies gravitate toward one another in proportion to their quantity of matter. This helped to unify what were once called superlunary and sublunary phenomena, a unification that was obviously crucial for later research in physics.

Despite his evident success in obtaining what we now call the law of universal gravitation, Newton admits that he lacks another kind of knowledge about gravity. In the General Scholium, he reminds his readers that gravity is proportional to a body's quantity of matter (its mass) and reaches across vast distances within our solar system, adding: "I have not as yet been able to deduce from phenomena the reason for these properties of gravity, and I do not feign hypotheses."[23] With this phrase, one of the most famous in all of Newton's writings, he returned to a key theme of his very first optical paper from forty years earlier, viz. the proper role of hypotheses and of hypothetical reasoning within natural philosophy.[24] Some of Newton's interpreters have regarded this phrase as signaling a strong commitment to the broad doctrine that all hypotheses concerning natural phenomena ought to be avoided on principle. This interpretation is sometimes coupled with the view that some British philosophers in the late seventeenth century regarded Cartesianism as overly reliant on hypotheses in reaching conclusions about phenomena. But this interpretation may be hard to square with Newton's texts. For instance, in the Scholium to proposition 96 of Book I of the *Principia*, Newton discusses hypotheses concerning light rays. Similarly, in query 21 of the *Opticks* (this volume, p. 170), he proposes that there might be an aether whose differential density accounts for the gravitational force acting between bodies. In light of such examples, one can read the General Scholium's pronouncement in this way: a philosopher concerned with explaining some feature of nature – such as the fact that gravity is inversely proportional to the *square* of spatial separation, rather than, say, the *cube* – may legitimately entertain and propose hypotheses for consideration by his readers, but he may not "feign" the hypothesis in the sense of taking it as having been established either through experiment, observation, or some form of reasoning. Hence Newton thinks that he has established the fact that gravity acts on all material bodies in proportion to their quantity of matter, but he has *not* established the existence of the aether. By the time of the General Scholium, Newton was increasingly embroiled in philosophical disputes with Leibniz. In order to account for the motions of the planetary bodies in his *Tentamen* of 1690, Leibniz introduces *ex hypothesi* the premise that some kind of fluid surrounds, and is contiguous to, the various planetary bodies, and then argues that this fluid must be in motion to account for

---

[23] We owe this translation of the phrase to Alexandre Koyré, who first noted that Newton uses the word "feign" in a parallel discussion in English: *From the Closed World to the Infinite Universe* (Baltimore, MD: Johns Hopkins University Press, 1957), 229 and 299 n. 12.

[24] For an influential discussion of the development in Newton's conception of hypotheses over time, see I. Bernard Cohen, "Hypotheses in Newton's Philosophy," *Physis: Rivista Internazionale di Storia della Scienza* 8 (1966), 163–84.

their orbits.[25] Newton would have argued that Leibniz had "feigned" the hypothesis of the vortices. A debate between the two philosophers on this score would bring them to the question of the mechanical philosophy: whereas Newton might object to Leibniz's reasoning on methodological grounds, Leibniz might reply that Newton's theory of gravity involves action at a distance, which his vortex hypothesis avoids (see below).

In addition to the General Scholium, the second edition of the *Principia* also included what Newton called "regulae philosophandi," or rules of philosophy (this volume, p. 108), which became the focal point of vigorous discussion and debate well into the eighteenth century. The first two rules concern causal reasoning, but it is the third rule that generated the most debate, for it involved both an aspect of Newton's controversial argument for universal gravity and also a rare public statement by Newton of what he regarded as the "foundation" of natural philosophy. The third rule concerns an induction problem: we have perceptions and experiments that provide us with knowledge of the objects and natural phenomena in our neck of the universe, but on what basis can we reach a conclusion concerning objects and phenomena throughout the *rest* of the universe? Newton himself reached such a conclusion about gravity in proposition 7 of Book III of the *Principia*. Part of Newton's answer is presented in rule 3: "Those qualities of bodies that cannot be intended and remitted [i.e., increased and diminished] and that belong to all bodies on which experiments can be made should be taken as qualities of all bodies universally" (this volume, p. 109). We know, say, that a clump of dirt has certain qualities such as extension and mobility, but how do we know that the entire earth has such qualities? It surely lies beyond the reach of our experiments, or at any rate, it did in Newton's day. Newton says that the sun and the earth interact according to his law of gravity, but how do we know that the sun contains a quantity of matter, that it is a material body with the same basic qualities that characterize the earth or the moon? Newton thinks that gravity reaches into the very center of the sun, but what did anyone in 1713 know about such things? Newton glosses his third rule in part as follows, connecting it with his laws of motion:

---

[25] See the *Tentamen* in Gottfried Wilhelm Leibniz, *Mathematische Schriften*, ed. C. Gerhardt (Berlin, 1849), vol. VI, 149, and Domenico Bertoloni Meli, *Equivalence and Priority: Newton vs. Leibniz* (Oxford University Press, 1993), 128–9.

That all bodies are movable and persevere in motion or in rest by means of certain forces (which we call forces of inertia) we infer from finding these properties in the bodies that we have seen. The extension, hardness, impenetrability, mobility, and force of inertia[26] of the whole arise from the extension, hardness, impenetrability, mobility, and force of inertia of each of the parts; and thus we conclude that every one of the least parts of all bodies is extended, hard, impenetrable, movable, and endowed with a force of inertia. And this is the foundation of all natural philosophy. (this volume, p. 109)

Many of Newton's readers in 1713 would have granted him the following inference: although we do not have any perceptions of, say, the interior of the earth, or even of many ordinary objects within our grasp, we can reasonably infer that everything with certain basic properties – something akin to what John Locke, borrowing a term of Robert Boyle's, called the "primary qualities" – at the macroscopic level is comprised of micro-particles that are characterized by those same basic properties. But at the end of his gloss of Rule 3, Newton applies this same (or analogous) reasoning to the force of gravity, arguing as follows: since we experience the fact that all bodies on or near the earth gravitate toward the earth – in cases such as free fall – and that the moon gravitates toward the earth, etc., we can infer that all bodies everywhere gravitate toward all other bodies. This argument would appear to suggest that gravity, which, as we have seen, is a kind of impressed force, an action, is somehow akin to qualities like extension and impenetrability. So is Newton suggesting that gravity is actually a *quality* of all bodies? This question became the subject of intense debate and remains so today.

The mechanical philosophy

Newton's second law indicates that a body moving rectilinearly will continue to do so unless a force is impressed on it. This is not equivalent to claiming that a body moving rectilinearly will continue to do so unless another body impacts upon it. A *vis impressa* – an impressed force – in Newton's system is not the same as a body, as we have seen; but what is

---

[26] This is a potentially confusing way of referring to the mass – specifically, what we would call the inertial mass – of a body. See Definition Three in this volume, p. 80.

more, some impressed forces need not involve contact between bodies at all. For instance, gravity is a kind of centripetal force, and the latter, in turn, is a species of impressed force. Hence a body moving in a straight line will continue to do so until it experiences a gravitational pull, even if no body impacts upon it. Indeed, the gravitational pull might originate with a mass that is millions of miles away. As we have seen, an impressed force is an action exerted on a body. Hence the gravity exerted on a moving body is an action (the Latin term is *actio*), which is obviously a causal notion. This is not an empirical claim per se; it is merely a reflection of Newton's laws, together with his notion of an impressed force, and his further idea that gravity is one kind of impressed force. These elements of the *Principia* make conceptual room for a causal interaction between two bodies separated by a vast distance. This became known in philosophical circles as the problem of action at a distance.[27]

Many of Newton's most influential contemporaries objected vigorously to the fact that his philosophy had made room for – if not explicitly defended – the possibility of distant action between material bodies. Leibniz and Huygens in particular rejected this aspect of Newton's work in the strongest terms, and it remained a point of contention between Newton and Leibniz for the rest of their lives (see below). Both Leibniz and Huygens were convinced that all natural change occurs through contact action, and that any deviation from this basic mechanist principle within natural philosophy would lead to serious difficulties, including the revival of outmoded Aristotelian ideas. By the seventh proposition of Book III of the *Principia*, as we have seen, Newton reached the following conclusion: "Gravity acts on all bodies universally and is proportional to the quantity of matter in each." Leibniz eventually accused Newton of regarding gravity as a kind of "occult quality," that is, as a quality of bodies that is somehow hidden within them and beyond the philosopher's understanding. Newton's gloss on Rule 3 only made matters worse from Leibniz's point of view, since it tacitly (or functionally) treats gravity as a kind of universal quality akin to extension or impenetrability. But unlike them, it was occult, imperceptible and unintelligible.

One would think that the criticisms of Leibniz and Huygens – both of whom were held in high regard by Newton early in his career – would

---

[27] For a classic treatment, see Mary Hesse, *Forces and Fields: The Concept of Action at a Distance in the History of Physics* (London: Nelson, 1961).

have pressed Newton into articulating an extensive defense of the possibility of action at a distance. Newton presented no such defense; moreover, there is actually evidence that Newton himself rejected the possibility of action at a distance, despite the fact that the *Principia* allows it as a conceptual possibility, if not an empirical reality. When Richard Bentley – later to become an important colleague of Newton and the Master of Newton's college in Cambridge – gave the first lectures on Christianity endowed by a bequest in Robert Boyle's will in late 1691, he sought Newton's advice in what became a celebrated correspondence (it is reproduced in this volume). Bentley's aim was to argue against atheism in part by appealing to the philosophical and theological consequences of what was at the time the newest theory of nature in England, viz., Newton's. In the course of explaining his views to Bentley, Newton made the following (now famous, if not infamous) pronouncement in a letter of 1693:

> It is inconceivable that inanimate brute matter should, without the mediation of something else which is not material, operate upon and affect other matter without mutual contact ... That gravity should be innate, inherent, and essential to matter, so that one body may act upon another at a distance through a vacuum, without the mediation of anything else, by and through which their action and force may be conveyed from one to another, is to me so great an absurdity that I believe no man who has in philosophical matters a competent faculty of thinking can ever fall into it. (This volume p. 137)

It certainly seems that Newton is uncomfortable with the very idea of action at a distance, although some historians and philosophers have argued strongly that there are other readings of the letter.[28] Rather than rejecting distant action between material bodies per se, he may have been rejecting a particular version of that idea. One motive for uncovering a

---

[28] Indeed, in recent years there has been a robust debate about the correspondence with Bentley in particular, and about Newton's attitude toward action at a distance in general, with many interpreters criticizing the account in Janiak, *Newton as Philosopher*. See, e.g., Steffen Ducheyne, "Newton on Action at a Distance and the Cause of Gravity," *Studies in History and Philosophy of Science* 42 (2011), 154–9; John Henry, "Gravity and *De Gravitatione*: The Development of Newton's Ideas on Action at a Distance," *Studies in History and Philosophy of Science* 42 (2011), 11–27; and Eric Schliesser, "Newton's Substance Monism, Distant Action, and the Nature of Newton's Empiricism," *Studies in History and Philosophy of Science* 42 (2011), 160–6. Cf. Janiak's reply to their criticisms in "Three Concepts of Cause in Newton," *Studies in History and Philosophy of Science* 44 (2013): 397–407.

nuanced interpretation of this letter is the obvious fact that Newton apparently regarded action at a distance as perfectly possible when writing the *Principia*. It is difficult to reconcile the *Principia* with the Bentley correspondence. One can argue that although he left open the possibility of action at a distance in his main work, Newton himself did not accept that possibility. The debate on such matters continues unabated.

Space and the divine

Unlike questions about Newton's methods and his apparent deviation from the norms established by mechanist philosophers like Descartes and Boyle, Newton's conception of space and time, along with his view of the divine being, did not immediately engender a philosophical debate. It was Leibniz more than any other philosopher who eventually succeeded in fomenting a philosophical debate in which the "Newtonian" conception of space, time, and the divine would play a central role (see below). But Leibniz's philosophical views were relatively unknown when Newton first formed his conception, and Newton never took Aristotelian philosophical views very seriously. It was instead Descartes's view of space, the world, and God, which he pondered in his youth, and like many contemporaries in Cambridge in those days, he encountered them within the context of Henry More's then famous discussions of Cartesianism (a term coined by More). Beginning with his correspondence with Descartes in 1648, and continuing with a series of publications in later years, many of which Newton owned in his personal library, More argued that Descartes made two fundamental mistakes: first, he wrongly contended that extension and matter are identical (and that the world is therefore a plenum); and second, he mistakenly believed that God and the mind were not extended substances, which made their causal interactions with such substances mysterious. Just as Princess Elisabeth of Bohemia raised fundamental objections to Cartesian dualism, More raised similar objections against the Cartesian view of the divine.[29] Descartes agreed with More's suggestion that God can act

---

[29] See Lisa Shapiro (ed.), *The Correspondence between Princess Elisabeth of Bohemia and René Descartes* (Chicago: University of Chicago Press, 2007), and Genevieve Lewis (ed.), *Descartes: Correspondance avec Arnauld et Morus, texte Latin et traduction* (Paris: Librairie philosophique Vrin, 1953).

anywhere on nature if he so chooses, and came very close to accepting More's contention that such a view entails that God must be present within the world wherever he in fact chooses to act. For how could God part the Red Sea, suggested More, unless God were present precisely where the Red Sea is located? Of course, More agreed that God is not made of parts, cannot be imagined, and cannot be affected by the causal activity of material bodies – the causal arrow flows only in one direction. But More concluded that God is extended in his own way. If one fixes Descartes's two basic mistakes, one obtains what More regarded as a proper philosophical view: space is distinct from matter because it is extended but penetrable, whereas matter is extended but impenetrable; and, in tandem, all substances are extended, but whereas some, such as tables and chairs, are impenetrable, others, such as the mind and even God, are penetrable and therefore not material.[30] Newton was deeply influenced both by More's criticisms of Descartes and by his positive philosophical conception of space and the divine.

In a number of texts, including *De Gravitatione*, the famous discussion of space and time in the Scholium to the *Principia*, and the discussion of God in the General Scholium, Newton made his generally Morean attitudes perfectly clear. He rejected the Cartesian identification of extension and matter, arguing that space itself exists independently of material objects and their relations, and he contended that all entities, including the human mind and even the divine being, are extended in the sense that they have spatial location, even if they are extended in ways that distinguish them from ordinary material bodies.[31] In Newton's hands, space becomes a fundamental concept of natural philosophy, which is foreign to Cartesians and (later) objectionable to Leibnizians. As Newton puts it in a famous

---

[30] For details of More's views, see the classic paper by Alan Gabbey, "Philosophia Cartesiana Triumphata: Henry More (1646–1671)," in *Problems of Cartesianism*, ed. Thomas Lennon et al. (Kingston and Montreal: McGill-Queen's University Press, 1982). For details on the Cartesian context, see the discussion in Jasper Reid, "The Spatial Presence of Spirits among the Cartesians," *Journal of the History of Philosophy* 46 (2008), 91–118. For further discussion of the Descartes-More correspondence and its possible influence on Newton, see Janiak, "Substance and Action in Newton and Descartes," *The Monist* 93 (October 2010), 657–77.

[31] This may mean that for Newton, two substances can be co-located: for discussion, see two recent papers by Hylarie Kochiras: "Gravity and Newton's Substance Counting Problem," *Studies in History and Philosophy of Science* 40 (2009), 267–80, and "Gravity's Cause and Substance Counting: Contextualizing the Problems," *Studies in History and Philosophy of Science* 42 (2011), 167–84.

passage from *De Gravitatione*: "No being exists or can exist which is not related to space in some way. God is everywhere, created minds are somewhere, and body is in the space that it occupies; and whatever is neither everywhere nor anywhere does not exist" (this volume, p. 40). For Newton, then, if one follows the Cartesians and thinks of the mind, or of God, as existing without any spatial location – as existing either "beyond" the natural world or somehow outside of it – then that is equivalent to conceiving of them as non-existent. Newton does not shy away from making this conception of the divine explicit in his public writings, despite the fact that it was anathema to his Cartesian and Leibnizian contemporaries. In the General Scholium, he writes of God:

> He endures always and is present everywhere, and by existing always and everywhere he constitutes duration and space. Since each and every particle of space is *always*, and each and every indivisible moment of duration is *everywhere*, certainly the maker and lord of all things will not be *never* or *nowhere*. (This volume p. 113)

For Newton, just as bodies are present in some spatial location, God, an infinite being, is present throughout all of space throughout all of time.

Newton's rejection of Cartesian views of space, and his embrace of space as a fundamental concept in philosophy following More's influence, aligns with his famous discussion of space and time in the Scholium that follows the opening definitions in the *Principia*. This text influenced nearly every subsequent philosophical discussion of space and time for the next three centuries, so its contours are well known.[32] In his *Principles of Philosophy* of 1644, Descartes had distinguished between the "ordinary" and the "proper" view of motion: whereas the ordinary view presents motion as a body's change of place, the philosopher knows that, properly speaking, motion is a body's change of relations to the bodies that surround it (recall Descartes's plenum). Newton contends in *De Gravitatione* that this idea of proper motion, according to which the motion of a body is at least partially a function of its relations to other bodies, is in tension with Descartes's own laws of nature, also presented in the *Principles*. For according to the principle of inertia that Descartes presents, a body moving rectilinearly will

---

[32] See Robert DiSalle, *Understanding Space-Time* (Cambridge University Press, 2006), ch. 2.

continue to do so unless caused to deviate from this path – hence a body's motion is not a function of its spatial relations to other bodies, but rather of its *causal* relations. Newton's Scholium reflects his idea that the concept of motion in the *Principia* ought to cohere with the laws of motion he endorses. He distinguishes between relative and absolute motion, true and apparent motion, and mathematical and common motion (the same distinctions hold for time, space and place), and the former item in each of these three pairings is a concept that coheres with the laws of motion. Newton's first law reflects Descartes's laws: it is a new version of the principle of inertia, one incorporating the concept of an impressed force. Since this law indicates that a body's motion is not a function of its spatial relations to other bodies, but rather of whether forces are impressed on it, Newton cannot rely on a body's motion relative to other bodies if he is to avoid the tension in the Cartesian view. Hence he indicates that a body's true or absolute motion – rather than its apparent motion, which depends on our perceptions, or its relative motion, which depends on its spatial relations – is a body's change of position within space itself. This means, in turn, that we must distinguish between the common idea of space, according to which space is conceived of as involving relations among various objects (like the space of our air), and the mathematical idea that space is independent of any objects or their relations. The famous "absolute space" is born.

Newton was perfectly well aware that the notion of absolute space was not unproblematic.[33] For instance, if a body's true motion just *is* its absolute motion, its motion with respect to space itself, then the imperceptibility of space would appear to render any detection of true motion difficult. Indeed, how would we detect any body's true motion? Newton's answer is ingenious. Under certain circumstances, we can detect a body's true motion by detecting its acceleration. We can do so when the body is rotating or has a circular motion, for such motions have certain effects. For instance, if a bucket full of water is spun around, we can detect the bucket's acceleration by the changing surface of the water. Or, if two balls are joined together by a rope and then spun

---

[33] In the Scholium, he notes explicitly that absolute space is not perceptible (this volume, p. 87), and in corollary five to the laws of motion (this volume, p. 99), he indicates that a system of bodies – for instance, on a ship's deck – will have the same motions among themselves whether the whole system is moving uniformly or is at rest. Hence he was perfectly aware that true motion is difficult to detect if it is absolute motion.

around, the changing tension in the rope will indicate that the balls are accelerated. Since any acceleration is a true motion – although not all true motions are accelerations, since a so-called inertial motion is not – each case indicates that we can detect a body's true motion even though space itself is imperceptible.

Newton's idea of space, then, enabled him to avoid the tension between the concept of true motion and the laws of motion of the kind found in Descartes, and it also enabled him to articulate what he took to be God's relation to the natural world. Many regard his achievements as an important advance over the Cartesian system. But the debate between Cartesians and Newtonians in the late seventeenth century was eclipsed after Leibniz and his followers began raising serious objections to Newton's conception of space in the 1710s. From Leibniz's point of view, Cartesian natural philosophy had many flaws, many of which he had characterized earlier in his career, but he came to believe that Newton had embraced a view of space, time, motion, and God that was equally flawed.

Newton's relation to Leibniz

Leibniz and Newton knew one another as mathematicians already in the 1670s, and, as we have seen, Leibniz discussed Newton's first optical work with Huygens, but after the publication of the *Principia* in 1687, their philosophical relationship, which was marked originally by respectful disagreement, began to develop in earnest. Just two years after the *Principia* appeared, Leibniz published his *Essay on the Causes of Celestial Motions* (or *Tentamen*), and then in 1693, the two corresponded with one another on both mathematical and philosophical issues (this volume, p. 141). Leibniz initiated their discussion in March of 1693: after highlighting Newton's "astonishing discovery" that the elliptical planetary orbits found by Kepler can be the result of gravitational attraction within the solar system, Leibniz contends that these motions must be caused by "the motion of a fluid medium" (this volume, p. 142). He had described such a fluid medium, or vortex, in detail in his *Essay*. The background to Leibniz's comment is his unwavering commitment – one shared by Huygens, whose theory of gravity's cause Leibniz mentions in the same letter – to the mechanical philosophy's requirement that all changes in motion must be the result of bits of matter impacting on one another. Thus for Leibniz, one can (e.g.) think of the sun as attracting the earth, but in fact the cause of the earth's acceleration, of its true motion around the sun, is its interaction with a fluid medium (Descartes was also a famous proponent of a vortex theory of planetary motion). In his reply in October of 1693, however, Newton insists that he has no need of a fluid medium, for all the phenomena of the heavens and the tides follow from gravity acting in accordance with the laws described in the *Principia*. That is, Newton contends that gravity itself – which is an impressed force, and therefore an "action" in Newton's system – causes the planetary orbits. It is not hard to divine why Leibniz and Huygens would have concluded that Newton had relinquished any commitment to the norms of the mechanical philosophy.

The Leibniz-Newton correspondence of 1693, albeit brief, is significant because it involves Newton's attempt to convince Leibniz that the theory of gravity in the *Principia* is sufficient to undermine the vortex theory favored by Leibniz. It is also significant because it represents an interaction between them that was not tainted by the controversy over the calculus; the latter did not seriously flare up until the English Newtonian John Keill claimed in 1708 that Leibniz had stolen the calculus from Newton. This controversy, with all its nationalist undertones and hyperbolic rhetoric, would taint much of the more famous correspondence between Leibniz and Clarke in 1715–16, and would eventually see Newton write and publish an anonymous response to a supposedly impartial review of the calculus affair by a committee convened under the auspices of the Royal Society (the "Account" – this volume, p. 166).

Nearly twenty years after their illuminating exchange in 1693, Leibniz and Newton narrowly missed a second opportunity to discuss their philosophical differences. In February of 1712, Leibniz wrote a letter to Nicholas Hartsoeker that was highly critical of the Newtonians; it was later published in the *Memoirs of Literature*, a journal to which Roger Cotes, the editor of the *Principia*'s second edition, held a subscription (see his reference to the journal in this volume, p. 158). After Cotes brought Leibniz's criticisms to Newton's attention – especially the claim that the *Principia* renders gravitation a "perpetual miracle" because it does not specify the physical mechanism underlying it – Newton wrote an intriguing, but only posthumously published, rebuttal. Here is part of Newton's paraphrase of Leibniz's original letter: "But he [i.e. Leibniz] goes on and tells us that God could not create planets that should move round of themselves without any cause that should prevent their removing through the tangent. For a miracle at least must keep the planet in" (see this volume p. 153). Newton's response to this Leibnizian charge is illuminating: "But certainly God could create planets that should move round of themselves without any other cause than gravity that should prevent their removing through the tangent. For gravity without a miracle may keep the planets in" (ibid.). Thus Newton repeats the view he mentions to Leibniz in 1693, viz., that the force of gravity itself causes the planets to follow their orbital paths rather than their inertial trajectories along the tangents to those orbits, independently of any fluid medium in the heavens. In his extensive correspondence with Clarke, Leibniz would emphasize the extent to which Newton had failed to live up to the mechanist commitment to intelligible causes.

By the time Newton wrote his "Account" of the Royal Society report concerning the calculus affair, the controversy between Newton and Leibniz had effected a significant rift between their followers in England and on the Continent. Not surprisingly, therefore, Newton's "Account" is highly polemical and includes many incendiary remarks, but it also includes several intriguing comparisons between what he takes to be the Newtonian "experimental philosophy" and the "metaphysics" promoted by Leibniz; we reproduce those remarks in this volume. The text indicates, among other things, that Newton was acquainted not just with Leibniz's contributions to mathematics and dynamics, but with at least some of his more narrowly metaphysical work, including his view of the so-called pre-established harmony. It reworks familiar themes from the 1693 correspondence with Leibniz, and from Leibniz's exchange with Clarke, such as their differing attitudes toward the mechanical philosophy, but it also highlights Newton's own conception of the important philosophical elements of the *Principia* and of the *Opticks* through extensive quotation from those texts. Each of the passages Newton singles out as salient is reprinted in this volume.

Chronology

1687	First edition of *Philosophiae Naturalis Principia Mathematica* is published in London under the imprimatur of the Royal Society
1689	Leibniz's *Tentamen* appears in *Acta Eruditorum*
1690	Newton corresponds with Locke; publication of Locke's *Essay Concerning Human Understanding* in London
1691	Death of Boyle; Boyle's will endows the Boyle Lectures, intended to assist in the explication and defense of Christianity
1692/3	Richard Bentley and Newton correspond extensively; Bentley delivers the first Boyle Lectures in London
1693	Leibniz and Newton correspond
1696	Newton appointed Warden of the Mint in London
1703	Newton elected President of the Royal Society (a position he retained until his death in 1727)
1704	First edition of the *Opticks* is published in London (with sixteen queries) by the printers to the Royal Society
1704/5	Samuel Clarke delivers the Boyle Lectures in London
1705	Newton is knighted by Queen Anne at a grand ceremony in Cambridge
1706	First edition of the Latin translation of the *Opticks*, prepared by Samuel Clarke, is published in London (with the original sixteen, plus seven new, queries)
1713	Second edition of the *Principia*, edited by Roger Cotes, is published in Cambridge
1713	The *Commercium Epistolicum*, a partisan account of the calculus controversy overseen by Newton, appears in the Royal Society's *Philosophical Transactions*
1715	Newton anonymously publishes "Account of the *Commercium Epistolicum*" in the *Philosophical Transactions*
1715–16	Clarke and Leibniz correspond extensively via Princess Caroline of Wales
1716	Death of Leibniz in November
1717	Clarke has his correspondence with Leibniz published in London
1718	Second edition of the *Opticks* is published in London (with thirty-one queries)

1721	Third edition of the *Opticks* is published in London (virtually unchanged from the second edition)
1726	Third edition of *Principia* published in London
1727	Death of Newton in March

Further reading

Classic works on Newton and his influence include Ferdinand Rosenberger's *Isaac Newton und seine physikalischen Principien* (Leipzig: J. A. Barth, 1895), Léon Bloch's *La Philosophie de Newton* (Paris: Libraires Félix Alcan, 1903), Alexandre Koyré's *Newtonian Studies* (Cambridge, MA: Harvard University Press, 1965), and I. Bernard Cohen's *The Newtonian Revolution* (Cambridge University Press, 1980). Influential treatments of somewhat more specialized topics include Mary Hesse, *Forces and Fields: The Concept of Action at a Distance in the History of Physics* (London: Thomas Nelson and Sons, 1961), Richard Westfall, *Force in Newton's Physics: The Science of Dynamics in the Seventeenth Century* (London: Macdonald, 1971), Ernan McMullin, *Newton on Matter and Activity* (Notre Dame, IN: University of Notre Dame Press, 1978), and A. I. Sabra, *Theories of Light from Descartes to Newton*, 2nd edition (Cambridge University Press, 1981), which is philosophically astute.

Because the field of Newtonian studies is flourishing, the relevant literature is vast. For excellent selections of papers and articles on diverse topics, see *The Annus Mirabilis of Sir Isaac Newton 1666–1966*, edited by Robert Palter (Cambridge, MA: MIT Press, 1970), and *Philosophical Perspectives on Newtonian Science*, edited by Philip Bricker and R. I. G. Hughes (Cambridge, MA: MIT Press, 1990); see also the more recent collections, *Isaac Newton's Natural Philosophy*, edited by Jed Buchwald and I. Bernard Cohen (Cambridge, MA: MIT Press, 2001), *The Cambridge Companion to Newton*, edited by I. Bernard Cohen and George Smith (Cambridge University Press, 2002), which contains an extensive bibliography of works by and about Newton, and *Interpreting Newton: Critical Essays*, edited by Andrew Janiak and Eric Schliesser (Cambridge University Press, 2012). Recent monographs about Newton's philosophical thought include Janiak, *Newton as Philosopher* (Cambridge University Press, 2008), William Harper, *Isaac Newton's Scientific Method: Turning Data into Evidence About Gravity and Cosmology* (Oxford University Press, 2011), and Steffen Ducheyne, *The Main Business of Natural Philosophy* (Dordrecht: Springer, 2012).

Important studies of the *Principia* and its background include John Herivel, *The Background to Newton's "Principia": A Study of Newton's Dynamical Researches in the Years 1664–1684* (Oxford: Clarendon Press, 1965), I. Bernard Cohen, *Introduction to Newton's "Principia"* (Cambridge, MA: Harvard University Press, 1971), Bruce Brakenridge, *The Key to Newton's Dynamics: The Kepler Problem and the "Principia,"* with translations by Mary Ann Rossi (Berkeley: University of California Press, 1995), Dana Densmore, *Newton's "Principia": The Central Argument*, with translations and illustrations by William Donahue (Santa Fe, NM: Green Lion Press, 1995), François DeGandt, *Force and Geometry in Newton's "Principia"*, translated by Curtis Wilson (Princeton University Press, 1995), and Niccolo Guicciardini, *Reading the "Principia": The Debate on Newton's Mathematical Methods for Natural Philosophy from 1687 to 1736* (Cambridge University Press, 1999). On Newton's optics, see Sabra's *Theories of Light from Descartes to Newton*, A. R. Hall's *And All Was Light: An Introduction to Newton's "Opticks"* (Oxford: Clarendon Press, 1993), and Alan Shapiro's *Fits, Passions, and Paroxysms: Physics, Method, and Chemistry and Newton's Theories of Colored Bodies and Fits of Easy Reflection* (Cambridge University Press, 1993).

The standard biography of Newton remains Richard Westfall's magisterial *Never at Rest* (Cambridge University Press, 1980), which is available in a condensed version as *The Life of Isaac Newton* (Cambridge University Press, 1993). A more concise account is available in Rob Iliffe, *Newton: A Very Short Introduction* (Oxford University Press, 2007). For early biographical views of Newton, see *Isaac Newton, Eighteenth-Century Perspectives*, edited by A. Rupert Hall (Oxford University Press, 1999). For a shorter discussion, see I. Bernard Cohen's entry on Newton in the *Dictionary of Scientific Biography*, volume x (New York: Scribner's, 1974). The best account of Newton's intellectual disputes with Leibniz is Domenico Bertoloni Meli's *Equivalence and Priority: Newton vs. Leibniz* (Oxford University Press, 1993). The broader cultural and historical context of Newton's work is explored in Betty Jo Teeter Dobbs and Margaret Jacobs, *Newton and the Culture of Newtonianism* (Atlantic Highlands, NJ: Humanities Press, 1995) and in Mordechai Feingold, *The Newtonian Moment: Isaac Newton and the Making of Modern Culture* (New York/Oxford: New York Public Library/Oxford University Press, 2004).

The principal sources for the scholarly study of Newton's oeuvre include: *Isaac Newton's "Philosophiae Naturalis Principia Mathematica," the Third Edition with Variant Readings*, edited by Alexandre Koyré and I. Bernard Cohen, with Anne Whitman (Cambridge, MA: Harvard University Press, 1972), along with the now standard translation, *The "Principia": Mathematical Principles of Natural Philosophy, a New Translation*, translated by I. Bernard Cohen and Anne Whitman, with Julia Budenz (Berkeley: University of California Press, 1999), and *Opticks: or, A Treatise of the Reflections, Refractions, Inflections and Colours of Light* (New York: Dover, 1952), which is based on the fourth edition of 1730. Some of the more important articles and papers written by Newton are available in these collections: *Isaac Newton's Theological Manuscripts*, edited by Herbert McLachlan (Liverpool University Press, 1950), *Isaac Newton's Papers and Letters on Natural Philosophy*, edited by I. Bernard Cohen and Robert Schofield, revised edition (Cambridge, MA: Harvard University Press, 1978), *Unpublished Scientific Papers of Isaac Newton*, edited by A. R. Hall and Marie Boas Hall (Cambridge University Press, 1962), *The Mathematical Papers of Isaac Newton*, edited by D. T. Whiteside (Cambridge University Press, 1967–81), and *The Optical Papers of Isaac Newton*, volume I: *The Optical Lectures of 1670–1672*, edited by Alan Shapiro (Cambridge University Press, 1984). Newton's undergraduate notebooks from Trinity College are available as *Certain Philosophical Questions: Newton's Trinity Notebook*, edited by J. E. McGuire and Martin Tamny (Cambridge University Press, 1983). For a complete reproduction of Newton's letters, see *The Correspondence of Isaac Newton*, edited by Herbert Turnbull, John Scott, A. R. Hall, and Laura Tilling (Cambridge University Press, 1959–77). The Newton Project is an ongoing program to make all of Newton's works, including extensive unpublished manuscript materials, available to the public via the Internet: www.newtonproject.sussex.ac.uk.

Note on texts and translations

I **"New Theory about Light and Colours" [1672]**. This is taken from the original version published in the *Philosophical Transactions*, volume VI (1672), 3075–87. The figures are reproduced from *Correspondence of Isaac Newton*, edited by H. W. Turnbull et al. (Cambridge University Press, 1959–), volume I, 96, 101.

II **Correspondence with Robert Boyle [1679]**. Newton's letter to Boyle of February 28, 1679 is taken from the version in *Correspondence of Isaac Newton*, volume II, 288–96.

III *De Gravitatione* **[date unknown]**. This section is expanded in the second edition: we have now included the complete text. With my assistance, Dr. Christian Johnson revised and corrected the translation of *De Gravitatione* in *Unpublished Scientific Writings of Isaac Newton*, edited by A. R. Hall and Marie Boas Hall (Cambridge University Press, 1962), which also includes a transcription of the original Latin text. Johnson and I have attempted to follow Newton's own English usage in other texts when translating the Latin of *De Gravitatione*. We have consulted two other editions: *De La Gravitation, ou, les Fondements de la Méchanique Classique*, edited by Marie-Françoise Biarnais (Paris: Les Belles Lettres, 1985), and, *Über die Gravitation . . . Texte zu den philosophischen Grundlagen der klassischen Mechanik*, edited and translated by Gernot Böhme (Frankfurt am Main: Vittorio Klostermann, 1988); the latter includes a facsimile of the original Latin manuscript. We also consulted Howard Stein's (partial) translation of the text; we are grateful to Stein for sharing his unpublished work with us.

IV The *Principia* [**1687, first edition**]. The excerpts are from *The "Principia": Mathematical Principles of Natural Philosophy*, translated by I. Bernard Cohen and Anne Whitman, with the assistance of Julia Budenz (Berkeley: University of California Press, 1999); this is based on the third (and last) edition of 1726. The excerpts are reprinted here with the kind permission of the University of California Press.

V **"An Account of the System of the World"** [**c. 1687**]. This text is an incomplete, unpublished manuscript written by Newton and held in the University Library at Cambridge (MS Add. 4005–7, ff. 39–42). I transcribed the original copy. It may have been written any time between 1687 and 1700.

VI **Correspondence with Richard Bentley** [**1692–3**]. This section is expanded in the second edition. Newton's letters to Bentley, written between December 10, 1692 and February 25, 1693, are from the version in *Correspondence of Isaac Newton*, volume III, 233–6, 238–40, 244, 253–6. Bentley's July 1691 description of Newton's advice for background reading to facilitate an understanding of the *Principia*, and his letter to Newton of February 18, 1692, are from the versions in *ibid.*, 155–6 and *ibid.*, 246–52, respectively.

VII **Correspondence with G. W. Leibniz** [**1693/1712**]. This section is expanded in the second edition.

(a) Leibniz's letter to Newton on March 7, 1693 and Newton's reply on October 16, 1693 are taken from the translation in *Correspondence of Isaac Newton*, volume III, 258–9 and 286–7, respectively. We have now included the complete texts.

(b) Leibniz's letter to Hartsoeker on February 10, 1711 is from the English translation in *Memoirs of Literature*, volume III, 453–60 (London, second edition, 1722, a reprint of the first edition of 1712); this is the version Cotes and Newton read. The letter is also available in *Die Philosophischen Schriften von Gottfried Wilhelm Leibniz*, edited by C. J. Gerhardt (Leipzig: Alfred Lorenz, 1931), volume III, 516–21.

(c) Newton's posthumously published response to (b), written to the editor of the *Memoirs of Literature* sometime after May 5, 1712, is from the version in *Correspondence of Isaac Newton*, volume V, 298–300.

VIII **Correspondence with Roger Cotes [1713]**. This section is expanded in the second edition. Each item in this section is from the version in *Correspondence of Isaac Newton*, volume V. Cotes's letter to Bentley of March 10, 1713 is from pp. 389–90; Bentley's letter to Cotes of March 12, 1713 is from pp. 390–91; Cotes's letter to Newton of March 18, 1713 is from pp. 391–3; Newton's letter to Cotes of March 28, 1713, along with a draft of that letter, are from pp. 396–7 and 398–9, respectively; Newton's letter to Cotes of March 31, 1713 is from p. 400; Cotes's letter to Clarke of June 25, 1713 is from pp. 412–13; and, Bentley's letter to Newton of June 30, 1713 is from pp. 413–14.

IX **An Account of the Book Entitled *Commercium Epistolicum* [1715]**. Newton's anonymously published review of the *Commercium Epistolicum*, the Royal Society's report concerning the calculus dispute with Leibniz, is taken from the version in *Philosophical Transactions*, volume XXIX (1714–16), 222–4.

X **Queries to the *Opticks* [1721]**. The excerpts from the queries are from the last edition published in Newton's lifetime, *Opticks, or, A Treatise of the Reflections, Refractions, Inflections, and Colours of Light* (London, 1721, 3rd edition), with the exception of the numbers provided on p. 175, which have been altered to match those of the 4th edition (London, 1730).

Chapter I
"New Theory about Light and Colours"

19 February 1672

Sir,

To perform my late promise to you, I shall without further ceremony acquaint you, that in the beginning of the year 1666 (at which time I applied myself to the grinding of optic glasses of other figures than *spherical*) I procured me a triangular glass prism, to try therewith the celebrated *phenomena* of *colours*. And in order thereto having darkened my chamber, and made a small hole in my window shuts, to let in a convenient quantity of the sun's light, I placed my prism at its entrance, that it might be thereby refracted to the opposite wall. It was at first a very pleasing divertisement, to view the vivid and intense colours produced thereby; but after a while applying myself to consider them more circumspectly, I became surprised to see them in an *oblong* form; which, according to the received laws of refraction, I expected should have been *circular*.

They were terminated at the sides with straight lines, but at the ends, the decay of light was so gradual, that it was difficult to determine justly, what was their figure; yet they seemed *semicircular*.

Comparing the length of this coloured *spectrum* with its breadth, I found it about five times greater; a disproportion so extravagant that it excited me to a more than ordinary curiosity of examining, from whence it might proceed. I could scarce think, that the various *thickness* of the glass, or the termination with shadow or darkness, could have any influence on light to produce such an effect; yet I thought it not amiss to examine first these circumstances, and so tried, what would happen by transmitting light through parts of the glass of diverse thicknesses, or through holes in the window of diverse bignesses, or by setting the prism without so that the light might pass through it, and be refracted before it was terminated by the hole: but I found none of these circumstances material. The fashion of the colours was in all these cases the same.

Then I suspected, whether by any *unevenness* in the glass, or other contingent irregularity, these colours might be thus dilated. And to try this, I took another prism like the former, and so placed it, that the light, passing through them both, might be refracted contrary ways, and so by the latter returned into that course, from which the former had diverted it. For, by this means I thought, the *regular* effects of the first prism would be destroyed by the second prism, but the *irregular* ones more augmented, by the multiplicity of refractions. The event was, that the light, which by the first prism was diffused into an *oblong* form, was by the second reduced into an *orbicular* one with as much regularity, as when it did not at all pass through them. So that, what ever was the cause of that length, 'twas not any contingent irregularity.

I then proceeded to examine more critically, what might be effected by the difference of the incidence of rays coming from diverse parts of the Sun; and to that end, measured the several lines and angles, belonging to the image. Its distance from the hole or prism was 22 foot; its utmost length 13¼ inches; its breadth 2⅝ inches; the diameter of the hole ¼ of an inch; the angle, which the rays, tending towards the middle of the image, made with those lines, in which they would have proceeded without refraction, 44 deg. 56'. And the vertical angle of the prism, 63 deg. 12'. Also the refractions on both sides of the prism, that is, of the incident, and emergent rays, were as near, as I could make them, equal, and consequently about 54 deg. 4'. And the rays fell perpendicularly upon the wall. Now subtracting the diameter of the hole from the length and breadth of the image, there remains 13 inches the length, and $2^{3/8}$ the breadth, comprehended by those rays, which passed through the centre of the said hole, and consequently the angle at the hole, which that breadth subtended, was about 31', answerable to the Sun's diameter; but the angle, which its length subtended, was more than five such diameters, namely 2 deg. 49'.

Having made these observations, I first computed from them the refractive power of that glass, and found it measured by the *ratio* of the sines, 20 to 31. And then, by that *ratio*, I computed the refractions of two rays flowing from opposite parts of the Sun's *discus*, so as to differ 31' in their obliquity of incidence, and found, that the emergent rays should have comprehended an angle of about 31', as they did, before they were incident.

But because this computation was founded on the hypothesis of the proportionality of the *sines* of incidence, and refraction, which though by my own experience I could not imagine to be so erroneous, as to make that angle but 31', which in reality was 2 deg. 49'; yet my curiosity caused me again to take my prism. And having placed it at my window, as before, I observed, that by turning it a little about its *axis* to and fro, so as to vary its obliquity to the light, more than by an angle of 4 or 5 degrees, the colours were not thereby sensibly translated from their place on the wall, and consequently by that variation of incidence, the quantity of refraction was not sensibly varied. By this experiment therefore, as well as by the former computation, it was evident, that the difference of the incidence of rays, flowing from diverse parts of the Sun, could not make them after intersection diverge at a sensibly greater angle, than that at which they before converged; which being, at most, but about 31 or 32 minutes, there still remained some other cause to be found out, from whence it could be 2 deg. 49'.

Then I began to suspect, whether the rays, after their trajection through the prism, did not move in curve lines, and according to their more or less curvature tend to diverse parts of the wall. And it increased my suspicion, when I remembered that I had often seen a tennis ball, struck with an oblique racket, describe such a curve line. For a circular as well as a progressive motion being communicated to it by that stroke, its parts on that side, where the motions conspire, must press and beat the contiguous air more violently than on the other, and there excite a reluctancy and reaction of the air proportionably greater. And for the same reason, if the rays of light should possibly be globular bodies, and by their oblique passage out of one medium into another acquire a circulating motion, they ought to feel the greater resistance from the ambient aether, on that side, where the motions conspire, and thence be continually bowed to the other. But notwithstanding this plausible ground of suspicion, when I came to examine it, I could observe no such curvature in them. And besides (which was enough for my purpose) I observed, that the difference between the length of the image, and diameter of the hole, through which the light was transmitted, was proportionable to their distance.

The gradual removal of these suspicions at length led me to the *experimentum crucis* [crucial experiment], which was this: I took two boards, and placed one of them close behind the prism at the window, so that the light might pass through a small hole, made in it for that purpose, and fall on the other board, which I placed at about 12 foot distance, having first made a small hole in it also, for some of that incident light to pass through. Then I placed another prism behind this second board, so that the light, trajected through both the boards, might pass through that also, and be again refracted before it arrived at the wall. This done, I took the first prism in my hand, and turned it to and fro slowly about its *Axis*, so much as to make the several parts of the image, cast on the second board, successively pass through the hole in it, that I might observe to what places on the wall the second prism would refract them. And I saw by the variations of those places, that the light, tending to that end of the image, towards which the refraction of the first prism was made, did in the second prism suffer a refraction considerably greater than the light tending to the other end. And so the true cause of the length of that image was detected to be no other, than that *light* consists of *rays differently refrangible*, which, without any respect to a difference in their incidence, were, according to their degrees of refrangibility, transmitted towards diverse parts of the wall.

When I understood this, I let off my aforesaid glass works; for I saw, that the perfection of telescopes was hitherto limited, not so much for want of glasses truly figured according to the prescriptions of optics authors (which all men have hitherto imagined) as because that light itself is a *heterogeneous mixture of differently refrangible rays*. So that, were a glass so exactly figured, as to collect any one sort of rays into one point, it could not collect those also into the same point, which having the same incidence upon the same medium are apt to suffer a different refraction. Nay, I wondered, that seeing the difference of refrangibility was so great, as I found it, telescopes should arrive to that perfection they are now at. For measuring the refractions in one of my prisms, I found, that supposing the common *sine* of incidence upon one of its planes was 44 parts, the *sine* of refraction of the utmost rays on the red end of the colours, made out of the glass into the air, would be 68 parts, and the *sine* of refraction of the utmost rays on the other end, 69 parts: so that the difference is about a 24th or 25th part of the whole refraction. And consequently, the object glass of any telescope cannot collect all the rays, which come from one point of an object, so as to make them convene at its *focus* in less room than in a circular space, whose diameter is the 50th part of the diameter of its aperture; which is an irregularity, some hundreds of times greater, than a circularly figured *lens*, of so small a section as the object glasses of long telescopes are, would cause by the unfitness of its figure, were light *uniform*.

This made me take *reflections* into consideration, and finding them regular, so that the angle of reflection of all sorts of rays was equal to their angle of incidence; I understood, that by their mediation, optics instruments might be brought to any degree of perfection imaginable, provided a *reflecting* substance could be found, which would polish as finely as glass, and *reflect* as much light, as glass *transmits*, and the art of communicating to it a parabolic figure be also attained. But these seemed very great difficulties, and I almost thought them insuperable, when I further considered, that every irregularity in a reflecting superficies makes the rays stray 5 or 6 times more out of their due course, than the like irregularities in a refracting one: so that a much greater curiosity would be here requisite, than in figuring glasses for refraction.

Amidst these thoughts I was forced from Cambridge by the intervening plague, and it was more than two years, before I proceeded further. But then having thought on a tender way of polishing, proper for metal, whereby, as I imagined, the figure also would be corrected to the last; I began to try, what might be effected in this kind, and by degrees so far perfected an instrument (in the essential parts of it like that I sent to *London*) by which I could discern Jupiter's 4 concomitants, and showed them diverse times to two others of my acquaintance. I could also discern the Moon-like phase of *Venus*, but not very distinctly, nor without some niceness in disposing the instrument.

From that time I was interrupted till this last Autumn, when I made the other. And as that was sensibly better than the first (especially for day objects) so I doubt not, but they will be still brought to a much greater perfection by their endeavours, who, as you inform me, are taking care about it at *London*.

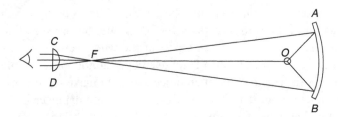

Figure 1.1

I have sometimes thought to make a microscope, which in like manner should have, instead of an object glass, a reflecting piece of metal. And this I hope they will also take into consideration. For those instruments seem as capable of improvement as *telescopes*, and perhaps more, because but one reflective piece of metal is requisite in them, as you may perceive by the annexed diagram, where *A B* represent the object metal, *C D* the eye glass, *F* their common focus, and *O* the other focus of the metal, in which the object is placed.

But to return from this digression, I told you, that light is not similar, or homogeneous, but consists of *difform* [diverse forms of] rays, some of which are more refrangible than others: so that of those, which are alike incident on the same medium, some shall be more refracted than others, and that not by any virtue of the glass, or other external cause, but from a predisposition, which every particular ray hath to suffer a particular degree of refraction.

I shall now proceed to acquaint you with another more notable difformity in its rays, wherein the *origin of colours* is unfolded: concerning which I shall lay down the *doctrine* first, and then, for its examination, give you an instance or two of the *experiments*, as a specimen of the rest.[1]

---

[1] In Newton's February 6 (1672) letter to Henry Oldenburg, Secretary of the Royal Society, which was the basis for the publication of "A New Theory" in the Society's *Philosophical Transactions*, the following passage was included (but removed for publication): "A naturalist would scarce expect to see the science of those become mathematical, & yet I dare affirm that there is as much certainty in it as in any other part of opticks. For what I shall tell concerning them is not an hypothesis but most rigid consequence, not conjectured by inferring 'tis thus because not otherwise or because it satisfies all phenomena (the philosophers' universal topic), but evinced by the mediation of experiments concluding directly & without any suspicion of doubt. To continue the historical narration of these experiments would make discourse too tedious & confused, & therefore I shall lay down the doctrine first ..." See *Correspondence*, vol. 1, 96–7.

The doctrine you will find comprehended and illustrated in the following propositions.

1. As the rays of light differ in degrees of refrangibility, so they also differ in their disposition to exhibit this or that particular colour. Colours are not *qualifications of light*, derived from refractions, or reflections of natural bodies (as 'tis generally believed) but *original* and *connate properties*, which in diverse rays are diverse. Some rays are disposed to exhibit a red colour and no other, some a yellow and no other, some a green and no other, and so of the rest. Nor are there only rays proper and particular to the more eminent colours, but even to all their intermediate gradations.

2. To the same degree of refrangibility ever belongs the same colour, and to the same colour ever belongs the same degree of refrangibility. The *least refrangible* rays are all disposed to exhibit a *red* colour, and contrarily those rays, which are disposed to exhibit a *red* colour, are all the least refrangible: so the most *refrangible* rays are all disposed to exhibit a deep *violet colour*, and contrarily those which are apt to exhibit such a violet colour, are all the most refrangible. And so to all the intermediate colours in a continued series belong intermediate degrees of refrangibility. And this analogy between colours, and refrangibility, is very precise and strict, the rays always either exactly agreeing in both, or proportionally disagreeing in both.

3. The species of colour, and degree of refrangibility proper to any particular sort of rays, is not mutable by refraction, nor by reflection from natural bodies, nor by any other cause, that I could yet observe. When any one sort of rays has been well parted from those of other kinds, it hath afterwards obstinately retained its colour, notwithstanding my utmost endeavours to change it. I have refracted it with prisms and reflected it with bodies, which in daylight were of other colours; I have intercepted it with the coloured film of air interceding two compressed plates of glass; transmitted it through coloured mediums, and through mediums irradiated with other sort of rays, and diversely terminated it, and yet could never produce any new colour out of it. It would by contracting or dilating

become more brisk, or faint, and by the loss of many rays, in some cases very obscure and dark; but I could never see it changed *in specie*.

4. Yet seeming transmutations of colours may be made where there is any mixture of diverse sorts of rays. For in such mixtures, the component colours appear not, but by their mutual allaying each other, constitute a middling colour. And therefore, if by refraction, or any other of the aforesaid causes, the difform rays, latent in such a mixture, be separated, there shall emerge colours different from the colour of the composition. Which colours are not new generated, but only made apparent by being parted; for if they be again entirely mixed and blended together, they will again compose that colour, which they did before separation. And for the same reason, transmutations made by the convening of diverse colours are not real; for when the difform rays are again severed, they will exhibit the very same colours, which they did before they entered the composition; as you see, blue and yellow powders, when finely mixed, appear to the naked eye green, and yet the colours of the component corpuscles are not thereby really transmuted, but only blended. For, when viewed with a good microscope, they still appear blue and yellow interspersedly.

5. There are therefore two sorts of colours. The one original and simple, the other compounded of these. The original or primary colours are, *red, yellow, green, blue*, and a *violet-purple*, together with orange, indigo, and an indefinite variety of intermediate gradations.

6. The same colours in *specie* with these primary ones may be also produced by composition: For, a mixture of *yellow* and *blue* makes *green*; of *red* and *yellow* makes *orange*; of *orange* and *yellowish green* makes *yellow*. And in general, if any two colours be mixed, which in the series of those, generated by the prism, are not too far distant one from another, they by their mutual alloy compound that colour, which in the said series appeareth in the mid-way between them. But those, which are situated at too great a distance, do not so. *Orange* and *indigo* produce not the intermediate green, nor scarlet and green the intermediate yellow.

7. But the most surprising and wonderful composition was that of *whiteness*. There is no one sort of rays which alone can exhibit this. 'Tis ever compounded, and to its composition are requisite all the aforesaid primary colours, mixed in a due proportion. I have often with admiration beheld, that all the colours of the prism being made to converge, and thereby to be again mixed as they were in the light before it was incident upon the prism, reproduced light, entirely and perfectly white, and not at all sensibly differing from a *direct* light of the Sun, unless when the glasses, I used, were not sufficiently clear; for then they would a little incline it to *their* colour.

8. Hence therefore it comes to pass, that whiteness is the usual colour of *light*; for, light is a confused aggregate of rays [endowed] with all sorts of colours, as they are promiscuously darted from the various parts of luminous bodies. And of such a confused aggregate, as I said, is generated whiteness, if there be a due proportion of the ingredients; but if any one predominate, the light must incline to that colour; as it happens in the blue flame of brimstone [sulphur]; the yellow flame of a candle; and the various colours of the fixed stars.

9. These things considered, the *manner*, how colours are produced by the prism, is evident. For of the rays, constituting the incident light, since those which differ in colour proportionally differ in refrangibility, *they* by their unequal refractions must be severed and dispersed into an oblong form in an orderly succession from the least refracted scarlet to the most refracted violet. And for the same reason it is, that objects, when looked upon through a prism, appear coloured. For the difform rays, by their unequal refractions, are made to diverge towards several parts of the *retina*, and there express the images of things coloured, as in the former case they did the Sun's image upon a wall. And by this inequality of refractions they become not only coloured, but also very confused and indistinct.

10. Why the colours of the *rainbow* appear in falling drops of rain, is also from hence evident. For those drops, which refract the rays, disposed to appear purple, in greatest quantity to the spectator's eye, refract the rays of other sorts so much less, as to make them pass beside it; and such are the drops on the inside of the

primary bow, and on the outside of the *second* or exterior one. So those drops, which refract in greatest plenty the rays, apt to appear red, towards the spectator's eye, refract those of other sorts so much more, as to make them pass beside it; and such are the drops on the exterior part of the *primary*, and interior part of the *secondary* bow.

11. The odd phenomena of an infusion of *lignum nephriticum*,[2] *leaf gold*, *fragments of coloured glass*, and some other transparently coloured bodies, appearing in one position of one colour, and of another in another, are on these grounds no longer riddles. For, those are substances apt to reflect one sort of light and transmit another; as may be seen in a dark room, by illuminating them with similar or uncompounded light. For then they appear of that colour only, with which they are illuminated, but yet in one position more vivid and luminous than in another, accordingly as they are disposed more or less to reflect or transmit the incident colour.

12. From hence also is manifest the reason of an unexpected experiment, which Mr *Hooke* somewhere in his *Micrographia*[3] relates to have made with two wedge-like transparent vessels, filled the one with a red, the other with a blue liquor [liquid]: namely, that though they were severally transparent enough, yet both together became opaque; for if one transmitted only red, and the other only blue, no rays could pass through both.

13. I might add more instances of this nature, but I shall conclude with this general one, that the colours of all natural bodies have no other origin than this, that they are variously qualified to reflect one sort of light in greater plenty than another. And this I have experimented in a dark room by illuminating those bodies with uncompounded light of diverse colours. For by that means

---

[2] *Lignum nephriticum* is nephritic wood, which was reputed in the seventeenth century to be useful in curing ailments such as kidney stones, and which would give water an unusual golden color under some circumstances.

[3] See Robert Hooke, *Micrographia: or some physiological descriptions of minute bodies made by magnifying glasses, with observations and inquiries thereupon* (London: Royal Society, 1665), 73–4; the work is available in a modern reprint, volume xx of *Historiae naturalis classica*, edited by J. Cramer and H. K. Swann (New York: Wheldon and Wesley, 1961). Hooke was the chief experimentalist at the Royal Society and had previously worked with Robert Boyle during the 1650s.

any body may be made to appear of any colour. They have there no appropriate colour, but ever appear of the colour of the light cast upon them, but yet with this difference, that they are most brisk and vivid in the light of their own daylight colour. *Minium* [red lead] appeareth there of any colour indifferently, with which 'tis illustrated, but yet most luminous in red, and so *bise*[4] appeareth indifferently of any colour with which 'tis illustrated, but yet most luminous in blue. And therefore *minium* reflects rays of any colour, but most copiously those [endowed] with red; and consequently when illustrated with daylight, that is, with all sorts of rays promiscuously blended, those qualified with red shall abound most in the reflected light, and by their prevalence cause it to appear of that colour. And for the same reason *bise*, reflecting blue most copiously, shall appear blue by the excess of those rays in its reflected light; and the like of other bodies. And that this is the entire and adequate cause of their colours, is manifest, because they have no power to change or alter the colour of any sort of rays incident apart, but put on all colours indifferently, with which they are enlightened.

These things being so, it can be no longer disputed, whether there be colours in the dark, nor whether they be the qualities of the objects we see, no nor perhaps, whether light be a body. For since colours are the *qualities* of light, having its rays for their entire and immediate subject, how can we think those rays *qualities* also, unless one quality may be the subject of and sustain another; which in effect is to call it *substance*. We should not know bodies for substances, were it not for their sensible qualities, and the principal of those being now found due to something else, we have as good reason to believe that to be a substance also.

Besides, whoever thought any quality to be a *heterogeneous* aggregate, such as light is discovered to be. But to determine more absolutely, what light is, after what manner refracted, and by what modes or actions it produces in our minds the phantasms of colours, is not so easy. And I shall not mingle conjectures with certainties.

---

[4] Bise is also called blue bice, which is short for a shade of blue made from smalt (glass or powder from glass).

Reviewing what I have written, I see the discourse itself will lead to divers experiments sufficient for its examination: and therefore I shall not trouble you further, than to describe one of those, which I have already insinuated.

In a darkened room make a hole in the shut of a window, whose diameter may conveniently be about a third part of an inch, to admit a convenient quantity of the Sun's light: And there place a clear and colourless prism, to refract the entering light towards the further part of the room, which, as I said, will thereby be diffused into an oblong and coloured image. Then place a *lens* of about three foot radius (suppose a broad object glass of a three foot telescope) at the distance of about four or five foot from thence, through which all those colours may at once be transmitted, and made by its refraction to convene at a further distance of about ten or twelve foot. If at that distance you intercept this light with a sheet of white paper, you will see the colours converted into whiteness again by being mingled. But it is requisite, that the prism and lens be placed steady, and that the paper, on which the colours are cast, be moved to and fro; for, by such motion, you will not only find, at what distance the whiteness is most perfect, but also see, how the colours gradually convene, and vanish into whiteness, and afterwards having crossed one another in that place where they compound whiteness, are again dissipated, and severed, and in an inverted order retain the same colours, which they had before they entered the composition. You may also see, that, if any of the colours at the *lens* be intercepted, the whiteness will be changed into the other colours. And therefore, that the composition of whiteness be perfect, care must be taken, that none of the colours fall besides the *lens*.

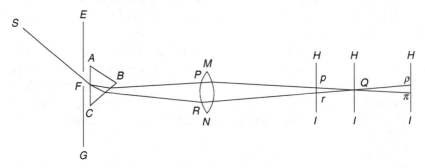

Figure 1.2

In the annexed design of this experiment, *A B C* expresseth the prism set endwise to sight, close by the hole *F* of the window *E G*. Its vertical angle *ACB* may conveniently be about 60 degrees: *M N* designates the *lens*. Its breadth 2½ or 3 inches. *SF* one of the straight lines, in which difform rays may be conceived to flow successively from the Sun. *F P* and *F R* two of those rays unequally refracted, which the *lens* makes to converge towards *Q*, and after decussation [crossing] to diverge again. And HI the paper, at diverse distances, on which the colours are projected: which in Q constitute whiteness, but are *red* and yellow in *R*, *r*, and *p*, and blue and *Purple* in *P*, *p*, and *π*.

If you proceed further to try the impossibility of changing any uncompounded colour (which I have asserted in the third and thirteenth propositions) 'tis requisite that the room be made very dark, lest any scattering light, mixing with the colour, disturb and allay it, and render it compound, contrary to the design of the experiment. 'Tis also requisite, that there be a more perfect separation of the colours, than, after the manner above described, can be made by the refraction of one single prism, and how to make such further separations, will scarce be difficult to them, that consider the discovered laws of refractions. But if trial shall be made with colours not thoroughly separated, there must be allowed changes proportionable to the mixture. Thus if compound yellow light fall upon blue *bise*, the bise will not appear perfectly yellow, but rather green, because there are in the yellow mixture many rays [endowed] with green, and green being less remote from the usual blue colour of bise than yellow, is the more copiously reflected by it.

In like manner, if any one of the prismatic colours, suppose red, be intercepted, on design to try the asserted impossibility of reproducing that colour out of the others, which are pretermitted [omitted]; 'tis necessary, either that the colours be very well parted before the red be intercepted, or that together with the red the neighbouring colours, into which any red is secretly dispersed (that is, the yellow, and perhaps green too) be intercepted, or else, that allowance be made for the emerging of so much red out of the yellow & green, as may possibly have been diffused, and scatteringly blended in those colours. And if these things be observed, the new production of red, or any intercepted colour will be found impossible.

This, I conceive, is enough for an introduction to experiments of this kind; which if any of the *Royal Society* shall be so curious as to prosecute, I should be very glad to be informed with what success: that, if anything seem to be defective, or to thwart this relation, I may have an opportunity of giving further direction about it, or of acknowledging my errors, if I have committed any.

So far this learned and very ingenious letter; which having been by that *illustrious company*, before whom it was read, with much applause committed to the consideration of some of their fellows, well versed in this argument, the reader may possibly in another *tract* be informed of some report given in upon this discourse.

Chapter II
Correspondence with Robert Boyle [1679]

NEWTON TO BOYLE

Cambridge, 28 February 1678/9

Honoured Sir,

I have so long deferred to send you my thoughts about the physical qualities we spoke of, that did I not esteem myself obliged by promise, I think I should be ashamed to send them at all. The truth is, my notions about things of this kind are so indigested, that I am not well satisfied myself in them; and what I am not satisfied in, I can scarce esteem fit to be communicated to others; especially in natural philosophy, where there is no end of fancying. But because I am indebted to you, and yesterday met with a friend, Mr Maulyverer,[1] who told me he was going to London, and intended to give you the trouble of a visit, I could not forbear to take the opportunity of conveying this to you by him.

1. It being only an explication of qualities, which you desire of me, I shall set down my apprehensions in the form of suppositions, as follows. And first, I suppose, that there is diffused through all places an aethereal substance, capable of contraction and dilatation [i.e. dilation], strongly elastic, and in a word much like air in all respects, but far more subtle.

---

[1] Newton most likely meant Thomas Mauliverer, who attended Trinity College, Cambridge as an undergraduate in the early 1660s, as did Newton.

2. I suppose this aether pervades all gross bodies, but yet so as to land rarer in their pores than in free spaces, and so much the rarer, as their pores are less. And this I suppose (with others) to be the cause, why light incident on those bodies is refracted towards the perpendicular; why two well polished metals cohere in a receiver exhausted of air; why mercury stands sometimes up to the top of a glass pipe, though much higher than 30 inches; and one of the main causes, why the parts of all bodies cohere; also the cause of filtration, and of the rising of water in small glass pipes above the surface of the stagnating water they are dipped into: for I suspect the other may stand rarer, not only in the insensible pores of bodies, but even in the very sensible cavities of those pipes. And the same principle may cause menstruums [i.e. solvents] to pervade with violence the pores of the bodies they dissolve, that surrounding [the] aether, as well as the atmosphere, pressing them together.

3. I suppose the rarer aether within bodies, and the denser without them, not to be terminated in a mathematical superficies, but to grow gradually into one another; the external aether beginning to grow rarer, and the internal to grow denser, at some little distance from the superficies of the body, and running through all intermediate degrees of density in the intermediate spaces. And this may be the cause why light, in Grimaldo's experiment, passing by the edge of a knife, or other opaque body, is turned aside and as it were refracted, and by that refraction makes several colours.[2]

Let ABCD be a dense body, whether opaque, or transparent, EFGH the outside of the uniform aether, which is within it, IKLM the inside of the uniform aether, which is without it; and conceive the aether, which is between EFGH and IKLM, to run through all intermediate degrees of density between that of the two uniform aethers on either side. This being supposed, the rays of the sun SB, SK, which pass by the edge of this body between B and K, ought in their passage through the unequally dense aether there, to receive a ply [bend] from the denser aether, which is on that side towards K, and that the more, by how much they pass nearer to the body, and thereby to be scattered through the space PQRST, as by experience they are found to be. Now the space

---

[2] Although it occurred years earlier, Francesco Maria Grimaldi's discovery of diffraction was published in 1665.

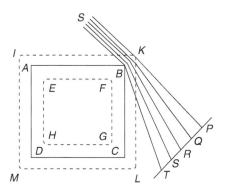

Figure 2.1

between the limits EFGH and IKLM, I shall call the space of the aether's graduated rarity.

4. When two bodies moving towards one another come near together, I suppose the aether between them to grow rarer than before, and the spaces of its graduated rarity to extend further from the superficies of the bodies towards one another; and this, by reason, that the aether cannot move and play up and down so freely in the straight passage between the bodies, as it could before they came so near together.

Thus, if the space of the aether's graduated rarity reach from the body ABCDFE only to the distance GHLMRS, when no other body is near it, yet may it reach farther, as to IK, when another body NOPQ approaches: and as the other body approaches more and more, I suppose the aether between them will grow rarer and rarer.

These suppositions I have so described, as if I thought the spaces of graduated aether had precise limits, as is expressed at I K L M in the first figure, and GMRS in the second: for thus I thought I could better express myself. But really I do not think they have such precise limits, but rather decay insensibly, and in so decaying, extend to a much greater distance than can easily be believed, or need be supposed.

5. Now from the fourth supposition it follows that when two bodies approaching one another come so near together as to make the aether between them begin to rarefy, they will begin to have a reluctance from being brought nearer together, and an endeavour to recede from one another: which reluctance and endeavour will increase, as they come

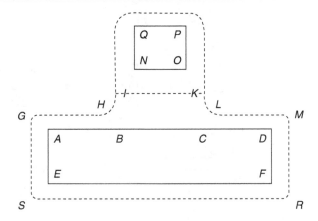

Figure 2.2

nearer together, because thereby they cause the interjacent aether to rarefy more and more. But at length, when they come so near together that the excess of pressure of the external aether which surrounds the bodies, above that of the rarefied aether, which is between them, is so great as to overcome the reluctance which the bodies have from being brought together, then will that excess of pressure drive them with violence together, and make them adhere strongly to one another, as was said in the second supposition. For instance, in the second figure, when the bodies ED and NP are so near together that the spaces of the aether's graduated rarity begin to reach to one another and meet in the line IK; the aether between them will have suffered much rarefaction, which rarefaction requires much force, that is, much pressing of the bodies together: and the endeavour, which the aether between them has to return to its former natural state of condensation, will cause the bodies to have an endeavour of receding from one another. But on the other hand, to counterpoise this endeavour, there will not yet be any excess of density of the aether which surrounds the bodies, above that of the aether which is between them at the line I K. But if the bodies come nearer together, so as to make the aether in the midway-line I K grow rarer than the surrounding aether, there will arise from the excess of density of the surrounding aether a compressure of the bodies towards one another: which when by the nearer approach of the bodies it becomes so great, as to overcome the aforesaid endeavour the bodies have to recede from one another, they will then go towards one another, and adhere together. And, on the contrary, if any power [should] force them asunder to that distance, where the endeavour to recede begins to overcome the endeavour to accede, they will again leap from one another. Now hence I conceive it is chiefly that a fly walks on water without wetting her feet, and consequently without touching the water; that two polished pieces of glass are not without pressure brought to contact, no, not though the one be plain, the other a little convex; that the particles of dust cannot by pressing be made to cohere, as they would do, if they did but fully touch; that the particles of tinging substances [a substance that tinges or colours][3] and salts dissolved in water do not of their own accord concrete and fall to the bottom, but diffuse themselves all over the liquor and expand still more, if you add more liquor to them. Also, that the particles of vapours, exhalations, and air, do stand at a distance from one another, and endeavour to recede as far from one another as the pressure of the incumbent atmosphere will let them: for I conceive the confused mass of vapours, air, and exhalations, which we call the atmosphere, to be nothing else but the particles of all sorts of bodies, of which the earth consists, separated from one another, and kept at a distance, by the said principle.

From these principles the actions of menstruums upon bodies may be thus explained. Suppose any tinging body, as cochineal, or logwood, be put into water;[4] so soon as the water sinks into its pores and wets on all sides any particle, which adheres to the body only by the principle in the second supposition, it takes off, or at least much diminishes the efficacy of that principle to hold the particle to the body, because it makes the aether on all sides of the particle to be of a more uniform density than before. And then the particle being shaken off, by any little motion, floats in the water, and with many such others makes a tincture [hue or colour]; which tincture will be of some lively colour, if the particles be all of the same size and density; otherwise of a dirty one. For the colours of all natural bodies whatever seem to depend on nothing but the various sizes and densities of their particles; as I think you have seen described

---

[3] Boyle himself employs the terms 'menstruum' and 'tinging' (to describe a powder) in *Usefulness of the Experimental and Natural Philosophy* (London, 1663), I.i.14.

[4] Newton discusses a case where an object changes the color of water into which it is placed.

by me more at large in another paper. If the particles be very small (as are those of salts, vitriols [sulfates of metals], and gums) they are transparent; and as they are supposed bigger and bigger, they put on these colours in order, black, white, yellow, red; violet, blue, pale green, yellow, orange, red; purple, blue, green, yellow, orange, red, etc. as is discerned by the colours, which appear at the several thicknesses of very thin plates of transparent bodies. Whence, to know the causes of the changes of colours, which are often made by the mixtures of several liquors [liquids], it is to be considered how the particles of any tincture may have their size or density altered by the infusion of another liquor.

When any metal is put into common water, the water cannot enter into its pores, to act on it and dissolve it. Not that water consists of too gross parts for this purpose, but because it is unsociable to metal. For there is a certain secret principle in nature, by which liquors are sociable to some things, and unsociable to others. Thus water will not mix with oil, but readily with spirit of wine, or with salts. It sinks also into wood, which quicksilver will not; but quicksilver sinks into metals which, as I said, water will not. So aqua fortis [nitric acid] dissolves silver and not gold, aqua regis [a mixture of nitric and hydrochloric acid] gold and not silver, etc.[5] But a liquor which is of itself unsociable to a body may, by the mixture of a convenient mediator, be made sociable. So molten lead, which alone will not mix with copper, or with regulus of Mars [a fusion of antimony sulphide with iron], by the addition of tin is made to mix with either. And water, by the mediation of saline spirits, will mix with metal. Now when any metal is put in water impregnated with such spirits, as into aqua fortis, aqua regis, spirit of vitriol [sulphuric acid], or the like, the particles of the spirits as they, in floating in the water, strike on the metal will by their sociableness enter into its pores and gather round its outside particles and, by advantage of the continual tremor the particles of the metal are in, hitch themselves in by degrees between those particles and the body, and loosen them from it; and the water entering into the pores together with the saline spirits, the particles of the metal will be thereby still more loosed, so as, by that motion the solution puts them into, to be easily shaken off, and made to float in the water: the saline particles still encompassing the metallic ones as a

---

[5] Here Newton employs standard alchemical symbols to denote silver, gold, etc.

Figure 2.3

coat or shell does a kernel, after the manner expressed in the annexed figure. In which figure I have made the particles round, though they may be cubical, or of any other shape.

If into a solution of metal thus made be poured a liquor abounding with particles, to which the former saline particles are more sociable than to the particles of the metal (suppose with particles of salt of tartar [potassium carbonate]) then so soon as they strike on one another in the liquor, the saline particles will adhere to those more firmly than to the metalline ones, and by degrees be wrought off from those to enclose these. Suppose A [is] a metalline particle, enclosed with saline ones of spirit of nitre [potassium nitrate], and E a particle of salt of tartar, contiguous to two of the particles of spirit of nitre b and c, and suppose the particle E is impelled by any motion towards d, so as to roll about the particle c, till it touch the particle d, the particle b adhering more firmly to E than to A, will be forced off from A.

And by the same means the particle E, as it rolls about A, will tear off the rest of the saline particles from A, one after another, till it has got them all, or almost all, about itself. And when the metallic particles are thus divested of the nitrous ones which, as a mediator between them and the water, held them floating in it, the alcalizate ones crowding for the room the metallic ones took up before, will press these towards one another, and make them come more easily together: so that by the motion they continually have in the water, they shall be made to strike on one another and then, by means of the principle in the second supposition, they will cohere and grow into clusters, and fall down by their weight to the bottom, which is called precipitation.

In the solution of metals, when a particle is loosing from the body, so soon as it gets to that distance from it where the principle of receding described in the fourth and fifth suppositions begins to overcome the principle of acceding described in the second supposition, the receding

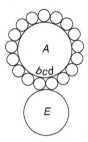

Figure 2.4

of the particle will be thereby accelerated, so that the particle shall as it were with violence leap from the body, and putting the liquor into a brisk agitation, beget and promote that heat we often find to be caused in solutions of metals. And if any particle happen to leap off thus from the body, before it be surrounded with water, or to leap off with that smartness, as to get loose from the water: the water, by the principle in the fourth and fifth suppositions, will be kept off from the particle and stand round about it, like a spherically hollow arch, not being able to come to a full contact with it any more. And several of these particles afterwards gathering into a cluster, so as by the same principle to stand at a distance from one another, without any water between them, will compose a bubble. Whence I suppose it is, that in brisk solutions there usually happens an ebullition [boiling].

This is one way of transmuting gross compact substances into aerial ones. Another way is by heat. For as fast as the motion of heat can shake off the particles of water from the surface of it, those particles by the said principle will float up and down in the air, at a distance both from one another, and from the particles of air, and make that substance we call vapour. Thus I suppose it is, when the particles of a body are very small (as I suppose those of water are) so that the action of heat alone may be sufficient to shake them asunder. But if the particles be much larger, they then require the greater force of dissolving menstruums to separate them, unless by any means the particles can be first broken into smaller ones. For the most fixed [non-volatile] bodies, even gold itself, some have said will become volatile only by breaking their parts smaller. Thus may the volatility and fixedness of bodies depend on the different sizes of their parts.

And on the same difference of size may depend the more or less permanency of aerial substances in their state of rarefaction. To

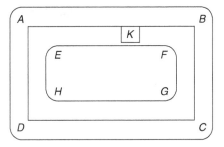

Figure 2.5

understand this let us suppose ABCD to be a large piece of any metal, EFGH the limit of the interior uniform aether, and K a part of the metal at the superficies AB. If this part or particle K be so little that it reaches not to the limit E F, it is plain that the aether at its centre must be less rare than if the particle were greater, for were it greater, its centre would be further from the superficies AB, that is, in a place where the aether (by supposition) is rarer.

The less the particle K, therefore, the denser the aether at its centre, because its centre comes nearer to the edge AB, where the aether is denser than within the limit EFGH. And if the particle were divided from the body, and removed to a distance from it, where the aether is still denser, the aether within it must proportionally grow denser. If you consider this you may apprehend how by diminishing the particle, the rarity of the aether within it will be diminished, till between the density of the aether without, and the density of the aether within it, there be little difference, that is, till the cause be almost taken away, which should keep this and other such particles at a distance from one another. For that cause, explained in the fourth and fifth suppositions, was the excess of density of the external aether above that of the internal. This may be the reason then why the small particles of vapours easily come together and are reduced back into water unless the heat which keeps them in agitation be so great as to dissipate them as fast as they come together: but the grosser particles of exhalations raised by fermentation keep their aerial form more obstinately, because the aether within them is rarer.

Nor does the size only but the density of the particles also conduce to the permanency of aerial substances. For the excess of density of the aether without such particles above that of the aether within them is still greater. Which has made me sometimes think that the true permanent air may be of a metallic original: the particles of no substances being more dense than those of metals. This, I think, is also favoured by experience, for I remember I once read in the *Philosophical Transactions*[6] how M. Huygens at Paris found that the air made by dissolving salt of tartar would in two or three days time condense and fall down again, but the air made by dissolving a metal continued without condensing or relenting in the least. If you consider then how by the continual fermentations made in the bowels of the earth there are aerial substances raised out of all kinds of bodies, all which together make the atmosphere, and that of all these the metallic are the most permanent, you will not perhaps think it absurd that the most permanent part of the atmosphere, which is the true air, should be constituted of these: especially since they are the heaviest of all other[s], and so must subside to the lower parts of the atmosphere and float upon the surface of the earth, and buoy up the lighter exhalation and vapours to float in greatest plenty above them. Thus I say it ought to be with the metallic exhalations raised in the bowels of the earth by the action of acid menstruums, and thus it is with the true permanent air. For this as in reason it ought to be esteemed the most ponderous [heavy] part of the atmosphere because the lowest: so it betrays its ponderosity by making vapours ascend readily in it, by sustaining mists and clouds of snow, and by buoying up gross and ponderous smoke. The air also is the most gross inactive part of the atmosphere affording living things no nourishment if deprived of the more tender exhalations and spirits that float in it: and what more inactive and remote from nourishment than metallic bodies?

I shall set down one conjecture more which came into my mind now as I was writing this letter. It is about the cause of gravity. For this end I will suppose aether to consist of parts differing from one another in subtlety by indefinite degrees: that in the pores of bodies there is less of the grosser aether, in proportion to the finer, than in open spaces, and consequently that in the great body of the earth there is much less of the grosser aether, in proportion to the finer, than in the regions of the air: and that yet the grosser aether in the air affects the upper regions of the

---

[6] Newton refers to "Some Experiments made in the Air-Pump by Monsieur Papin, as directed by Monsieur *Hugens*," *Philosophical Transactions* 10 (1675), 443–7. Here and elsewhere, we find a variant spelling of Christiaan Huygens's name.

earth, and the finer aether in the earth the lower regions of the air, in such a manner that from the top of the air to the surface of the earth, and again from the surface of the earth to the centre thereof, the aether is insensibly finer and finer. Imagine now any body suspended in the air, or lying on the earth, and the aether being by the hypothesis grosser in the pores, which are in the upper parts of the body, than in those which are in its lower parts, and that grosser aether being less apt to be lodged in those pores, than the finer aether below, it will endeavour to get out and give way to the finer aether below, which cannot be without the bodies descending to make room above for it to go out into.

From this supposed gradual subtlety of the parts of aether some things above might be further illustrated, and made more intelligible, but by what has been said you will easily discern whether in these conjectures there be any degree of probability, which is all I aim at. For my own part, I have so little fancy to things of this nature that, had not your encouragement moved me to it, I should never I think have thus far set pen to paper about them. What is amiss, therefore, I hope you will the more easily pardon in

Your most humble servant and honourer,
ISAAC NEWTON

Chapter III
De Gravitatione [date unknown]

It is fitting to treat the science of the weight and of the equilibrium of fluids and solids in fluids by a twofold method. To the extent that it appertains to the mathematical sciences, it is reasonable that I largely abstract it from physical considerations. And for this reason I have undertaken to demonstrate its individual propositions from abstract principles, sufficiently well known to the student, strictly and geometrically. Since this doctrine may be judged to be somewhat akin to natural philosophy, in so far as it may be applied to making clear many of the phenomena of natural philosophy and in order, moreover, that its usefulness may be particularly apparent and the certainty of its principles perhaps confirmed, I shall not be reluctant to illustrate the propositions abundantly from experiments as well, in such a way, however, that this freer method of discussion, disposed in scholia, may not be confused with the former, which is treated in lemmas, propositions and corollaries.

The foundations from which this science may be demonstrated are either definitions of certain words, or axioms and postulates no one denies. And of these I treat directly.

Definitions

The terms 'quantity', 'duration', and 'space' are too well known to be susceptible of definition by other words.[1]

---

[1] Cf. Newton's discussion in the Scholium to the *Principia* in this volume (p. 84).

Definition 1. Place is a part of space which something fills completely.
Definition 2. Body is that which fills place.
Definition 3. Rest is remaining in the same place.
Definition 4. Motion is change of place.

Note. I said that a body fills place, that is, it so completely fills it that it wholly excludes other things of the same kind or other bodies, as if it were an impenetrable being. Place could be said, however, to be a part of space into which a thing enters completely; but as only bodies are here considered and not penetrable things, I have preferred to define [place] as the part of space that a thing fills.

Moreover, since body is here proposed for investigation not in so far as it is a physical substance endowed with sensible qualities, but only in so far as it is extended, mobile, and impenetrable, I have not defined it in a philosophical manner, but abstracting the sensible qualities (which philosophers also should abstract, unless I am mistaken, and assign to the mind as various ways of thinking excited by the motions of bodies),[2] I have postulated only the properties required for local motion. So that instead of physical bodies you may understand abstract figures in the same way that they are considered by geometers when they assign motion to them, as is done in Euclid's *Elements*, Book I, 4 and 8. And in the demonstration of the tenth definition, Book XI, this should be done, since it is mistakenly included among the definitions and ought rather to be demonstrated among the propositions, unless perhaps it should be taken as an axiom.[3]

Moreover, I have defined motion as change of place because motion, transition, translation, migration, and so forth seem to be synonymous words. If you prefer, let motion be transition or translation of a body from place to place.

---

[2] Newton refers here to the distinction between what came to be known as primary and secondary qualities, a distinction first articulated, in the modern period, by Galileo in his *Assayer* and expanded on by Boyle and Locke, among others.

[3] In Book I, proposition 4, Euclid's proof of the congruence of two triangles involves the motion of one triangle such that it achieves superposition with the other; proposition 8 similarly employs the so-called method of superposition. Definition 10 of Book XI reads as follows: "Equal and similar solid figures are those contained by similar planes equal in multitude and in magnitude" (*The Thirteen Books of Euclid's Elements*, ed. and trans. Thomas Heath (Cambridge University Press, 1926), vol. III, 261). Newton takes the familiar position that this is properly understood to be a theorem rather than a definition. Some take it to be demonstrable as a theorem through the method of superposition, which may be why Newton mentions it in tandem with the above propositions from Book I.

For the rest, when I suppose in these definitions that space is distinct from body, and when I determine that motion is with respect to the parts of that space, and not with respect to the position of neighbouring bodies, lest this should be taken as being gratuitously contrary to the Cartesians, I shall venture to dispose of his fictions.

I can summarize his doctrine in the following three propositions:

(1) That from the truth of things only one proper motion[4] fits each body (*Principles*, Part II, articles 28, 31, 32), which may be defined as being the translation of one part of matter or of one body from the vicinity of those bodies that immediately adjoin it, and which are regarded as being at rest, to the vicinity of others (*Principles*, Part II, article 25; Part III, article 28).[5]

(2) That by a body – transferred in its proper motion according to this definition – may be understood not only some particle of matter, or a body composed of parts relatively at rest, but all that is transferred simultaneously, although this may, of course, consist of many parts which have different relative motions (*Principles*, Part II, article 25).

(3) That besides this motion particular to each body there can arise in it innumerable other motions through participation (or in so far as it is part of other bodies having other motions) (*Principles*, Part II, article 31), which, however, are not motions in the philosophical sense and rationally speaking (Part III, article 29) and according to the truth of things (Part II, article 25 and Part III, article 28), but only improperly and according to common sense (Part II, articles 24, 25, 28, 31; Part III, article 29). That kind of motion he seems to describe (Part II, article 24; Part III, article 28) as the action by which any body migrates from one place to another.

---

[4] Newton refers here, and elsewhere, to Descartes's distinction in the *Principles* between the "common" (literally, "vulgar" or "loose") and the "proper" understanding of motion (Part II, articles 34–5); cf. Newton's own distinction between "mathematical" and "common" conceptions of space, time, and motion in the Scholium to the *Principia* (pp. 84–91 below).

[5] In these sections of Part II of his *Principles*, Descartes defines and discusses motion, continuing on to present his laws of nature, where he articulates, among other things, an early version of the principle of inertia. In the sections of Part III cited by Newton, Descartes claims that, properly speaking, the earth does not move, given his earlier definition of motion in the *Principles*.

And just as he formulates two types of motion, namely proper and derivative, so he assigns two types of place from which these motions proceed, and these are the surfaces of immediately surrounding bodies (Part II, article 15), and the position among any other bodies (Part II, article 13; Part III, article 29).

Indeed, not only do its absurd consequences convince us how confused and incongruous with reason this doctrine is, but Descartes seems to acknowledge the fact by contradicting himself. For he says that speaking properly and according to philosophical sense, the earth and the other planets do not move, and that he who claims they are moved because of their translation with respect to the fixed stars speaks without reason and only in the common fashion (Part III, articles 26, 27, 28, 29). Yet later he attributes to the earth and planets a tendency to recede from the sun as though from a centre about which they are moved circularly, by which they are balanced at their own distances from the sun by a similar tendency of the gyrating vortex (Part III, article 140). What, then? Is this tendency to be derived from the (according to Descartes) true and philosophical rest of the planets, or rather from [their] common and non-philosophical motion? But Descartes says further that a comet has a lesser tendency to recede from the sun when it first enters the vortex, and maintaining a position among the fixed stars does not yet obey the impetus of the vortex, but with respect to it is transferred from the vicinity of the contiguous aether and so philosophically speaking gyrates round the sun, after which the matter of the vortex carries the comet along with it and so renders it at rest, according to strict philosophical sense (Part III, articles 119–20). And so the philosopher is hardly consistent who uses as the basis of philosophy the common motion which he had rejected a little before, and now rejects that motion as fit for nothing which alone was formerly said to be true and philosophical, according to the nature of things. And since the gyrating of the comet around the sun in his philosophical sense does not cause a tendency to recede from the centre, which a gyration in the common sense can do, surely motion ought to be acknowledged in the common sense, rather than the philosophical.

Secondly, he seems to contradict himself when he postulates that to each body corresponds a strict motion, according to the nature of things; and yet he asserts that motion to be a product of our imagination, defining it as translation from the vicinity of bodies which are not at rest but only are seen to be at rest, even though they may instead be moving, as is more fully explained in Part II, articles 29–30. And by this he aims to avoid the difficulties concerning the mutual translation of bodies, namely, why one body is said to move rather than another, and why a boat on a flowing stream is said to be at rest when it does not change its position with respect to the banks (Part II, article 15). But so that the contradiction may be evident, imagine that someone sees the matter of the vortex to be at rest, and that the earth, philosophically speaking, is at rest at the same time; imagine also that at the same time someone else sees that the same matter of the vortex is moving in a circle, and that the earth, philosophically speaking, is not at rest. In the same way, a ship at sea will simultaneously move and not move; and that is so without taking motion in the looser common sense, according to which there are innumerable motions for each body, but in his philosophical sense, according to which, he says, there is but one in each body, and that one proper to it and corresponding to the nature of things and not to our imagination.

Thirdly, he seems hardly consistent when he posits a single motion that corresponds to each body according to the truth of things, and yet (Part II, article 31) posits innumerable motions that really are in each body. For the motions that really are in any body are in fact natural motions, and thus [are] motions in the philosophical sense and according to the truth of things, even though he would contend that they are motions in the common sense only. Add that when a whole thing moves, all the parts that constitute the whole and are translated together are really at rest, unless it is truly conceded that they move by participating in the motion of the whole, and then indeed they have innumerable motions according to the truth of things.

But besides this, we may see from its consequences how absurd this doctrine of Descartes is. And first, just as he pointedly contends that the earth does not move because it is not transferred from the vicinity of the contiguous aether, so from these very same principles it would follow that the internal particles of hard bodies, while they are not transferred from the vicinity of immediately contiguous particles, do not have motion in the strict sense, but move only by participating in the motion of the external particles. It rather appears that the interior parts of the external particles do not move with a proper motion because they are not transferred from the vicinity of the internal parts, and I submit that only the external surface of each body moves with a proper motion and that the whole internal substance, that is the whole body, moves through participation in the motion of the external surface. The fundamental definition of motion errs, therefore, that attributes to bodies that which is suitable only to surfaces, and which denies that there can have been a more proper motion of any body at all.

Secondly, if we regard only article 25 of Part II, each body has not merely a single proper motion but innumerable ones, provided that they are said to be moved properly and according to the truth of things by which the whole is properly moved. And that is because by the body whose motion he defines, he understands all that which is transferred simultaneously, and yet this may consist of parts having other motions among themselves: [for example] a vortex together with all the planets, or a ship along with everything in it floating on the sea, or a man walking on a ship together with the things he carries with him, or the wheel[s] of a clock together with its constituent metallic particles. For unless you say that the motion of the whole aggregate is not posited as proper motion and as belonging to the parts according to the truth of things, it will have to be admitted that all these motions of the wheels of the clock, of the man, of the ship, and of the vortex, are truly and philosophically speaking in the particles of the wheels [of the man, of the ship, and of the vortex].

From both of these consequences it appears further that no one motion can be said to be true, absolute and proper in preference to others, but that all – whether with respect to contiguous bodies or remote ones – are equally philosophical; and nothing more absurd than that can be imagined. For unless it is conceded that there can be a single physical motion of any body, and that the rest of its changes of relation and position with respect to other bodies are just external designations, it follows that the earth (for example) endeavours to recede[6] from the centre of the sun on account of a motion relative to the fixed stars, and endeavours the less to recede on account of a lesser motion relative to Saturn and the aetherial orbit in which it is carried, and still less relative

---

[6] We have translated Newton's "conatus" throughout as "endeavour" for two reasons. First, when writing in English and expressing related points, Newton himself uses "endeavour"; see, for instance, the letter to Boyle (this volume, p. 18). Second, Cohen translates it in this way in his "Guide to the *Principia*" (pp. 14–15), which is prefixed to the new standard translation of that work, from which we have reprinted excerpts here – see Note on texts and translations above.

to Jupiter and the swirling aether which occasions its orbit, and also less relative to Mars and its aetherial orbit, and much less relative to other orbits of aetherial matter which, although not bearing planets, are closer to the annual orbit of the earth; and indeed relative to its own orbit it has no endeavour, because it does not move in it. Since all these endeavours and non-endeavours cannot absolutely coincide, it is rather to be said that only the natural and the absolute motion of the earth coincide, on account of which it endeavours to recede from the sun, and because of which its translations with respect to external bodies are just external designations.

Thirdly, it follows from the Cartesian doctrine that motion can be generated where there is no force acting. For example, if God should suddenly cause the spinning of our vortex to stop, without applying any force to the earth which could stop it at the same time, Descartes would say that the earth is moving in a philosophical sense – on account of its translation from the vicinity of the contiguous fluid – whereas before he said it was at rest, in the same philosophical sense.

Fourthly, it also follows from the same doctrine that God himself could not generate motion in some bodies even though he impelled them with the greatest force. For example, if God impelled the starry heaven together with all the most remote part of creation with any very great force so as to cause it to revolve around the earth (suppose with a diurnal motion): yet by this, according to Descartes, the earth alone and not the sky would be truly said to move (Part III, article 38), as if it would be the same whether, with a tremendous force, he would cause the skies to turn from east to west, or with a small force turn the earth in the opposite direction. But who will suppose that the parts of the earth endeavour to recede from its centre on account only of a force impressed upon the heavens? Or is it not more agreeable to reason that when a force imparted to the heavens makes them endeavour to recede from the centre of the gyration thus caused, they are for that reason the sole bodies properly and absolutely moved; and that when a force impressed upon the earth makes its parts endeavour to recede from the centre of gyration thus caused, for that reason it is the sole body properly and absolutely moved, although there is the same relative motion of the bodies in both cases. And thus physical and absolute motion is to be designated by considerations other than translation, such translation being a merely external designation.

Fifthly, it seems repugnant to reason that bodies should change their relative distances and positions without physical motion; but Descartes says that the earth and the other planets and the fixed stars are properly speaking at rest, and nevertheless they change their relative positions.

Sixthly, on the other hand, it seems no less repugnant to reason that of several bodies maintaining the same relative positions one should move physically while others are at rest. But if God should cause any planet to stand still and make it continually maintain the same position with respect to the fixed stars, would not Descartes say that although the stars are not moving, the planet now moves physically on account of a translation from the matter of the vortex?

Seventhly, I ask by what reason any body is properly said to move when other bodies from whose vicinity it is transferred are not seen to be at rest, or rather when they cannot be seen to be at rest. For example, in what way can our own vortex be said to move circularly on account of the translation of matter near the circumference, from the vicinity of similar matter in other surrounding vortices, since the matter of surrounding vortices cannot be seen to be at rest, and this not only with respect to our vortex, but also in so far as those vortices are not at rest with respect to each other. For if the philosopher refers this translation not to the numerical corporeal particles of the vortices, but to the generic space (as he calls it) in which those vortices exist, at last we do agree, for he admits that motion ought to be referred to space in so far as it is distinguished from bodies.

Lastly, that the absurdity of this position may be disclosed in full measure, I say that it follows furthermore that a moving body has no determinate velocity and no definite line in which it moves. And, what is worse, that the velocity of a body moving without resistance cannot be said to be uniform, nor the line said to be straight in which its motion is accomplished. On the contrary, there can be no motion since there can be none without a certain velocity and determination.

But that this may be clear, it is first of all to be shown that when a certain motion is finished it is impossible, according to Descartes, to assign a place in which the body was at the beginning of the motion; it cannot be said from where the body moved. And the reason is that according to Descartes, the place cannot be defined or assigned except with respect to the position of the surrounding bodies, and after the completion of some motion the position of the surrounding bodies no longer stays the same as it was before. For example, if the place of the planet Jupiter a year ago were sought now, by what procedure, I ask, can the Cartesian philosopher describe it? Not by means of the positions of the particles of the fluid matter, for the positions of these particles have greatly changed since a year ago. Nor can he describe it by the positions of the sun and fixed stars, for the unequal influx of subtle matter through the poles of the vortices towards the central stars (Part III, article 104), the undulation (article 114), inflation (article 111) and absorption of the vortices, and other more true causes, such as the rotation of the sun and stars around their own centres, the generation of spots, and the passage of comets through the heavens, change both the magnitude and positions of the stars so much that they may be adequate to designate the place sought only with an error of several miles; and still less can the place be accurately described and determined by their help, as geometry would require it to be described. Truly there are no bodies in the world whose relative positions remain unchanged with the passage of time, and certainly none which do not move in the Cartesian sense: that is, which are neither transported from the vicinity of contiguous bodies, nor are parts of other bodies so translated. And thus there is no basis from which we can at the present moment designate a place which was in the past, or say that such a place is any longer discoverable in nature. For since, according to Descartes, place is nothing but the surface of surrounding bodies or position among some other more distant bodies, it is impossible (according to his doctrine) that it should exist in nature any longer than those bodies maintain the same positions from which he takes the individual designation. And so, reasoning as in the question of Jupiter's position a year ago, it is clear that if one follows Cartesian doctrine, not even God himself could define the past position of any moving body accurately and geometrically now that a fresh state of things prevails since, on account of the changed positions of the bodies, the place does not exist in nature any longer.

Now since it is impossible to pick out the place in which a motion began – that is, the beginning of the space traversed – for this place no longer exists after the motion is completed, that traversed space, having no beginning, can have no length; and since velocity depends upon the length of the space passed over in a given time, it follows that the moving body can have no velocity, just as I wished to show at first. Moreover, what was said regarding the beginning of the space passed over should be understood concerning all the intermediate places; and thus, as the space has no beginning nor intermediate parts, it follows that there was no space passed over and thus no determinate motion, which was my second point. It follows indubitably that Cartesian motion is not motion, for it has no velocity, no determination, and there is no space or distance traversed by it. So it is necessary that the definition of places, and hence of local motion, be referred to some motionless being such as extension alone or space in so far as it is seen to be truly distinct from bodies. And this the Cartesian philosopher may the more willingly allow, if only he notices that Descartes himself had an idea of extension as distinct from bodies, which he wished to distinguish from corporeal extension by calling it generic (*Principles*, Part II, articles 10, 12, 18). And also that the rotations of the vortices, from which he deduced the force of the aether in receding from their centres, and thus the whole of his mechanical philosophy, are tacitly referred to generic extension.

In addition, since Descartes in Part II, articles 4 and 11, seems to have demonstrated that body does not differ at all from extension, abstracting hardness, colour, weight, cold, heat, and the remaining qualities which body can lack, so that at last there remains only its extension in length, width, and depth, which therefore alone pertain to its essence. And as this has been taken by many as proved, and is in my view the only reason for having confidence in this opinion, and lest any doubt should remain about the nature of motion, I shall reply to this argument by saying what extension and body are, and how they differ from each other. For since the distinction of substances into thinking and extended [entities], or rather into thoughts and extensions, is the principal foundation of Cartesian philosophy, which he contends to be known more exactly than mathematical demonstrations: I consider it most important to overthrow [that philosophy] as regards extension, in order to lay truer foundations of the mechanical sciences.[7]

Perhaps now it may be expected that I should define extension as substance, or accident, or else nothing at all. But by no means, for it has its own manner of existing which is proper to it and which fits neither substances nor accidents. It is not substance: on the one hand, because it

---

[7] The distinction between thinking and extended substances is obviously crucial in Descartes's *Meditations*, which Newton read. At the beginning of this paragraph, Newton may have had the wax example from the Second Meditation in mind.

is not absolute in itself, but is as it were an emanative effect of God and an affection of every kind of being; on the other hand, because it is not among the proper affections that denote substance, namely actions, such as thoughts in the mind and motions in body. For although philosophers do not define substance as an entity that can act upon things, yet everyone tacitly understands this of substances, as follows from the fact that they would readily allow extension to be substance in the manner of body if only it were capable of motion and of sharing in the actions of body. And on the contrary, they would hardly allow that body is substance if it could not move, nor excite any sensation or perception in any mind whatsoever. Moreover, since we can clearly conceive extension existing without any subject, as when we may imagine spaces outside the world or places empty of any body whatsoever, and we believe [extension] to exist wherever we imagine there are no bodies, and we cannot believe that it would perish with the body if God should annihilate a body, it follows that [extension] does not exist as an accident inhering in some subject. And hence it is not an accident. And much less may it be said to be nothing, since it is something more than an accident, and approaches more nearly to the nature of substance. There is no idea of nothing, nor has nothing any properties, but we have an exceptionally clear idea of extension by abstracting the dispositions and properties of a body so that there remains only the uniform and unlimited stretching out of space in length, breadth and depth. And furthermore, many of its properties are associated with this idea; these I shall now enumerate not only to show that it is something, but also to show what it is.

1. In all directions, space can be distinguished into parts whose common boundaries we usually call surfaces; and these surfaces can be distinguished in all directions into parts whose common boundaries we usually call lines; and again these lines can be distinguished in all directions into parts which we call points. And hence surfaces do not have depth, nor lines breadth, nor points dimension, unless you say that coterminous spaces penetrate each other as far as the depth of the surface between them, namely what I have said to be the boundary of both or the common limit; and the same applies to lines and points. Furthermore, spaces are everywhere contiguous to spaces, and extension is everywhere placed next to extension, and so there are everywhere common boundaries of contiguous parts; that is, there are everywhere surfaces acting as boundaries to solids on this side and that; and everywhere lines in which

parts of the surfaces touch each other; and everywhere points in which the continuous parts of lines are joined together. And hence there are everywhere all kinds of figures, everywhere spheres, cubes, triangles, straight lines, everywhere circular, elliptical, parabolical, and all other kinds of figures, and those of all shapes and sizes, even though they are not disclosed to sight. For the delineation of any material figure is not a new production of that figure with respect to space, but only a corporeal representation of it, so that what was formerly insensible in space now appears before the senses. For thus we believe all those spaces to be spherical through which any sphere ever passes, being progressively moved from moment to moment, even though a sensible trace of that sphere no longer remains there. We firmly believe that the space was spherical before the sphere occupied it, so that it could contain the sphere; and hence as there are everywhere spaces that can adequately contain any material sphere, it is clear that space is everywhere spherical. And so of other figures. In the same way we see no material shapes in clear water, yet there are many in it which merely introducing some colour into its parts will cause to appear in many ways. However, if the colour were introduced, it would not constitute material shapes, but only cause them to be visible.

2. Space is extended infinitely in all directions. For we cannot imagine any limit anywhere without at the same time imagining that there is space beyond it. And hence all straight lines, paraboloids, hyperboloids, and all cones and cylinders and other figures of the same kind continue to infinity and are bounded nowhere, even though they are crossed here and there by lines and surfaces of all kinds extending transversely, and with them form segments of figures in all directions. So that you may indeed have an instance of infinity, imagine any triangle whose base and one side are at rest and the other side turns about the contiguous end of its base in the plane of the triangle so that the triangle is by degrees opened at the vertex, and meanwhile take a mental note of the point where the two sides meet, if they are produced that far: it is obvious that all these points are found on the straight line along which the fixed side lies, and that they become perpetually more distant as the moving side turns further until the two sides become parallel and can no longer meet anywhere. Now, I ask, what was the distance of the last point where the sides met? It was certainly greater than any assignable distance, or rather none of the points was the last,

and so the straight line in which all those meeting points lie is in fact greater than finite. Nor can anyone say that this is infinite only in imagination, and not in fact; for if a triangle is actually drawn, its sides are always, in fact, directed towards some common point, where both would meet if produced, and therefore there is always such an actual point where the produced sides would meet, although it may be imagined to fall outside the limits of the physical universe. And so the line traced by all these points will be real, though it extends beyond all distance.

If anyone now objects that we cannot imagine extension to be infinite, I agree. But at the same time I contend that we can understand it. We can imagine a greater extension, and then a greater one, but we understand that there exists a greater extension than any we can imagine. And here, incidentally, the faculty of understanding is clearly distinguished from imagination.

Should one say further that we do not understand what an infinite being is, save by negating the limitations of a finite being, and that this is a negative and faulty conception, I deny this. For the limit or boundary is the restriction or negation of greater reality or existence in the limited being, and the less we conceive any being to be constrained by limits, the more we observe something to be attributed to it, that is, the more positively we conceive it. And thus by negating all limits the conception becomes maximally positive. 'End' [*finis*] is a word negative with respect to perception, and thus 'infinity', since it is the negation of a negation (that is, of ends), will be a word maximally positive with respect to our perception and understanding, though it seems grammatically negative. Add [also] that positive and finite quantities of many surfaces infinite in length are accurately known to geometers. And so I can positively and accurately determine the solid quantities of many solids infinite in length and breadth and compare them to given finite solids. But this is irrelevant here.

If Descartes should now say that extension is not infinite but rather indefinite, he should be corrected by the grammarians. For the word 'indefinite' ought never to be applied to that which actually is, but always looks to a future possibility, signifying only something which is not yet determined and definite. Thus before God had decreed anything about the creation of the world (if ever he was not decreeing), the quantity of matter, the number of the stars, and all other things were indefinite; once the world was created, they were defined. Thus matter is indefinitely divisible, but is always divided either finitely or infinitely (Part I, article 26; Part II, article 34). Thus an indefinite line is one whose future length is still undetermined. And so an indefinite space is one whose future magnitude is not yet determined; for indeed that which actually is, is not to be defined, but either does or does not have boundaries and so is either finite or infinite. Nor may Descartes object that he takes space to be indefinite in relation to us; that is, we just do not know its limits and do not know positively that there are none (Part I, article 27). This is because although we are ignorant beings, God at least understands that there are no limits, not merely indefinitely but certainly and positively, and because although we negatively imagine it to transcend all limits, yet we positively and most certainly understand that it does so. But I see what Descartes feared, namely that if he should consider space infinite, it would perhaps become God because of the perfection of infinity. But by no means, for infinity is not perfection except when it is attributed to perfect things. Infinity of intellect, power, happiness, and so forth is the height of perfection; but infinity of ignorance, impotence, wretchedness, and so on is the height of imperfection; and infinity of extension is so far perfect as that which is extended.

3. The parts of space are motionless. If they moved, it would have to be said either that the motion of each part is a translation from the vicinity of other contiguous parts, as Descartes defined the motion of bodies, and it has been sufficiently demonstrated that this is absurd; or that it is a translation out of space into space, that is out of itself, unless perhaps it is said that two spaces everywhere coincide, a moving one and a motionless one. Moreover, the immobility of space will be best exemplified by duration. For just as the parts of duration are individuated by their order, so that (for example) if yesterday could change places with today and become the later of the two, it would lose its individuality and would no longer be yesterday, but today; so the parts of space are individuated by their positions, so that if any two could change their positions, they would change their individuality at the same time and each would be converted numerically into the other. The parts of duration and space are understood to be the same as they really are only because of their mutual order and position; nor do they have any principle of individuation apart from that order and position, which consequently cannot be altered.

4. Space is an affection of a being just as a being. No being exists or can exist which is not related to space in some way. God is everywhere, created minds are somewhere, and body is in the space that it occupies; and whatever is neither everywhere nor anywhere does not exist. And hence it follows that space is an emanative effect of the first existing being, for if any being whatsoever is posited, space is posited. And the same may be asserted of duration: for certainly both are affections or attributes of a being according to which the quantity of any thing's existence is individuated to the degree that the size of its presence and persistence is specified. So the quantity of the existence of God is eternal in relation to duration, and infinite in relation to the space in which he is present; and the quantity of the existence of a created thing is as great in relation to duration as the duration since the beginning of its existence, and in relation to the size of its presence, it is as great as the space in which it is present.

Moreover, lest anyone should for this reason imagine God to be like a body, extended and made of divisible parts, it should be known that spaces themselves are not actually divisible, and furthermore, that any being has a manner proper to itself of being present in spaces. For thus the relation of duration to space is very different from that of body to space. For we do not ascribe various durations to the different parts of space, but say that all endure simultaneously. The moment of duration is the same at Rome and at London, on the earth and on the stars, and throughout all the heavens. And just as we understand any moment of duration to be diffused throughout all spaces, according to its kind, without any concept of its parts, so it is no more contradictory that mind also, according to its kind, can be diffused through space without any concept of its parts.

5. The positions, distances, and local motions of bodies are to be referred to the parts of space. And this appears from the properties of space enumerated as 1 and 4 above, and will be more manifest if you conceive that there are vacuities scattered between the particles, or if you pay heed to what I have formerly said about motion. To this it may be further added that in space there is no force of any kind that might impede, assist, or in any way change the motions of bodies. And hence projectiles describe straight lines with a uniform motion unless they meet with an impediment from some other source. But more of this later.

6. Lastly, space is eternal in duration and immutable in nature because it is the emanative effect of an eternal and immutable being. If ever space had not existed, God at that time would have been nowhere; and hence he either created space later (where he was not present himself), or else, which is no less repugnant to reason, he created his own ubiquity. Next, although we can possibly imagine that there is nothing in space, yet we cannot think that space does not exist, just as we cannot think that there is no duration, even though it would be possible to suppose that nothing whatever endures. This is manifest from the spaces beyond the world, which we must suppose to exist (since we imagine the world to be finite), although they are neither revealed to us by God, nor known through perception, nor does their existence depend upon that of the spaces within the world. But it is usually believed that these spaces are nothing; yet indeed they are spaces. Although space may be empty of body, nevertheless it is not in itself a void; and something is there, because spaces are there, although nothing more than that. Yet in truth it must be acknowledged that space is no more space where the world exists, than where there is no world, unless perchance you would say that when God created the world in this space he at the same time created space in itself, or that if God should afterwards annihilate the world in this space, he would also annihilate the space in it. Whatever has more reality in one space than in another space belongs to body rather than to space; the same thing will appear more clearly if we lay aside that puerile and jejune prejudice according to which extension is inherent in bodies like an accident in a subject without which it cannot actually exist.

Now that extension has been described, it remains to give an explanation of the nature of body. Of this, however, the explanation must be more uncertain, for it does not exist necessarily but by divine will, because it is hardly given to us to know the limits of the divine power, that is to say, whether matter could be created in one way only, or whether there are several ways by which different beings similar to bodies could be produced. And although it scarcely seems credible that God could create beings similar to bodies which display all their actions and exhibit all their phenomena, and yet would not be bodies in essential and metaphysical constitution, as I have no clear and distinct perception[8]

---

[8] Here Newton has adopted Cartesian terminology familiar to his readers.

of this matter I should not dare to affirm the contrary, and hence I am reluctant to say positively what the nature of bodies is, but I would rather describe a certain kind of being similar in every way to bodies, and whose creation we cannot deny to be within the power of God, so that we can hardly say that it is not body.

Since each man is conscious that he can move his body at will, and believes further that other men enjoy the same power of similarly moving their bodies by thought alone, the free power of moving bodies at will can by no means be denied to God, whose faculty of thought is infinitely greater and more swift. And for the same reason it must be agreed that God, by the sole action of thinking and willing, can prevent a body from penetrating any space defined by certain limits.

If he should exercise this power, and cause some space projecting above the earth, like a mountain or any other body, to be impervious to bodies and thus stop or reflect light and all impinging things, it seems impossible that we should not consider this space really to be a body from the evidence of our senses (which constitute our sole judges in this matter); for it ought to be regarded as tangible on account of its impenetrability, and visible, opaque, and coloured on account of the reflection of light, and it will resonate when struck because the adjacent air will be moved by the blow.

Thus we may suppose that there are empty spaces scattered through the world, one of which, defined by certain limits, happens by divine power to be impervious to bodies, and by hypothesis it is manifest that this would resist the motions of bodies and perhaps reflect them, and assume all the properties of a corporeal particle, except that it will be regarded as motionless. If we should suppose that that impenetrability is not always maintained in the same part of space but can be transferred here and there according to certain laws, yet so that the quantity and shape of that impenetrable space are not changed, there will be no property of body which it does not possess. It would have shape, be tangible and mobile, and be capable of reflecting and being reflected, and constitute no less a part of the structure of things than any other corpuscle, and I do not see why it would not equally operate upon our minds and in turn be operated upon, because it would be nothing other than the effect of the divine mind produced in a definite quantity of space. For it is certain that God can stimulate our perception by means of his own will, and thence apply such power to the effects of his will.

In the same way, if several spaces of this kind should be impervious to bodies and to each other, they would all sustain the vicissitudes of corpuscles and exhibit the same phenomena. And so if all of this world were constituted out of these beings, it would hardly seem to be inhabited differently. And hence these beings will either be bodies, or very similar to bodies. If they are bodies, then we can define bodies as *determined quantities of extension which omnipresent God endows with certain conditions.* These conditions are: (1) that they be mobile, and therefore I did not say that they are numerical parts of space which are absolutely immobile, but only definite quantities which may be transferred from space to space; (2) that two of this kind cannot coincide anywhere, that is, that they may be impenetrable, and hence that oppositions obstruct their mutual motions and they are reflected in accord with certain laws; (3) that they can excite various perceptions of the senses and the imagination in created minds, and conversely be moved by them, which is not surprising since the description of their origin is founded on this.

Moreover, it will help to note the following points concerning the matters already explained.

1. That for the existence of these beings it is not necessary that we suppose some unintelligible substance to exist in which as subject there may be an inherent substantial form; extension and an act of the divine will are enough. Extension takes the place of the substantial subject in which the form of the body is conserved by the divine will; and that product of the divine will is the form or formal reason of the body denoting every dimension of space in which the body is to be produced.

2. These beings will not be less real than bodies, nor (I say) are they less able to be called substances. For whatever reality we believe to be present in bodies is conferred on account of their phenomena and sensible qualities. And hence we would judge these beings, since they can receive all qualities of this kind and can similarly exhibit all these phenomena, to be no less real, if they should exist in this manner. Nor will they be any less than substances, since they will likewise subsist and acquire accidents through God alone.

3. Between extension and its impressed form there is almost the same analogy that the Aristotelians posit between prime matter and substantial forms, namely when they say that the same matter is capable of assuming all forms, and borrows the denomination of numerical body from its

form.[9] For so I posit that any form may be transferred through any space, and everywhere denote the same body.

4. They differ, however, in that extension (since it [involves] 'what' and 'how constituted' and 'how much') has more reality than prime matter, and also in that it can be understood in the same way as the form that I assigned to bodies. For if there is any difficulty in this conception it is not in the form that God imparts to space, but in the manner by which he imparts it. But that is not to be regarded as a difficulty, since the same question arises with regard to the way we move our bodies, and nevertheless we do believe that we can move them. If that were known to us, by like reasoning we should also know how God can move bodies, and expel them from a certain space bounded in a given figure, and prevent the expelled bodies or any others from being able to enter it again, that is, cause that space to be impenetrable and assume the form of body.

5. Thus I have deduced a description of this corporeal nature from our faculty of moving our bodies, so that all the difficulties of the conception may at length be reduced to that; and further, so that God may appear (to our innermost consciousness) to have created the world solely by the act of will, just as we move our bodies by an act of will alone; and, moreover, so that I might show that the analogy between the divine faculties and our own may be shown to be greater than has formerly been perceived by philosophers. That we were created in God's image, holy writ testifies. And his image would shine more clearly in us if only he simulated in the faculties granted to us the power of creation in the same degree as his other attributes; nor is it an objection that we ourselves are created beings and so a share of this attribute could not have been equally granted to us. For if for this reason the power of creating minds is not delineated in any faculty of created mind, nevertheless created mind (since it is the image of God) is of a far more noble nature than body, so that perhaps it may eminently contain [body] in itself. Moreover, in moving bodies we create nothing, nor can we create anything, but we only simulate the power of creation. For we cannot

---

[9] A doctrine of so-called prime matter, according to which a type of "formless" matter would underlie various fundamental kinds of change that bodies, or elements, can undergo, is sometimes attributed to Aristotle. The attribution remains controversial: see *Physics* (190b and 193a), and *Generation and Corruption* (332a).

make any space impervious to bodies, but we only move bodies; and at that not any we choose, but only our own bodies, to which we are united not by our own will, but by divine constitution; nor can we move bodies in any way but only in accord with those laws which God has imposed on us. If anyone, however, prefers this our power to be called the finite and lowest level of the power which makes God the creator, this no more detracts from the divine power than it detracts from his intellect that intellect belongs to us in a finite degree, particularly since we do not move our bodies by a proper and independent power but by laws imposed on us by God. Rather, if anyone should think it possible that God may produce some intellectual creature so perfect that it could, by divine accord, in turn produce creatures of a lower order, this I submit does not detract from the divine power, it posits an infinitely greater power, by which creatures would be brought forth not only directly but by other intermediate creatures. And so some may perhaps prefer to posit a soul of the world created by God, upon which he imposes the law that definite spaces are endowed with corporeal properties, rather than to believe that this function is directly discharged by God. To be sure, the world should not be called the creature of that soul but of God alone, who creates it by constituting the soul of such a nature that the world necessarily emanates [from it]. But I do not see why God himself does not directly inform space with bodies, so long as we distinguish between the formal reason of bodies and the act of divine will. For it is contradictory that it [body] should be the act of willing or anything other than the effect which that act produces in space, which effect does not even differ less from that act than Cartesian space, or the substance of body according to the common concept; if only we suppose that they are created, that is, that they borrow existence from the will, or that they are beings of the divine reason.

Lastly, the usefulness of the idea of body that I have described is brought out by the fact that it clearly involves the principal truths of metaphysics and thoroughly confirms and explains them. For we cannot posit bodies of this kind without at the same time positing that God exists, and has created bodies in empty space out of nothing, and that they are beings distinct from created minds, but able to be united with minds. Say, if you can, which of the views, now common, elucidates any one of these truths or rather is not opposed to all of them, and leads to obscurity. If we say with Descartes that extension is body, do we not manifestly offer a path to atheism, both because extension is not created but has existed eternally, and because we have an idea of it without any relation to God, and so in some circumstances it would be possible for us to conceive of extension while supposing God not to exist? Nor is the distinction between mind and body in his philosophy intelligible, unless at the same time we say that mind has no extension at all, and so is not substantially present in any extension, that is, exists nowhere; which seems the same as if we were to say that it does not exist, or at least renders its union with body thoroughly unintelligible and impossible. Moreover, if the distinction of substances between thinking and extended is legitimate and complete, God does not eminently contain extension within himself and therefore cannot create it; but God and extension would be two separate, complete, absolute substances, and in the same sense. But on the contrary if extension is eminently contained in God, or the highest thinking being, certainly the idea of extension will be eminently contained within the idea of thinking, and hence the distinction between these ideas will not be such that both may fit the same created substance, that is, but that a body may think, and a thinking being be extended. But if we adopt the common idea (or rather lack of it) of body, according to which there resides in bodies some unintelligible reality that they call substance, in which all the qualities of the bodies are inherent, this (apart from its unintelligibility) is exposed to the same problems as the Cartesian view. Since it cannot be understood, it is impossible that its distinction from the substance of the mind should be understood. For the distinction drawn from substantial form or the attributes of substances is not enough: if bare substances do not have an essential difference, the same substantial forms or attributes can fit both, and render them by turns, if not at one and the same time, mind and body. And so if we do not understand that difference of substances deprived of attributes, we cannot knowingly assert that mind and body differ substantially. Or if they do differ, we cannot discover any basis for their union. Further, they attribute no less reality in concept (though less in words) to this corporeal substance regarded as being without qualities and forms, than they do to the substance of God, abstracted from his attributes. They conceive of both, when considered simply, in the same way; or rather they do not conceive of them, but confound them in some common apprehension of an unintelligible reality. And hence it is not surprising that atheists arise ascribing to corporeal substances that which solely belongs to the divine. Indeed, however we cast about we find almost no other reason for atheism than this notion of bodies having, as it were, a complete, absolute, and independent reality in themselves, such as almost all of us, through negligence, are accustomed to have in our minds from childhood (unless I am mistaken), so that it is only verbally that we call bodies created and dependent. And I believe that this prejudice explains why the same word, substance, is applied univocally in the schools to God and his creatures, and what philosophers, in forming the idea of body, cling to and ramble on about, when they try to form an independent idea of a thing dependent upon God. For certainly whatever cannot exist independently of God cannot be truly understood independently of the idea of God. God does not sustain his creatures any less than they sustain their accidents, so that created substance, whether you consider its degree of dependence or its degree of reality, is of an intermediate nature between God and accident. And hence the idea of it no less involves the concept of God, than the idea of accident involves the concept of created substance. And so it ought to embrace no other reality in itself than a derivative and incomplete reality. Thus the prejudice just mentioned must be laid aside, and substantial reality is to be ascribed to these kinds of attributes, which are real and intelligible things in themselves and do not need to be inherent in a subject, rather than to the subject which we cannot conceive as dependent, much less form any idea of it. And this we can manage without difficulty if (besides the idea of body expounded above) we reflect that we can conceive of space existing without any subject when we think of a vacuum. And hence some substantial reality fits this. But if, moreover, the mobility of the parts (as Descartes supposed) should be involved in the idea of vacuum, everyone would freely concede that it is corporeal substance. In the same way, if we should have an idea of that attribute or power by which God, through the action of his will alone, can create beings, we should readily conceive of that attribute as subsisting by itself without any substantial subject and [thus as] involving the rest of his attributes. But while we cannot form an idea of this attribute, nor even of our proper power by which we move our bodies, it would be rash to say what may be the substantial basis of mind.

So much for the nature of bodies, which in explicating I judge that I have sufficiently proved that such a creation as I have expounded is most clearly the work of God, and that if this world were not constituted from that creation, at least another very like it could be constituted. And since there is no difference between the materials as regards their properties and nature, but only in the method by which God created one and the other, the distinction between body and extension is certainly brought to light from this. For extension is eternal, infinite, uncreated, uniform throughout, not in the least mobile, nor capable of inducing change of motion in bodies or change of thought in the mind; whereas body is opposite in every respect, at least if God did not please to create it always and everywhere. For I should not dare to deny God that power. And if anyone thinks otherwise, let him say where he could have created prime matter, and whence the power of creating was granted to God. Or if there was no beginning to that power, but he had the same eternally that he has now, then he could have created from eternity. For it is the same to say that there never was in God an impotence to create, or that he always had the power to create and could have created, and that he could always create matter. In the same way, either a space may be assigned in which matter could not be created from the beginning, or it must be conceded that God could have created it everywhere.

Moreover, so that I may respond more concisely to Descartes's argument: let us abstract from body (as he demands) gravity, hardness, and all sensible qualities, so that nothing remains except what pertains to its essence. Will extension alone then remain? By no means. For we may also reject that faculty or power by which they [the qualities] stimulate the perceptions of thinking things. For since there is so great a distinction between the ideas of thought and of extension that it is not obvious that there is any basis of connection or relation [between them], except that which is caused by divine power, the above capacity of bodies can be rejected while preserving extension, but not while preserving their corporeal nature. Clearly the changes which can be induced in bodies by natural causes are only accidental and they do not denote that substance is really changed. But if any change is induced that transcends natural causes, it is more than accidental and radically affects the substance. And according to the sense of the demonstration, only those things are to be rejected which bodies can be deprived of, and made to lack, by the force of nature. But should anyone object that bodies not united to minds cannot directly arouse perceptions in minds, and that since there are bodies not united to minds, it follows that this power is not essential to them, it should be noticed that there is no suggestion here of an actual union, but only of a capacity of bodies by which they are capable of such a union through the forces of nature. From the fact that the parts of the brain, especially the more subtle ones to which the mind is united, are in a continual flux, new ones succeeding those which fly away, it is manifest that that capacity is in all bodies. And whether you consider divine action or corporeal nature, to remove this is no less than to remove that other faculty by which bodies are enabled to transfer mutual actions from one to another, that is, to reduce body into empty space.

However, as water offers less resistance to the motion of solid bodies passing through it than quicksilver does, and air much less than water, and aetherial spaces even less than air-filled ones, if we set aside altogether every force of resistance to the passage of bodies, we must also set aside the corporeal nature [of the medium] utterly and completely. In the same way, if the subtle matter were deprived of all forces of resistance to the motion of globules, I should no longer believe it to be subtle matter but a scattered vacuum. And so if there were any aerial or aetherial space of such a kind that it yielded without any resistance to the motions of comets or any other projectiles, I should believe that it was utterly empty. For it is impossible that a corporeal fluid should not impede the motion of bodies passing through it, assuming that (as I supposed before) it is not disposed to move at the same speed as the body.[10]

However, it is manifest that every force can be removed from space only if space and body differ from one another; and hence that each can be removed is not to be denied before it has been proved that they do not differ, lest an error be let in by begging the question.

But lest any doubt remain, it should be observed from what was said earlier that there are empty spaces in nature. For if the aether were a corporeal fluid entirely without vacuous pores, however subtle its parts are made by division, it would be as dense as any other fluid, and it

---

[10] Part II, Epistle 96 to Mersenne. (Editor's note: Newton probably means Descartes's letter to Mersenne of 9 January 1639, in which Descartes discusses the motion of bodies through various kinds of media. The original letter is available in *Oeuvres de Descartes*, ed. Charles Adam and Paul Tannery (Paris: Vrin, 1996), vol. II: 479–92, and is partially translated in *The Philosophical Writings of Descartes*, ed. John Cottingham et al. (Cambridge University Press, 1991), vol. III, 131–3. Thanks to Alan Gabbey for this reference.)

would yield to the motion of passing bodies with no less inertia; indeed with a much greater inertia if the projectile were porous, because then the aether would enter its internal pores, and encounter and resist not only the whole of its external surface, but also the surfaces of all the internal parts. Since the resistance of the aether is on the contrary so small when compared with the resistance of quicksilver as to be over ten or a hundred thousand times less, there is all the more reason for thinking that by far the largest part of the aetherial space is empty, scattered between the aetherial particles. The same may also be conjectured from the various gravities of these fluids, for the descent of heavy bodies and the oscillations of pendulums show that these are in proportion to their densities, or as the quantities of matter contained in equal spaces. But this is not the place to go into this.

Thus you see how fallacious and unsound this Cartesian argumentation is, for when the accidents of bodies have been rejected, there remains not extension alone, as he supposed, but also the capacities by which they can stimulate perceptions in the mind by means of various bodies. If we further reject these capacities and every power of moving, so that there only remains a precise conception of uniform space, will Descartes fabricate any vortices, any world, from this extension? Surely not, unless he first invokes God, who alone can generate new bodies in those spaces (or by restoring those capacities to the corporeal nature, as I explained above). And so in what has gone before I was correct in assigning the corporeal nature to the capacities already enumerated.

And so finally, since spaces are not the very bodies themselves, but are only the places in which bodies exist and move, I think that what I laid down concerning local motion is sufficiently confirmed. Nor do I see what more could be desired in this matter, unless perhaps I warn those for whom this is not satisfactory that by the space whose parts I have defined as places filled by bodies, they should understand the Cartesian generic space in which spaces regarded singularly, or Cartesian bodies, are moved, and so they will find hardly anything to object to in our definitions.

I have already digressed enough; let us return to the main theme.

Definition 5. Force is the causal principle of motion and rest. And it is either an external one that generates, destroys, or otherwise changes impressed motion in some body, or it is an internal principle by which existing motion or rest is conserved in a body, and by which any being endeavours to continue in its state and opposes resistance.

Definition 6 *Conatus* [endeavour] is resisted force, or force in so far as it is resisted.

Definition 7. *Impetus* is force in so far as it is impressed on a thing.

Definition 8. *Inertia* is the inner force of a body, lest its state should be easily changed by an external exciting force.

Definition 9. Pressure is the endeavour [conatus] of contiguous parts to penetrate into each other's dimensions. For if they could penetrate [each other] the pressure would cease. And pressure is only between contiguous parts, which in turn press upon others contiguous to them, until the pressure is transferred to the most remote parts of any body, whether hard, soft, or fluid. And upon this action is based the communication of motion by means of a point or surface of contact.

Definition 10. Gravity is the force in a body impelling it to descend. Here, however, by descent is not only meant a motion towards the centre of the earth, but also towards any point or region, or even from any point. In this way if the endeavour [conatus] of the aether gyrating about the sun to recede from its centre be taken for gravity, in receding from the sun the aether could be said to descend. And so by analogy, that plane should be called horizontal that is directly opposed to the direction of gravity or conatus. Moreover, the quantity of these powers, namely motion, force, conatus, impetus, inertia, pressure, and gravity, may be reckoned by a twofold account: that is, according to either its intension or extension.

Definition 11. The intension of any of the above mentioned powers is the degree of its quality.

Definition 12. Its extension is the quantity of space or time in which it operates.

Definition 13. Its absolute quantity is the product of its intension and its extension. So, if the quantity of the intension is 2, and the quantity of the extension 3, multiply the two together and you will have the absolute quantity 6.

Moreover, it will be helpful to illustrate these definitions via individual powers. And thus motion is either more intense or more remiss, as the space traversed in the same time is greater or less, for which reason a body is usually said to move more swiftly or more slowly. Again, motion is more or less extended as the body moved is greater or less, or as it is diffused through a larger or smaller body. And the absolute quantity of motion is composed of both the velocity and the magnitude of the moving body. So force, conatus, impetus, or inertia are more intense as they are greater in the same or an equivalent body: they are more extensive when the body is larger, and their absolute quantity arises from both. So the intension of pressure is proportional to the increase of pressure upon the surface area; its extension proportional to the surface pressed. And the absolute quantity results from the intension of the pressure and the quantity of the surface pressed. So, lastly, the intension of gravity is proportional to the specific gravity of the body; its extension is proportional to the size of the heavy body, and absolutely speaking the quantity of gravity is the product of the specific gravity and mass of the gravitating body. And whoever fails to distinguish these clearly, necessarily falls into many errors concerning the mechanical sciences.

In addition, the quantity of these powers may sometimes be reckoned according to the period of duration; for which reason there will be an absolute quantity which will be the product of intension, extension, and duration. In this way, if a body [of size] 2 is moved with a velocity 3 for a time 4, the whole motion will be $2 \times 3 \times 4$ or 24.[11]

Definition 14. Velocity is the intension of motion, slowness is remission.
Definition 15. Bodies are denser when their inertia is more intense, and rarer when it is more remiss.

The rest of the above mentioned powers have no names. It is, however, to be noted that if, with Descartes or Epicurus, we suppose rarefaction and condensation to be accomplished in the manner of relaxed or compressed sponges, that is, by the dilation and contraction of pores which are either filled with, or empty of, some very subtle matter, then we ought to estimate the size of the whole body from the quantity of both its parts and its pores as in Definition 15; so that one may consider inertia to be remitted by the increase of the pores and intensified by their diminution, as though the pores, which offer no inertial resistance to change, and whose mixtures with the truly corporeal parts give rise to all the various degrees of inertia, bear some ratio to the parts.

But in order that you may conceive of this composite body as a uniform one, suppose its parts to be infinitely divided and dispersed everywhere throughout the pores, so that in the whole composite body there is not the least particle of extension without an absolutely perfect mixture of infinitely divided parts and pores. Certainly such reasoning is suitable for contemplation by mathematicians; or if you prefer the manner of the peripatetics: things seem to be captured differently in physics.

---

[11] The original manuscript erroneously has "12" in place of "24."

Definition 16. An elastic body is one that can be condensed by the force of pressure or compressed within the limits of a narrower space; and a nonelastic body is one that cannot be condensed by that force.

Definition 17. A hard body is one whose parts do not yield to pressure.

Definition 18. A fluid body is one whose parts yield to an overwhelming pressure. Moreover, the pressures by which the fluid is driven in any direction whatsoever (whether these are exerted merely on the external surface, or on the internal parts by the action of gravity or any other cause), are said to be balanced when the fluid rests in equilibrium. This situation obtains if the pressure is exerted in some one direction and not towards all directions at once.

Definition 19. The limits defining the surface of the body (such as wood or glass) containing the fluid, or defining the surface of the external part of the same fluid containing some internal part, constitute the vessel of fluid.

In these definitions, however, I refer only to absolutely hard or fluid bodies, for one cannot reason mathematically concerning bodies that are partially so, on account of the innumerable figures, motions, and connections of the least particles. Thus I suppose that a fluid does not consist of hard particles, but that it is of such a kind that it has no small portion or particle which is not likewise fluid. And moreover, since the physical cause of fluidity is not to be examined here, I define the parts, not as being in motion among themselves, but only as capable of motion, that is, as being everywhere so divided one from another that, although they may be supposed to be in contact and at rest with respect to one another, yet they do not cohere as though stuck together, but can be moved separately by any impressed force and can change the state of rest as easily as the state of motion if they move relatively. Indeed, I suppose that the parts of hard bodies do not merely touch each other and remain at relative rest, but that they also so strongly and firmly cohere, and are so bound together – as it were by glue – that no one of them can be moved without all the rest being drawn along with it; or rather that a hard body is not made up of conglomerate parts, but is a single undivided and uniform body which preserves its shape most resolutely, whereas a fluid body is uniformly divided at all points.

And thus I have accommodated these definitions not to physical things but to mathematical reasoning, after the manner of the geometers who do not accommodate their definitions of figures to the irregularities of physical bodies. And just as the dimensions of physical bodies are best determined by their geometry – as with the dimension of a field by plane geometry, although a field is not a true plane; and the dimension of the earth by the doctrine of the sphere, even though the earth is not precisely spherical – so the properties of physical fluids and solids are best known from this mathematical doctrine, even though they are not perhaps absolutely nor uniformly fluid or solid as I have defined them here.

Axioms

1. From like postulates like consequences ensue.
2. Bodies in contact press one another equally.

Propositions on non-elastic fluids

Prop. 1. All the parts of a non-gravitating fluid, compressed with the same intension in all directions, press each other equally (or with equal intension).

Prop. 2. And compression does not cause motion between the parts.

Demonstration of both

Let us first suppose that the fluid is contained and uniformly compressed by the spherical boundary *AB* whose centre is *K* (Figure 3.1). Any small portion of it *CGEH* is bounded by the two spherical surfaces *CD* and *EF* described about the same centre *K* and by the conical surface *GKH* whose vertex is at *K*. And it is manifest that *CGEH* cannot in any way approach the centre *K* because all the matter between the spherical surfaces *CD* and *EF* would everywhere approach the same centre for the same reason,[12] and so would penetrate the volume of the fluid contained within the sphere *EF*.[13] Nor can *CGEH* recede in any direction towards the circumference *AB* because all that shell of fluid between *CD* and *EF* would similarly recede for the same reason,[14] and so would penetrate the volume of fluid between the spherical surfaces *AB* and *CD*.[15] Nor can it be squeezed out sideways, say towards *H*, since if we imagine another little section Hγ, terminated in every direction by the same spherical surfaces and a similar conical surface and contiguous to *GH* at *H*, this

---

[12] Axiom 1.   [13] Contrary to the definition.   [14] Axiom 1.
[15] Contrary to the definition.

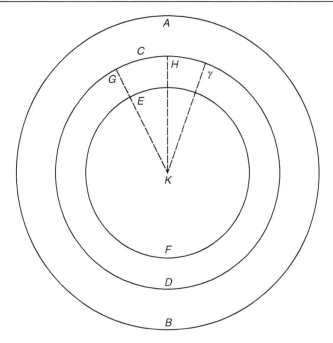

Figure 3.1

section Hγ may for the same reason be squeezed out towards H,[16] and so effect a penetration of volume by the mutual approach of contiguous parts.[17] And so it is that no portion of fluid CGEH can exceed its limits because of pressure. And hence all the parts remain in equilibrium. Which is what I wished to demonstrate first.

I saw also that all parts press each other equally, and with the same intension of pressure that the external surface is pressed. To show this, imagine that *PSQR* is a part of the said fluid *AB* contained by similar spherical segments *PRQ* and *PSQ*, and that its compression upon the internal surface *PSQ* is as great as that upon the external surface *PRQ* (Figure 3.2). For I have already shown that this part of the fluid remains in equilibrium, and so the effects of the pressures acting on both of its surfaces are equal, and hence the pressures are equal.[18,19]

---

[16] Axiom 1.   [17] Contrary to the definition.
[18] Axiom.   [19] Definition.

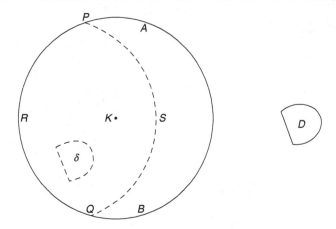

Figure 3.2

And thus since spherical surfaces such as *PSQ* can be described anywhere in the fluid *AB*, and can touch any other given surfaces in any points whatever, it follows that the intension of the pressure of the parts along the surfaces, wherever placed, is as great as the pressure on the external surface of the fluid. Which is the second point I wished to demonstrate.

Moreover, as the force of this argument is based on the equality of the surfaces *PRQ* and *PSQ*, lest it should seem that there is some disparity, in that one is within the fluid and the other is a segment of the external surface, it will help to imagine that the whole sphere *AB* is a part of an indefinitely larger volume of fluid, in which it is contained as within a vessel, and is everywhere compressed just as its part *PRQS* is pressed upon the surface *PSQ* by another part *PABQS*. For the method by which the sphere *AB* is compressed is of no significance, so long as its compression is supposed to be equal everywhere.

Now that these things have been demonstrated for a fluid sphere, I say lastly that all the parts of the fluid *D* (bounded in any manner at all, and compressed with the same intension in all directions) press each other equally and are not made to move relatively by the compression. For let *AB* be an indefinitely greater fluid sphere compressed with the same degree of intension; and let δ be some part of it equal and similar to *D*. From what has already been demonstrated it follows that this part δ is compressed with an equal intension in all directions and that the intension of the pressure is the same as that of the sphere AB, that is (by hypothesis) as that which compressed the fluid D. Thus the compression of the similar and equal fluids, D and δ, is equal; and hence the effects will be equal.[20] But all the parts of the sphere AB[21] and so of the fluid δ contained in it, press each other equally, and the pressure does not cause a relative motion of the parts. For which reason the same is true of the fluid D.[22] Q.E.D.

Corollary 1. The internal parts of a fluid press each other with the same intension as that by which the fluid is pressed on its external surface.

Corollary 2. If the intension of the pressure is not everywhere the same, the fluid does not remain in equilibrium. For since it stays in equilibrium because the pressure is everywhere uniform, if the pressure is anywhere increased, it will predominate there and cause the fluid to recede from that region.[23]

Corollary 3. If no motion is caused in a fluid by pressure, the intension of the pressure is everywhere the same. Since if it is not the same, motion will be caused by the predominant pressure.[24]

Corollary 4. A fluid presses on whatever bounds it with the same intension as the fluid is pressed by whatever bounds it, and vice versa. Since the parts of a fluid are certainly the bounds of contiguous parts and press each other with an equal intension, conceive the aforesaid fluid to be part of a greater fluid, or similar and equal to such a part, and similarly compressed, and the assertion will be evident.[25]

Corollary 5. A fluid everywhere presses all its bounds, if they are capable of withstanding the pressure applied, with that intension with which it is itself pressed in any place. For otherwise it would not be pressed everywhere with the same intension.[26] On which assumption it yields to the more intense pressure.[27] And so it will either be condensed or it will break through the bounds where the pressure is less.[28]

---

[20] Axiom.   [21] According to what has been demonstrated.
[22] Axiom.   [23] Definition.   [24] Corollary 2.   [25] Axiom.   [26] Corollary 4.
[27] Corollary 2.   [28] Contrary to the hypothesis.

Scholium

I have proposed all this about fluids, not as contained in hard and rigid vessels, but within soft and quite flexible bounds (say within the internal surface of a homogeneous exterior fluid), so that I might more clearly show that their equilibrium is caused only by an equal degree of pressure in all directions. But once a fluid is put into equilibrium by an equal pressure, it is equal whether you imagine it to be contained within rigid or yielding bounds.

Chapter IV
The *Principia* [1687, first edition]
Author's Preface to the Reader, First Edition

Since the ancients (according to Pappus) considered *mechanics* to be of the greatest importance in the investigation of nature and science and since the moderns – rejecting substantial forms and occult qualities – have undertaken to reduce the phenomena of nature to mathematical laws, it has seemed best in this treatise to concentrate on *mathematics* as it relates to natural philosophy. The ancients divided *mechanics* into two parts: the *rational*, which proceeds rigorously through demonstrations, and the *practical*. *Practical mechanics* is the subject that comprises all the manual arts, from which the subject of *mechanics* as a whole has adopted its name. But since those who practise an art do not generally work with a high degree of exactness, the whole subject of *mechanics* is distinguished from *geometry* by the attribution of exactness to *geometry* and of anything less than exactness to *mechanics*. Yet the errors do not come from the art but from those who practise the art. Anyone who works with less exactness is a more imperfect mechanic, and if anyone could work with the greatest exactness, he would be the most perfect mechanic of all. For the description of straight lines and circles, which is the foundation of *geometry*, appertains to *mechanics*. *Geometry* does not teach how to describe these straight lines and circles, but postulates such a description. For *geometry* postulates that a beginner has learned to describe lines and circles exactly before he approaches the threshold of *geometry*, and then it teaches how problems are solved by these operations. To describe straight lines and to describe circles are problems, but not problems in *geometry*. *Geometry* postulates the solution of these problems from *mechanics* and teaches the use of the problems thus solved. And *geometry* can boast that with so few principles obtained from other fields, it can do so much. Therefore *geometry* is founded on mechanical practice and is nothing other than that part of *universal mechanics* which reduces the art of measuring to exact propositions and demonstrations. But since the manual arts are applied especially to making bodies move, *geometry* is commonly used in reference to magnitude, and *mechanics* in reference to motion. In this sense *rational mechanics* will be the science, expressed in exact propositions and demonstrations, of the motions that result from any forces whatever and of the forces that are required for any motions whatever. The ancients studied this part of *mechanics* in terms of the *five powers* that relate to the manual arts [i.e. the five mechanical powers] and paid hardly any attention to gravity (since it is not a manual power) except in the moving of weights by these powers. But since we are concerned with natural philosophy rather than manual arts, and are writing about natural rather than manual powers, we concentrate on aspects of gravity, levity, elastic forces, resistance of fluids, and forces of this sort, whether attractive or impulsive. And therefore our present work sets forth mathematical principles of natural philosophy. For the basic problem of philosophy seems to be to discover the forces of nature from the phenomena of motions and then to demonstrate the other phenomena from these forces. It is to these ends that the general propositions in books 1 and 2 are directed, while in book 3 our explanation of the system of the world illustrates these propositions. For in book 3, by means of propositions demonstrated mathematically in books 1 and 2, we derive from celestial phenomena the gravitational forces by which bodies tend towards the sun and towards the individual planets. Then the motions of the planets, the comets, the moon, and the sea are deduced from these forces by propositions that are also mathematical. If only we could derive the other phenomena of nature from mechanical principles by the same kind of reasoning! For many things lead me to have a suspicion that all phenomena may depend on certain forces by which the particles of bodies, by causes not yet known, either are impelled towards one another and cohere in regular figures, or are repelled from one another and recede. Since these forces are unknown, philosophers have hitherto made trial of nature in vain. But I hope that the principles set down here will shed some light on either this mode of philosophizing or some truer one.

In the publication of this work, Edmond Halley, a man of the greatest intelligence and of universal learning, was of tremendous assistance; not only did he correct the typographical errors and see to the making of the woodcuts, but it was he who started me off on the road to this publication. For when he had obtained my demonstration of the shape of the celestial orbits, he never stopped asking me to communicate it to the Royal Society, whose subsequent encouragement and kind patronage made me begin to think about publishing it. But after I began to work on the inequalities of the motions of the moon, and then also began to explore other aspects of the laws and measures of gravity and of other forces, the curves that must be described by bodies attracted according to any given laws, the motions of several bodies with respect to one another, the motions of bodies in resisting mediums, the forces and densities and motions of mediums, the orbits of comets, and so forth, I thought that publication should be put off to another time, so that I might investigate these other things and publish all my results together. I have grouped them together in the corollaries of proposition 66 the inquiries (which are imperfect) into lunar motions, so that I might not have to deal with these things one by one in propositions and demonstrations, using a method more prolix than the subject warrants, which would have interrupted the sequence of the remaining propositions. There are a number of things that I found afterwards which I preferred to insert in less suitable places rather than to change the numbering of the propositions and the cross-references. I earnestly ask that everything be read with an open mind and that the defects in a subject so difficult may be not so much reprehended as investigated, and kindly supplemented, by new endeavours of my readers.

Trinity College, Cambridge   Is. Newton
8 May 1686

Editor's Preface, Second Edition (1713)

THE LONG-AWAITED NEW EDITION of Newton's *Principles of Natural Philosophy* is presented to you, kind reader, with many corrections and additions. The main topics of this celebrated work are listed in the table of contents and the index prepared for this edition. The major additions or changes are indicated in the author's preface. Now something must be said about the method of this philosophy.

Those who have undertaken the study of natural science can be divided into roughly three classes. There have been those who have endowed the individual species of things with specific occult qualities, on which – they have then alleged – the operations of individual bodies depend in some unknown way. The whole of Scholastic doctrine derived from Aristotle and the Peripatetics is based on this. Although they affirm that individual effects arise from the specific natures of bodies, they do not tell us the causes of those natures, and therefore they tell us nothing. And since they are wholly concerned with the names of things rather than with the things themselves, they must be regarded as inventors of what might be called philosophical jargon, rather than as teachers of philosophy.

Therefore, others have hoped to gain praise for greater carefulness by rejecting this useless hodgepodge of words. And so they have held that all matter is homogeneous, and that the variety of forms that is discerned in bodies all arises from certain very simple and easily comprehensible attributes of the component particles. And indeed they are right to set up a progression from simpler things to more compounded ones, so long as they do not give those primary attributes of the particles any character-istics other than those given by nature itself. But when they take the liberty of imagining that the unknown shapes and sizes of the particles are whatever they please, and of assuming their uncertain positions and motions, and even further of feigning certain occult fluids that permeate the pores of bodies very freely, since they are endowed with an omnipo-tent subtlety and are acted on by occult motions: when they do this, they are drifting off into dreams, ignoring the true constitution of things, which is obviously to be sought in vain from false conjectures, when it can scarcely be found out even by the most certain observations. Those who take the foundation of their speculations from hypotheses, even if they then proceed most rigorously according to mechanical laws, are merely putting together a romance [i.e. fiction], elegant perhaps and charming, but nevertheless a romance.

There remains then the third type, namely, those whose natural philosophy is based on experiment. Although they too hold that the causes of all things are to be derived from the simplest possible principles, they assume nothing as a principle that has not yet been thoroughly proved from phenomena. They do not contrive hypotheses, nor do they admit them into natural science otherwise than as questions whose truth may be discussed. Therefore they proceed by a twofold method, analytic and synthetic. From certain selected phenomena they deduce by analysis the forces of nature and the simpler laws of those forces, from which they then give the constitution of the rest of the phenomena by synthesis. This is that incomparably best way of philosophizing which our most celebrated author thought should be justly embraced in preference to all others. This alone he judged worthy of being cultivated and enriched by the expenditure of his labour. Of this therefore he has given a most illustrious example, namely, the explication of the system of the world most successfully deduced from the theory of gravity. That the force of gravity is in all bodies universally, others have suspected or imagined; Newton was the first and only one who was able to demonstrate it from phenomena and to make it a solid foundation for his brilliant theories.

I know indeed that some men, even of great reputation, unduly influenced by certain prejudices, have found it difficult to accept this new principle and have repeatedly preferred uncertainties to certainties. It is not my intention to carp at their reputation; rather, I wish to give you in brief, kind reader, the basis for making a fair judgement of the issue for yourself.

Therefore, to begin our discussion with what is simplest and nearest to us, let us briefly consider what the nature of gravity is in terrestrial bodies, so that when we come to consider celestial bodies, so very far removed from us, we may proceed more securely. It is now agreed among all philosophers that all bodies on or near the earth universally gravitate towards the earth. Manifold experience has long confirmed that there are no truly light bodies. What is called relative levity is not true levity, but only apparent, and arises from the more powerful gravity of contiguous bodies.

Furthermore, just as all bodies universally gravitate towards the earth, so the earth in turn gravitates equally towards the bodies; for the action of gravity is mutual and is equal in both directions. This is shown as follows. Let the whole body of the earth be divided into any two parts, whether equal or in any way unequal; now, if the weights of the parts towards each other were not equal, the lesser weight would yield to the greater, and the parts, joined together, would proceed to move straight on without limit in the direction towards which the greater weight tends, entirely contrary to experience. Therefore the necessary conclusion is that the weights of the parts are in equilibrium – that is, that the action of gravity is mutual and equal in both directions.

The weights of bodies equally distant from the centre of the earth are as the quantities of matter in the bodies. This is gathered from the equal acceleration of all bodies falling from rest by the force of their weights; for the forces by which unequal bodies are equally accelerated must be proportional to the quantities of matter to be moved. Now, that all falling bodies universally are equally accelerated is evident from this, that in the vacuum produced by Boyle's air pump (that is, with the resistance of the air removed), they describe, in falling, equal spaces in equal times, and this is proved more exactly by experiments with pendulums.

The attractive forces of bodies, at equal distances, are as the quantities of matter in the bodies. For, since bodies gravitate towards the earth, and the earth in turn gravitates towards the bodies, with equal moments [i.e. strengths or powers], the weight of the earth towards each body, or the force by which the body attracts the earth, will be equal to the weight of the body towards the earth. But, as mentioned above, this weight is as the quantity of matter in the body, and so the force by which each body attracts the earth, or the absolute force of the body, will be as its quantity of matter.

Therefore the attractive force of entire bodies arises and is compounded from the attractive force of the parts, since (as has been shown), when the amount of matter is increased or diminished, its force is proportionally increased or diminished. Therefore the action of the earth must result from the combined actions of its parts; hence all terrestrial bodies must attract one another by absolute forces that are proportional to the attracting matter. This is the nature of gravity on earth; let us now see what it is in the heavens.

Every body perseveres in its state either of being at rest or of moving uniformly straight forwards, except insofar as it is compelled by impressed forces to change that state: this is a law of nature accepted by all philosophers. It follows that bodies that move in curves, and so continually deviate from straight lines tangent to their orbits, are kept in a curvilinear path by some continually acting force. Therefore, for the planets to revolve in curved orbits, there will necessarily be some force by whose repeated actions they are unceasingly deflected from the tangents.

Now, it is reasonable to accept something that can be found by mathematics and proved with the greatest certainty: namely, that all bodies moving in some curved line described in a plane, which by a radius drawn to a point (either at rest or moving in any way) describe areas about that point proportional to the times, are urged by forces that tend towards that same point. Therefore, since it is agreed among astronomers that the primary planets describe areas around the sun proportional to the times, as do the secondary planets around their own primary planets, it follows that the force by which they are continually pulled away from rectilinear tangents and are compelled to revolve in curvilinear orbits is directed towards the bodies that are situated in the centres of the orbits. Therefore this force can, appropriately, be called centripetal with respect to the revolving body, and attractive with respect to the central body, from whatever cause it may in the end be imagined to arise.

The following rules must also be accepted and are mathematically demonstrated. If several bodies revolve with uniform motion in concentric circles, and if the squares of the periodic times are as the cubes of the distances from the common centre, then the centripetal forces of the revolving bodies will be inversely as the squares of the distances. Again, if the bodies revolve in orbits that are very nearly circles, and if the apsides of the orbits are at rest, then the centripetal forces of the revolving bodies will be inversely as the squares of the distances. Astronomers agree that one or the other case holds for all the planets [both primary and secondary]. Therefore the centripetal forces of all the planets are inversely as the squares of the distances from the centres of the orbits. If anyone objects that the apsides of the planets, especially the apsides of the moon, are not completely at rest but are carried progressively forwards [or in consequentia] with a slow motion, it can be answered that even if we grant that this very slow motion arises from a slight deviation of the centripetal force from the proportion of the inverse square, this difference can be found by mathematical computation and is quite insensible. For the ratio of the moon's centripetal force itself, which should deviate most of all from the square, will indeed exceed the square by a very little, but it will be about sixty times closer to it than to the cube. But our answer to the objection will be truer if we say that this progression of the apsides does not arise from a deviation from the proportion of the [inverse] square but from another and entirely different cause, as is admirably shown in Newton's philosophy. As a result, the centripetal forces by which the primary planets tend towards the sun, and the secondary planets towards their primaries, must be exactly as the squares of the distances inversely.

From what has been said up to this point, it is clear that the planets are kept in their orbits by some force continually acting upon them, that this force is always directed towards the centres of the orbits, and that its efficacy is increased in approaching the centre and decreased in receding from the centre – actually increased in the same proportion in which the square of the distance is decreased, and decreased in the same proportion in which the square of the distance is increased. Let us now, by comparing the centripetal forces of the planets and the force of gravity, see whether or not they might be of the same kind. They will be of the same kind if the same laws and the same attributes are found in both. Let us first, therefore, consider the centripetal force of the moon, which is closest to us.

When bodies are let fall from rest, and are acted on by any forces whatever, the rectilinear spaces described in a given time at the very beginning of the motion are proportional to the forces themselves; this of course follows from mathematical reasoning. Therefore the centripetal force of the moon revolving in its orbit will be to the force of gravity on the earth's surface as the space that the moon would describe in a minimally small time in descending towards the earth by its centripetal force – supposing it to be deprived of all circular motion – is to the space that a heavy body describes in the same minimally small time in the vicinity of the earth, in falling by the force of its own gravity. The first of these spaces is equal to the versed sine of the arc described by the moon during the same time, inasmuch as this versed sine measures the depart-ure of the moon from the tangent caused by centripetal force and thus can be calculated if the moon's periodic time and its distance from the centre of the earth are both given. The second space is found by experiments with pendulums, as Huygens has shown. Therefore, the result of the calculation will be that the first space is to the second space, or the centripetal force of the moon revolving in its orbit is to the force of gravity on the surface of the earth, as the square of the semidiameter of the earth is to the square of the semidiameter of the orbit. By what is shown above, the same ratio holds for the centripetal force of the moon revolving in its orbit and the centripetal force of the moon if it were near the earth's surface. Therefore this centripetal force near the earth's surface is equal to the force of gravity. They are not, therefore, different forces, but one and the same; for if they were different, bodies acted on by both forces together would fall to the earth twice as fast as from the force of gravity alone. And therefore it is clear that this centripetal force by which the moon is continually either drawn or impelled from the tangent and is kept in its orbit is the very force of terrestrial gravity extending as far as the moon. And indeed it is reasonable for this force to extend itself to enormous distances, since one can observe no sensible diminution of it even on the highest peaks of mountains. Therefore the moon gravitates towards the earth. Further, by mutual action, the earth in turn gravitates equally towards the moon, a fact which is abundantly confirmed in this philosophy, when we deal with the tide of the sea and the precession of the equinoxes, both of which arise from the action of both the moon and the sun upon the earth. Hence finally we learn also by what law the force of gravity decreases at greater distances from the earth. For since gravity is not different from the moon's centripetal force, which is inversely proportional to the square of the distance, gravity will also be diminished in the same ratio.

Let us now proceed to the other planets. The revolutions of the primary planets about the sun and of the secondary planets about Jupiter and Saturn are phenomena of the same kind as the revolution of the moon about the earth; furthermore, it has been demonstrated that the centripetal forces of the primary planets are directed towards the centre of the sun, and those of the secondary planets towards the centres of Jupiter and of Saturn, just as the moon's centripetal force is directed towards the centre of the earth; and, additionally, all these forces are inversely as the squares of the distances from the centres, just as the force of the moon is inversely as the square of the distance from the earth. Therefore it must be concluded that all of these primary and secondary planets have the same nature. Hence, as the moon gravitates towards the earth, and the earth in turn gravitates towards the moon, so also all the secondary planets will gravitate towards their primaries, and the primaries in turn towards the secondaries, and also all the primary planets will gravitate towards the sun, and the sun in turn towards the primary planets.

Therefore the sun gravitates towards all the primary and secondary planets, and all these towards the sun. For the secondary planets, while accompanying their primaries, revolve with them around the sun. By the same argument, therefore, both kinds of planets gravitate towards the sun, and the sun towards them. Additionally, that the secondary planets gravitate towards the sun is also abundantly clear from the inequalities of the moon, concerning which a most exact theory is presented with marvellous sagacity in the third book of this work.

The motion of the comets shows very clearly that the attractive force of the sun is propagated in every direction to enormous distances and is diffused to every part of the surrounding space, since the comets, starting out from immense distances, come into the vicinity of the sun and sometimes approach so very close to it that in their perihelia they all seemingly touch its globe. Astronomers until now have tried in vain to find the theory of these comets; now at last, in our time, our most illustrious author has succeeded in finding the theory and has demonstrated it with the greatest certainty from observations. It is therefore evident that the comets move in conic sections having their foci in the centre of the sun and by radii drawn to the sun describe areas proportional to the times. From these phenomena it is manifest and it is mathematically proved that the forces by which the comets are kept in their orbits are directed towards the sun and are inversely as the squares of their distances from its centre. Thus the comets gravitate towards the sun; and so the attractive force of the sun reaches not only to the bodies of the planets, which are at fixed distances and in nearly the same plane, but also to the comets, which are in the most diverse regions of the heavens and at the most diverse distances. It is the nature of gravitating bodies, therefore, that they propagate their forces at all distances to all other gravitating bodies. From this it follows that all planets and comets universally attract one another and are heavy towards one another – which is also confirmed by the perturbation of Jupiter and Saturn, known to astronomers and arising from the actions of these planets upon each other; it is also confirmed by the very slow motion of the apsides that was mentioned above and that arises from an entirely similar cause.

We have at last reached the point where it must be acknowledged that the earth and the sun and all the celestial bodies that accompany the sun attract one another. Therefore every least particle of each of them will have its own attractive force in proportion to the quantity of matter, as was shown above for terrestrial bodies. And at different distances their forces will also be in the squared ratio of the distances inversely; for it is mathematically demonstrated that particles attracting by this law must constitute globes attracting by the same law.

The preceding conclusions are based upon an axiom which is accepted by every philosopher, namely, that effects of the same kind – that is, effects whose known properties are the same – have the same causes, and their properties which are not yet known are also the same. For if gravity is the cause of the fall of a stone in Europe, who can doubt that in America the cause of the fall is the same? If gravity is mutual between a stone and the earth in Europe, who will deny that it is mutual in America? If in Europe the attractive force of the stone and the earth is compounded of the attractive forces of the parts, who will deny that in America the force is similarly compounded? If in Europe the attraction of the earth is propagated to all kinds of bodies and to all distances, why should we not say that in America it is propagated in the same way? All philosophy is based on this rule, inasmuch as, if it is taken away, there is then nothing we can affirm about things universally. The constitution of individual things can be found by observations and experiments; and proceeding from there, it is only by this rule that we make judgements about the nature of things universally.

Now, since all terrestrial and celestial bodies on which we can make experiments or observations are heavy, it must be acknowledged without exception that gravity belongs to all bodies universally. And just as we must not conceive of bodies that are not extended, mobile, and impenetrable, so we should not conceive of any that are not heavy. The extension, mobility, and impenetrability of bodies are known only through experiments; it is in exactly the same way that the gravity of bodies is known. All bodies for which we have observations are extended and mobile and impenetrable; and from this we conclude that all bodies universally are extended and mobile and impenetrable, even those for which we do not have observations. Thus all bodies for which we have observations are heavy; and from this we conclude that all bodies universally are heavy, even those for which we do not have observations. If anyone were to say that the bodies of the fixed stars are not heavy, since their gravity has not yet been observed, then by the same argument one would be able to say that they are neither extended nor mobile nor impenetrable, since these properties of the fixed stars have not yet been observed. Need I go on? Among the primary qualities of all bodies universally, either gravity will have a place, or extension, mobility, and impenetrability will not. And the nature of things either will be correctly explained by the gravity of bodies or will not be correctly explained by the extension, mobility, and impenetrability of bodies.

I can hear some people disagreeing with this conclusion and muttering something or other about occult qualities. They are always prattling on and on to the effect that gravity is something occult, and that occult causes are to be banished completely from philosophy. But it is easy to answer them: occult causes are not those causes whose existence is very clearly demonstrated by observations, but only those whose existence is occult, imagined, and not yet proved. Therefore gravity is not an occult cause of celestial motions, since it has been shown from phenomena that this force really exists.[1] Rather, occult causes are the refuge of those who assign the governing of these motions to some sort of vortices of a certain matter utterly fictitious and completely imperceptible to the senses.

But will gravity be called an occult cause and be cast out of natural philosophy on the grounds that the cause of gravity itself is occult and not yet found? Let those who so believe take care lest they believe in an absurdity that, in the end, may overthrow the foundations of all philosophy. For causes generally proceed in a continuous chain from compound to more simple; when you reach the simplest cause, you will not be able to proceed any further. Therefore no mechanical explanation can be given for the simplest cause; for if it could, the cause would not yet be the simplest. Will you accordingly call these simplest causes occult, and banish them? But at the same time the causes most immediately depending on them, and the causes that in turn depend on these causes, will also be banished, until philosophy is emptied and thoroughly purged of all causes.

Some say that gravity is preternatural and call it a perpetual miracle.[2] Therefore they hold that it should be rejected, since preternatural causes have no place in physics. It is hardly worth spending time on

---

[1] Newton makes the same claim in the General Scholium to the *Principia*, reprinted in this volume (p. 114).

[2] See Leibniz's 1711 letter to Hartsoeker, printed in the *Memoirs of Literature*, and reprinted in this volume (p. 145).

demolishing this utterly absurd objection, which of itself undermines all of philosophy. For either they will say that gravity is not a property of all bodies – which cannot be maintained – or they will assert that gravity is preternatural on the grounds that it does not arise from other affections of bodies and thus not from mechanical causes. Certainly there are primary affections of bodies, and since they are primary, they do not depend on others. Therefore let them consider whether or not all these are equally preternatural, and so equally to be rejected, and let them consider what philosophy will then be like.

There are some who do not like all this celestial physics just because it seems to be in conflict with the doctrines of Descartes and seems scarcely capable of being reconciled with these doctrines. They are free to enjoy their own opinion, but they ought to act fairly and not deny to others the same liberty that they demand for themselves. Therefore, we should be allowed to adhere to the Newtonian philosophy, which we consider truer, and to prefer causes proved by phenomena to causes imagined and not yet proved. It is the province of true philosophy to derive the natures of things from causes that truly exist, and to seek those laws by which the supreme artificer willed to establish this most beautiful order of the world, not those laws by which he could have, had it so pleased him. For it is in accord with reason that the same effect can arise from several causes somewhat different from one another; but the true cause will be the one from which the effect truly and actually does arise, while the rest have no place in true philosophy. In mechanical clocks one and the same motion of the hour hand can arise from the action of a suspended weight or an internal spring. But if the clock under discussion is really activated by a weight, then anyone will be laughed at if he imagines a spring and on such a premature hypothesis undertakes to explain the motion of the hour hand; for he ought to have examined the internal workings of the machine more thoroughly, in order to ascertain the true principle of the motion in question. The same judgement or something like it should be passed on those philosophers who have held that the heavens are filled with a certain most subtle matter, which is endlessly moved in vortices. For even if these philosophers could account for the phenomena with the greatest exactness on the basis of their hypotheses, still they cannot be said to have given us a true philosophy and to have found the true causes of the celestial motions until they have demonstrated either that these causes really do exist or at least that others do not exist. Therefore if it can be shown that the attraction of all bodies universally has a true place in the nature of things, and if it further can be shown how all the celestial motions are solved by that attraction, then it would be an empty and ridiculous objection if anyone said that those motions should be explained by vortices, even if we gave our fullest assent to the possibility of such an explanation.[3] But we do not give our assent; for the phenomena can by no means be explained by vortices, as our author fully proves with the clearest arguments. It follows that those who devote their fruitless labour to patching up a most absurd figment of their imagination and embroidering it further with new fabrications must be overly indulging their fantasies.

If the bodies of the planets and the comets are carried around the sun by vortices, the bodies carried around must move with the same velocity and in the same direction as the immediately surrounding parts of the vortices, and must have the same density or the same force of inertia in proportion to the bulk of the matter. But it is certain that planets and comets, while they are in the same regions of the heavens, move with a variety of velocities and directions. Therefore it necessarily follows that those parts of the celestial fluid that are at the same distances from the sun revolve in the same time in different directions with different velocities; for there will be need of one direction and velocity to permit the planets to move through the heavens, and another for the comets. Since this cannot be accounted for, either it will have to be confessed that all the celestial bodies are not carried by the matter of a vortex, or it will have to be said that their motions are to be derived not from one and the same vortex, but from more than one, differing from one another and going through the same space surrounding the sun.

If it is supposed that several vortices are contained in the same space and penetrate one another and revolve with different motions, then – since these motions must conform to the motions of the bodies being carried around, motions highly regular in conic sections that are sometimes extremely eccentric and sometimes very nearly circular – it will be right to ask how it can happen that these same vortices keep their integrity without being in the least perturbed through so many centuries

---

[3] See Newton's 1693 letter to Leibniz, reprinted in this volume (pp. 143–45).

by the interactions of their matter. Surely, if these imaginary motions are more complex and more difficult to explain than the true motions of the planets and comets, I think it pointless to admit them into natural philosophy; for every cause must be simpler than its effect. Granted the freedom to invent any fiction, let someone assert that all the planets and comets are surrounded by atmospheres, as our earth is, a hypothesis that will certainly seem more reasonable than the hypothesis of vortices. Let him then assert that these atmospheres, of their own nature, move around the sun and describe conic sections, a motion that can surely be much more easily conceived than the similar motion of vortices penetrating one another. Finally, let him maintain that it must be believed that the planets themselves and the comets are carried around the sun by their atmospheres, and let him celebrate his triumph for having found the causes of the celestial motions. Anyone who thinks that this fiction should be rejected will also reject the other one; for the hypothesis of atmospheres and the hypothesis of vortices are as alike as two peas in a pod.

Galileo showed that when a stone is projected and moves in a parabola, its deflection from a rectilinear path arises from the gravity of the stone towards the earth, that is, from an occult quality. Nevertheless it can happen that some other philosopher, even more clever, may contrive another cause. He will accordingly imagine that a certain subtle matter, which is not perceived by sight or by touch or by any of the senses, is found in the regions that are most immediately contiguous to the surface of the earth. He will argue, moreover, that this matter is carried in different directions by various and – for the most part – contrary motions and that it describes parabolic curves. Finally he will beautifully show how the stone is deflected and will earn the applause of the crowd. The stone, says he, floats in that subtle fluid and, by following the course of that fluid, cannot but describe the same path. But the fluid moves in parabolic curves; therefore the stone must move in a parabola. Who will not now marvel at the most acute genius of this philosopher, brilliantly deducing the phenomena of nature from mechanical causes – at a level comprehensible even to ordinary people! Who indeed will not jeer at that poor Galileo, who undertook by a great mathematical effort once more to bring back occult qualities, happily excluded from philosophy! But I am ashamed to waste any more time on such trifles.

It all finally comes down to this: the number of comets is huge; their motions are highly regular and observe the same laws as the motions of the planets. They move in conic orbits; these orbits are very, very eccentric. Comets go everywhere into all parts of the heavens and pass very freely through the regions of the planets, often contrary to the order of the signs. These phenomena are confirmed with the greatest certainty by astronomical observations and cannot be explained by vortices. Further, these phenomena are even inconsistent with planetary vortices. There will be no room at all for the motions of the comets unless that imaginary matter is completely removed from the heavens.

For if the planets are carried around the sun by vortices those parts of the vortices that most immediately surround each planet will be of the same density as the planet, as has been said above. Therefore all the matter that is contiguous to the perimeter of the earth's orbit will have the same density as the earth, while all the matter that lies between the earth's orbit and the orbit of Saturn will have either an equal or a greater density. For, in order that the constitution of a vortex may be able to last, the less dense parts must occupy the centre, and the more dense parts must be further away from the centre. For since the periodic times of the planets are as the powers of the distances from the sun, the periods of the parts of the vortex should keep the same ratio. It follows that the centrifugal forces of these parts will be inversely as the squares of the distances. Therefore those parts that are at a greater distance from the centre strive to recede from it by a smaller force; accordingly, if they should be less dense, it would be necessary for them to yield to the greater force by which the parts nearer to the centre endeavour to ascend. Therefore the denser parts will ascend, the less dense will descend, and a mutual exchange of places will occur, until the fluid matter of the whole vortex has been arranged in such order that it can now rest in equilibrium [i.e. its parts are completely at rest with respect to one another or no longer have any motion of ascent or descent]. If two fluids of different density are contained in the same vessel, certainly it will happen that the fluid whose density is greater will go to the lowest place under the action of its greater force of gravity, and by similar reasoning it must be concluded that the denser parts of the vortex will go to the highest place under the action of their greater centrifugal force. Therefore the whole part of the vortex that lies outside the earth's orbit (much the greatest

74

part) will have a density and so a force of inertia (proportional to the quantity of matter) that will not be smaller than the density and force of inertia of the earth. From this will arise a huge and very noticeable resistance to the comets as they pass through, not to say a resistance that rightly seems to be able to put a complete stop to their motion and absorb it entirely. It is however clear from the altogether regular motion of comets that they encounter no resistance that can be in the least perceived, and thus that they do not come upon any matter that has any force of resistance, or accordingly that has any density or force of inertia. For the resistance of mediums arises either from the inertia of fluid matter or from its friction. That which arises from friction is extremely slight and indeed can scarcely be observed in commonly known fluids, unless they are very tenacious like oil and honey. The resistance that is encountered in air, water, quicksilver, and non-tenacious fluids of this sort is almost wholly of the first kind and cannot be decreased in subtlety by any further degree, if the fluid's density or force of inertia – to which this resistance is always proportional – remains the same. This is most clearly demonstrated by our author in his brilliant theory of the resistance of fluids, which in this second edition is presented in a somewhat more accurate manner and is more fully confirmed by experiments with falling bodies.

As bodies move forwards, they gradually communicate their motion to a surrounding fluid, and by communicating their motion lose it, and by losing it are retarded. Therefore the retardation is proportional to the motion so communicated, and the motion communicated (where the velocity of the moving body is given) is as the density of the fluid; therefore the retardation or resistance will also be as the density of the fluid and cannot be removed by any means unless the fluid, returning to the back of the body, restores the lost motion. But this cannot be the case unless the force of the fluid on the rear of the body is equal to the force the body exerts on the fluid in front, that is, unless the relative velocity with which the fluid pushes the body from behind is equal to the velocity with which the body pushes the fluid, that is, unless the absolute velocity of the returning fluid is twice as great as the absolute velocity of the fluid pushed forwards, which cannot happen. Therefore there is no way in which the resistance of fluids that arises from their density and force of inertia can be taken away. And so it must be concluded that the celestial fluid has no force of inertia, since it has no force of resistance; it has no force by which motion may be communicated, since it has no force of inertia; it has no force by which any change may be introduced into one or more bodies, since it has no force by which motion may be communicated; it has no efficacy at all, since it has no faculty to introduce any change. Surely, therefore, this hypothesis, plainly lacking in any foundation and not even marginally useful to explain the nature of things, may well be called utterly absurd and wholly unworthy of a philosopher. Those who hold that the heavens are filled with fluid matter, but suppose this matter to have no inertia, are saying there is no vacuum but in fact are assuming there is one. For, since there is no way to distinguish a fluid matter of this sort from empty space, the whole argument comes down to the names of things and not their natures. But if anyone is so devoted to matter that he will in no way admit a space void of bodies, let us see where this will ultimately lead him.

For such people will say that this constitution of the universe as everywhere full, which is how they imagine it, has arisen from the will of God, so that a very subtle aether pervading and filling all things would be there to facilitate the operations of nature; this cannot be maintained, however, since it has already been shown from the phenomena of comets that this aether has no efficacy. Or they will say that this constitution has arisen from the will of God for some unknown purpose, which ought not to be said either, since a different constitution of the universe could equally well be established by the same argument. Or finally they will say that it has not arisen from the will of God but from some necessity of nature. And so at last they must sink to the lowest depths of degradation, where they have the fantasy that all things are governed by fate and not by providence, that matter has existed always and everywhere of its own necessity and is infinite and eternal. On this supposition, matter will also be uniform everywhere, for variety of forms is entirely inconsistent with necessity. Matter will also be without motion; for if by necessity matter moves in some definite direction with some definite velocity, by a like necessity it will move in a different direction with a different velocity; but it cannot move in different directions with different velocities; therefore it must be without motion. Surely, this world – so beautifully diversified in its forms and motions – could not have arisen except from the perfectly free will of God, who provides and governs all things.

From this source, then, have all the laws that are called laws of nature come, in which many traces of the highest wisdom and counsel certainly appear, but no traces of necessity. Accordingly we should not seek these laws by using untrustworthy conjectures, but learn them by observing and experimenting. He who is confident that he can truly find the principles of physics, and the laws of things, by relying only on the force of his mind and the internal light of his reason[4] should maintain either that the world has existed from necessity and follows the said laws from the same necessity, or that although the order of nature was constituted by the will of God, nevertheless a creature as small and insignificant as he is has a clear understanding of the way things should be. All sound and true philosophy is based on phenomena, which may lead us – however unwilling and reluctant – to principles in which the best counsel and highest dominion of an all-wise and all-powerful being are most clearly discerned; these principles will not be rejected because certain men may perhaps not like them. These men may call the things that they dislike either miracles or occult qualities, but names maliciously given are not to be blamed on the things themselves, unless these men are willing to confess at last that philosophy should be based on atheism. Philosophy must not be overthrown for their sake, since the order of things refuses to be changed.

Therefore honest and fair judges will approve the best method of natural philosophy, which is based on experiments and observations. It need scarcely be said that this way of philosophizing has been illumined and dignified by our illustrious author's well-known book; his tremendous genius, enodating [clarifying or solving] each of the most difficult problems and reaching out beyond the accepted limits of the human, is justly admired and esteemed by all who are more than superficially versed in these matters. Having unlocked the gates, therefore, he has opened our way to the most beautiful mysteries of nature. He has finally so clearly revealed a most elegant structure of the system of the world for our further scrutiny that even were King Alfonso himself to come to life again, he would not find it wanting either in simplicity or in grace of harmony.[5]

---

[4] This is intended as a criticism of Descartes's procedure in the *Principles of Philosophy*.

[5] Alfonso X, the Spanish King of Castile and Leon (1252–82), compiled the so-called Alfonsine Tables in astronomy, and was reputed to have claimed that if he had been given a few simple principles he could have created a simpler system of the world than that depicted by then–current Ptolemaic astronomy.

And hence it is now possible to have a closer view of the majesty of nature, to enjoy the sweetest contemplation, and to worship and venerate more zealously the maker and lord of all; and this is by far the greatest fruit of philosophy. He must be blind who does not at once see, from the best and wisest structures of things, the infinite wisdom and goodness of their almighty creator; and he must be mad who refuses to acknowledge them.

Therefore Newton's excellent treatise will stand as a mighty fortress against the attacks of atheists; nowhere else will you find more effective ammunition against that impious crowd. This was understood long ago, and was first splendidly demonstrated in learned discourses in English and in Latin, by a man of universal learning and at the same time an outstanding patron of the arts, Richard Bentley, a great ornament of his time and of our academy, the worthy and upright master of our Trinity College.[6] I must confess that I am indebted to him on many grounds; you as well, kind reader, will not deny him due thanks. For, as a long-time intimate friend of our renowned author (he considers being celebrated by posterity for this friendship to be of no less value than becoming famous for his own writings, which are the delight of the learned world), he worked simultaneously for the public recognition of his friend and for the advancement of the sciences. Therefore, since the available copies of the first edition were extremely rare and very expensive, he tried with persistent demands to persuade Newton (who is distinguished as much by modesty as by the highest learning) and finally – almost scolding him – prevailed upon Newton to allow him to get out this new edition, under his auspices and at his own expense, perfected throughout and also enriched with significant additions. He authorized me to undertake the not unpleasant duty of seeing to it that all this was done as correctly as possible.

Cambridge, 12 May 1713

Roger Cotes, Fellow of Trinity College, Plumian Professor of Astronomy and Experimental Philosophy

---

[6] See Newton's letters to Bentley in this volume.

Definitions

Definition 1

Quantity of matter is a measure of matter that arises from its density and volume jointly.

If the density of air is doubled in a space that is also doubled, there is four times as much air, and there is six times as much if the space is tripled. The case is the same for snow and powders condensed by compression or liquefaction, and also for all bodies that are condensed in various ways by any causes whatsoever. For the present, I am not taking into account any medium, if there should be any, freely pervading the interstices between the parts of bodies. Furthermore, I mean this quantity whenever I use the term 'body' or 'mass' in the following pages. It can always be known from a body's weight, for – by making very accurate experiments with pendulums – I have found it to be proportional to the weight, as will be shown below.

Definition 2

Quantity of motion is a measure of motion that arises from the velocity and the quantity of matter jointly.

The motion of a whole is the sum of the motions of the individual parts, and thus if a body is twice as large as another and has equal velocity there is twice as much motion, and if it has twice the velocity there is four times as much motion.

Definition 3

Inherent force of matter is the power of resisting by which every body, so far as it is able, perseveres in its state either of resting or of moving uniformly straight forwards.

This force is always proportional to the body and does not differ in any way from the inertia of the mass except in the manner in which it is conceived. Because of the inertia of matter, every body is only with difficulty put out of its state either of resting or of moving. Consequently, inherent force may also be called by the very significant name of force of inertia. Moreover, a body exerts this force only during a change of its state, caused by another force impressed upon it, and this exercise of force is, depending on the viewpoint, both resistance and impetus: resistance insofar as the body, in order to maintain its state, strives against the impressed force, and impetus insofar as the same body, yielding only with difficulty to the force of a resisting obstacle, endeavours to change the state of that obstacle. Resistance is commonly attributed to resting bodies and impetus to moving bodies; but motion and rest, in the popular sense of the terms, are distinguished from each other only by point of view, and bodies commonly regarded as being at rest are not always truly at rest.

Definition 4

Impressed force is the action exerted on a body to change its state either of resting or of moving uniformly straight forwards.

This force consists solely in the action and does not remain in a body after the action has ceased. For a body perseveres in any new state solely by the force of inertia. Moreover, there are various sources of impressed force, such as percussion, pressure, or centripetal force.

Definition 5

Centripetal force is the force by which bodies are drawn from all sides, are impelled, or in any way tend, towards some point as to a centre.

One force of this kind is gravity, by which bodies tend towards the centre of the earth; another is magnetic force, by which iron seeks a lodestone; and yet another is that force, whatever it may be, by which the planets are continually drawn back from rectilinear motions and compelled to revolve around curved lines. A stone whirled in a sling endeavours to leave the hand that is whirling it, and by its endeavour it stretches the sling, doing so the more strongly the more swiftly it revolves; and as soon as it is released, it flies away. The force opposed to that endeavour, that is, the force by which the sling continually draws the stone back towards the hand and keeps it in an orbit, I call centripetal, since it is directed towards the hand as towards the centre of an orbit. And the same applies to all bodies that are made to move in orbits. They all endeavour to recede from the centres of their orbits, and unless some force opposed to that endeavour is present, restraining them and keeping them in orbits and hence called by me centripetal, they will go off in straight lines with uniform motion. If a projectile were deprived of the force of gravity, it would not be deflected towards the earth but would go off in a straight line into the heavens and do so with uniform motion, provided that the resistance of the air were removed. The projectile, by its gravity, is drawn back from a rectilinear course and continually deflected towards the earth, and this is so to a greater or lesser degree in proportion to its gravity and its velocity of motion. The less its gravity in proportion to its quantity of matter, or the greater the velocity with which it is projected, the less it will deviate from a rectilinear course and the farther it will go. If a lead ball were projected with a given velocity along a horizontal line from the top of some mountain by the force of gunpowder and went in a curved line for a distance of two miles before falling to the earth, then the same ball projected with twice the velocity would go about twice as far and with ten times the velocity about ten times as far, provided that the resistance of the air were removed. And by increasing the velocity, the distance to which it would be projected could be increased at will and the curvature of the line that it would describe could be decreased, in such a way that it would finally fall at a distance of 10 or 30 or 90 degrees or even go around the whole earth or, lastly, go off into the heavens and continue indefinitely in this motion. And in the same way that a projectile could, by the force of gravity, be deflected into an orbit and go around the whole earth, so too the moon, whether by the force of gravity – if it has gravity – or by any other force by which it may be urged towards the earth, can always be drawn back towards the earth from a rectilinear course and deflected into its orbit; and without such a force the moon cannot be kept in its orbit. If this force were too small, it would not deflect the moon sufficiently from a rectilinear course; if it were too great, it would deflect the moon excessively and draw it down from its orbit towards the earth. In fact, it must be of just the right magnitude, and mathematicians have the task of finding the force by which a body can be kept exactly in any given orbit with a given velocity and, alternatively, to find the curvilinear path into which a body leaving any given place with a given velocity is deflected by a given force.

The quantity of centripetal force is of three kinds: absolute, accelerative, and motive.

Definition 6

The absolute quantity of centripetal force is the measure of this force that is greater or less in proportion to the efficacy of the cause propagating it from a centre through the surrounding regions.

An example is magnetic force, which is greater in one lodestone [i.e. magnet] and less in another, in proportion to the bulk or potency of the lodestone.

Definition 7

The accelerative quantity of centripetal force is the measure of this force that is proportional to the velocity which it generates in a given time.

One example is the potency of a lodestone, which, for a given lodestone, is greater at a smaller distance and less at a greater distance. Another example is the force that produces gravity, which is greater in valleys and less on the peaks of high mountains and still less (as will be made clear below) at greater distances from the body of the earth, but which is everywhere the same at equal distances, because it equally accelerates all falling bodies (heavy or light, great or small), provided that the resistance of the air is removed.

Definition 8

The motive quantity of centripetal force is the measure of this force that is proportional to the motion which it generates in a given time.

An example is weight, which is greater in a larger body and less in a smaller body; and in one and the same body is greater near the earth and less out in the heavens. This quantity is the centripetency, or propensity towards a centre, of the whole body, and (so to speak) its weight, and it may always be known from the force opposite and equal to it, which can prevent the body from falling.

These quantities of forces, for the sake of brevity, may be called motive, accelerative, and absolute forces, and, for the sake of differentiation, may be referred to bodies seeking a centre, to the places of the bodies, and to the centre of the forces: that is, motive force may be referred to a body as an endeavour of the whole directed towards a centre and compounded of the endeavours of all the parts; accelerative force, to the place of the body as a certain efficacy diffused from the centre through each of the surrounding places in order to move the bodies that are in those places; and absolute force, to the centre as having some cause without which the motive forces are not propagated through the surrounding regions, whether this cause is some central body (such as a lodestone in the centre of a magnetic force or the earth in the centre of a force that produces gravity) or whether it is some other cause which is not apparent. This concept is purely mathematical, for I am not now considering the physical causes and sites of forces.

Therefore, accelerative force is to motive force as velocity to motion. For quantity of motion arises from velocity and quantity of matter jointly, and motive force from accelerative force and quantity of matter jointly. For the sum of the actions of the accelerative force on the individual particles of a body is the motive force of the whole body. As a consequence, near the surface of the earth, where the accelerative gravity, or the force that produces gravity, is the same in all bodies universally, the motive gravity, or weight, is as the body, but in an ascent to regions where the accelerative gravity becomes less, the weight will decrease proportionately and will always be as the body and the accelerative gravity jointly. Thus, in regions where the accelerative gravity is half as great, a body one-half or one-third as great will have a weight four or six times less.

Further, it is in this same sense that I call attractions and impulses accelerative and motive. Moreover, I use interchangeably and indiscriminately words signifying attraction, impulse, or any sort of propensity towards a centre, considering these forces not from a physical but only from a mathematical point of view. Therefore, let the reader beware of thinking that by words of this kind I am anywhere defining a species or mode of action or a physical cause or reason, or that I am attributing forces in a true and physical sense to centres (which are mathematical points) if I happen to say that centres attract or that centres have forces.

Scholium

Thus far it has seemed best to explain the senses in which less familiar words are to be taken in this treatise. Although time, space, place, and motion are very familiar to everyone, it must be noted that these quantities are popularly conceived solely with reference to the objects of sense perception. And this is the source of certain preconceptions; to eliminate them it is useful to distinguish these quantities into absolute and relative, true and apparent, mathematical and common.

1. Absolute, true, and mathematical time, in and of itself and of its own nature, without reference to anything external, flows uniformly and by another name is called duration. Relative, apparent, and common time is any sensible and external measure (precise or imprecise) of duration by means of motion; such a measure – for example, an hour, a day, a month, a year – is commonly used instead of true time.

2. Absolute space, of its own nature without reference to anything external, always remains homogeneous and immovable. Relative space is any movable measure or dimension of this absolute space; such a measure or dimension is determined by our senses from the situation of the space with respect to bodies and is popularly used for immovable space, as in the case of space under the earth or in the air or in the heavens, where the dimension is determined from the situation of the space with respect to the earth. Absolute and relative space are the same in species and in magnitude, but they do not always remain the same numerically. For example, if the earth moves, the space of our air, which in a relative sense and with respect to the earth always remains the same, will now be one part of the absolute space into which the air passes, now another part of it, and thus will be changing continually in an absolute sense.

3. Place is the part of space that a body occupies, and it is, depending on the space, either absolute or relative. I say the part of space, not the position of the body or its outer surface. For the places of equal solids are always equal, while their surfaces are for the most part unequal because of the dissimilarity of shapes; and positions, properly speaking, do not have quantity and are not so much places as attributes of places. The motion of a whole is the same as the sum of the motions of the parts; that is, the change in position of a whole from its place is the same as the sum of the changes in position of its parts from their places, and thus the place of a whole is the same as the sum of the places of the parts and therefore is internal and in the whole body.

4. Absolute motion is the change of position of a body from one absolute place to another; relative motion is change of position from one relative place to another. Thus, in a ship under sail, the relative place

of a body is that region of the ship in which the body happens to be or that part of the whole interior of the ship which the body fills and which accordingly moves along with the ship, and relative rest is the continuance of the body in that same region of the ship or same part of its interior. But true rest is the continuance of a body in the same part of that unmoving space in which the ship itself, along with its interior and all its contents, is moving. Therefore, if the earth is truly at rest, a body that is relatively at rest on a ship will move truly and absolutely with the velocity with which the ship is moving on the earth. But if the earth is also moving, the true and absolute motion of the body will arise partly from the true motion of the earth in unmoving space and partly from the relative motion of the ship on the earth. Further, if the body is also moving relatively on the ship, its true motion will arise partly from the true motion of the earth in unmoving space and partly from the relative motions both of the ship on the earth and of the body on the ship, and from these relative motions the relative motion of the body on the earth will arise. For example, if that part of the earth where the ship happens to be is truly moving eastward with a velocity of 10,010 units, and the ship is being borne westward by sails and wind with a velocity of 10 units, and a sailor is walking on the ship towards the east with a velocity of 1 unit, then the sailor will be moving truly and absolutely in unmoving space towards the east with a velocity of 10,001 units and relatively on the earth towards the west with a velocity of 9 units.

In astronomy, absolute time is distinguished from relative time by the equation of common time. For natural days, which are commonly considered equal for the purpose of measuring time, are actually unequal. Astronomers correct this inequality in order to measure celestial motions on the basis of a truer time. It is possible that there is no uniform motion by which time may have an exact measure. All motions can be accelerated and retarded, but the flow of absolute time cannot be changed. The duration or perseverance of the existence of things is the same, whether their motions are rapid or slow or null; accordingly, duration is rightly distinguished from its sensible measures and is gathered from them by means of an astronomical equation. Moreover, the need for using this equation in determining when phenomena occur is proved by experience with a pendulum clock and also by eclipses of the satellites of Jupiter.

Just as the order of the parts of time is unchangeable, so, too, is the order of the parts of space. Let the parts of space move from their places, and they will move (so to speak) from themselves. For times and spaces are, as it were, the places of themselves and of all things. All things are placed in time with reference to order of succession and in space with reference to order of position. It is of the essence of spaces to be places, and for primary places to move is absurd. They are therefore absolute places, and it is only changes of position from these places that are absolute motions.

But since these parts of space cannot be seen and cannot be distinguished from one another by our senses, we use sensible measures in their stead. For we define all places on the basis of the positions and distances of things from some body that we regard as immovable, and then we reckon all motions with respect to these places, insofar as we conceive of bodies as being changed in position with respect to them. Thus, instead of absolute places and motions we use relative ones, which is not inappropriate in ordinary human affairs, although in philosophy abstraction from the senses is required. For it is possible that there is no body truly at rest to which places and motions may be referred.

Moreover, absolute and relative rest and motion are distinguished from each other by their properties, causes, and effects. It is a property of rest that bodies truly at rest are at rest in relation to one another. And therefore, since it is possible that some body in the regions of the fixed stars or far beyond is absolutely at rest, and yet it cannot be known from the position of bodies in relation to one another in our regions whether or not any of these maintains a given position with relation to that distant body, true rest cannot be defined on the basis of the position of bodies in relation to one another.[7]

It is a property of motion that parts which keep given positions in relation to wholes participate in the motions of such wholes. For all the parts of bodies revolving in orbit endeavour to recede from the axis of motion, and the impetus of bodies moving forwards arises from the joint impetus of the individual parts. Therefore, when bodies containing

---

[7] This is intended as a criticism of Descartes; cf. the extended discussion in *De Gravitatione* in this volume.

others move, whatever is relatively at rest within them also moves. And thus true and absolute motion cannot be determined by means of change of position from the vicinity of bodies that are regarded as being at rest. For the exterior bodies ought to be regarded not only as being at rest but also as being truly at rest. Otherwise all contained bodies, besides being subject to change of position from the vicinity of the containing bodies, will participate in the true motions of the containing bodies and, if there is no such change of position, will not be truly at rest but only be regarded as being at rest. For containing bodies are to those inside them as the outer part of the whole to the inner part or as the shell to the kernel. And when the shell moves, the kernel also, without being changed in position from the vicinity of the shell, moves as a part of the whole.

A property akin to the preceding one is that when a place moves, whatever is placed in it moves along with it, and therefore a body moving away from a place that moves participates also in the motion of its place. Therefore, all motions away from places that move are only parts of whole and absolute motions, and every whole motion is compounded of the motion of a body away from its initial place, and the motion of this place away from its place, and so on, until an unmoving place is reached, as in the abovementioned example of the sailor. Thus, whole and absolute motions can be determined only by means of unmoving places, and therefore in what has preceded I have referred such motions to unmoving places and relative motions to movable places. Moreover, the only places that are unmoving are those that all keep given positions in relation to one another from infinity to infinity and therefore always remain immovable and constitute the space that I call immovable.

The causes which distinguish true motions from relative motions are the forces impressed upon bodies to generate motion. True motion is neither generated nor changed except by forces impressed upon the moving body itself, but relative motion can be generated and changed without the impression of forces upon this body. For the impression of forces solely on other bodies with which a given body has a relation is enough, when the other bodies yield, to produce a change in that relation which constitutes the relative rest or motion of this body. Again, true motion is always changed by forces impressed upon a moving body, but relative motion is not necessarily changed by such forces. For if the same forces are impressed upon a moving body and also upon other bodies with which it has a relation, in such a way that the relative position is maintained, the relation that constitutes the relative motion will also be maintained. Therefore, every relative motion can be changed while the true motion is preserved, and can be preserved while the true one is changed, and thus true motion certainly does not consist in relations of this sort.

The effects distinguishing absolute motion from relative motion are the forces of receding from the axis of circular motion. For in purely relative circular motion these forces are null, while in true and absolute circular motion they are larger or smaller in proportion to the quantity of motion. If a bucket is hanging from a very long cord and is continually turned around until the cord becomes twisted tight, and if the bucket is thereupon filled with water and is at rest along with the water and then, by some sudden force, is made to turn around in the opposite direction and, as the cord unwinds, perseveres for a while in this motion; then the surface of the water will at first be level, just as it was before the vessel began to move. But after the vessel, by the force gradually impressed upon the water, has caused the water also to begin revolving perceptibly, the water will gradually recede from the middle and rise up the sides of the vessel, assuming a concave shape (as experience has shown me), and, with an ever faster motion, will rise further and further until, when it completes its revolutions in the same times as the vessel, it is relatively at rest in the vessel. The rise of the water reveals its endeavour to recede from the axis of motion, and from such an endeavour one can find out and measure the true and absolute circular motion of the water, which here is the direct opposite of its relative motion. In the beginning, when the relative motion of the water in the vessel was greatest, that motion was not giving rise to any endeavour to recede from the axis; the water did not seek the circumference by rising up the sides of the vessel but remained level, and therefore its true circular motion had not yet begun. But afterwards, when the relative motion of the water decreased, its rise up the sides of the vessel revealed its endeavour to recede from the axis, and this endeavour showed the true circular motion of the water to be continually increasing and finally becoming greatest when the water was relatively at rest in the vessel. Therefore, that endeavour does not depend on the change of position of the water with respect to surrounding bodies, and thus true circular motion cannot be determined by means of such changes of position. The truly circular motion of each revolving body is unique, corresponding to a unique endeavour as its proper and sufficient effect, while relative motions are innumerable in accordance with their varied relations to external bodies and, like relations, are completely lacking in true effects except insofar as they participate in that true and unique motion. Thus, even in the system of those who hold that our heavens revolve below the heavens of the fixed stars and carry the planets around with them, the individual parts of the heavens, and the planets that are relatively at rest in the heavens to which they belong, are truly in motion. For they change their positions relative to one another (which is not the case with things that are truly at rest), and as they are carried around together with the heavens, they participate in the motions of the heavens and, being parts of revolving wholes, endeavour to recede from the axes of those wholes.

Relative quantities, therefore, are not the actual quantities whose names they bear but are those sensible measures of them (whether true or erroneous) that are commonly used instead of the quantities being measured. But if the meanings of words are to be defined by usage, then it is these sensible measures which should properly be understood by the terms 'time', 'space', 'place', and 'motion', and the manner of expression will be out of the ordinary and purely mathematical if the quantities being measured are understood here. Accordingly those who there interpret these words as referring to the quantities being measured do violence to the Scriptures. And they no less corrupt mathematics and philosophy who confuse true quantities with their relations and common measures.

It is certainly very difficult to find out the true motions of individual bodies and actually to differentiate them from apparent motions, because the parts of that immovable space in which the bodies truly move make no impression on the senses. Nevertheless, the case is not utterly hopeless. For it is possible to draw evidence partly from apparent motions, which are the differences between the true motions, and partly from the forces that are the causes and effects of the true motions. For example, if two balls, at a given distance from each other with a cord connecting them, were revolving about a common centre of gravity, the endeavour of the balls to recede from the axis of motion could be known from the tension of the cord, and thus the quantity of circular motion could be computed. Then, if any equal forces were simultaneously impressed upon the alternate faces of the balls to increase or decrease their circular motion, the increase or decrease of the motion could be known from the increased or decreased tension of the cord, and thus, finally, it could be discovered which faces of the balls the forces would have to be impressed upon for a maximum increase in the motion, that is, which were the posterior faces, or the ones that are in the rear in a circular motion. Further, once the faces that follow and the opposite faces that precede were known, the direction of the motion would be known. In this way both the quantity and the direction of this circular motion could be found in any immense vacuum, where nothing external and sensible existed with which the balls could be compared. Now if some distant bodies were set in that space and maintained given positions with respect to one another, as the fixed stars do in the regions of the heavens, it could not, of course, be known from the relative change of position of the balls among the bodies whether the motion was to be attributed to the bodies or to the balls. But if the cord was examined and its tension was discovered to be the very one which the motion of the balls required, it would be valid to conclude that the motion belonged to the balls and that the bodies were at rest, and then, finally, from the change of position of the balls among the bodies, to determine the direction of this motion. But in what follows, a fuller explanation will be given of how to determine true motions from their causes, effects, and apparent differences, and, conversely, of how to determine from motions, whether true or apparent, their causes and effects. For this was the purpose for which I composed the following treatise.

Axioms, or the Laws of Motion

Law 1

Every body perseveres in its state of being at rest or of moving uniformly straight forwards, except insofar as it is compelled to change its state by forces impressed.

Projectiles persevere in their motions, except insofar as they are retarded by the resistance of the air and are impelled downwards by the force of gravity. A spinning hoop, which has parts that by their cohesion continually draw one another back from rectilinear motions, does not cease to rotate, except insofar as it is retarded by the air. And larger bodies – planets and comets – preserve for a longer time both their progressive and their circular motions, which take place in spaces having less resistance.

Law 2

A change in motion is proportional to the motive force impressed and takes place along the straight line in which that force is impressed.

If some force generates any motion, twice the force will generate twice the motion, and three times the force will generate three times the motion, whether the force is impressed all at once or successively by degrees. And if the body was previously moving, the new motion (since motion is always in the same direction as the generative force) is added to the original motion if that motion was in the same direction or is subtracted from the original motion if it was in the opposite direction or, if it was in an oblique direction, is combined obliquely and compounded with it according to the directions of both motions.

Law 3

To any action there is always an opposite and equal reaction; in other words, the actions of two bodies upon each other are always equal and always opposite in direction.

Whatever presses or draws something else is pressed or drawn just as much by it. If anyone presses a stone with a finger, the finger is also pressed by the stone. If a horse draws a stone tied to a rope, the horse will (so to speak) also be drawn back equally towards the stone, for the rope, stretched out at both ends, will urge the horse towards the stone and the stone towards the horse by one and the same endeavour to go slack and will impede the forward motion of the one as much as it promotes the forward motion of the other. If some body impinging upon another body changes the motion of that body in any way by its own force, then, by the force of the other body (because of the equality of their mutual pressure), it also will in turn undergo the same change in its own motion in the opposite direction. By means of these actions, equal changes occur in the motions, not in the velocities – that is, of course, if the bodies are not impeded by anything else. For the changes in velocities that likewise occur in opposite directions are inversely proportional to the bodies because the motions are changed equally. This law is valid also for attractions, as will be proved in the next Scholium.

Corollary 1

A body acted on by [two] forces acting jointly describes the diagonal of a parallelogram in the same time in which it would describe the sides if the forces were acting separately.

Let a body in a given time, by force M alone impressed in A, be carried with uniform motion from A to B, and, by force N alone impressed in the same place, be carried from A to C; then complete the parallelogram ABDC, and by both forces the body will be carried in the same time along the diagonal from A to D. For, since force N acts along the line AC parallel to BD, this force, by law 2, will make no change at all in the velocity towards the line BD which is generated by the other force. Therefore, the body will reach the line BD in the same time whether force N is impressed or not, and so at the end of that time will be found somewhere on the line BD. By the same argument, at the end of the same time it will be found somewhere on the line CD, and accordingly it is necessarily found at the intersection D of both lines. And, by law 1, it will go with [uniform] rectilinear motion from A to D.

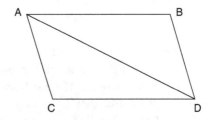

Figure 4.1

Corollary 2

And hence the composition of a direct force AD out of any oblique forces AB and BD is evident, and conversely the resolution of any direct force AD into any oblique forces AB and BD. And this kind of composition and resolution is indeed abundantly confirmed from mechanics.

For example, let OM and ON be unequal spokes going out from the centre O of any wheel, and let the spokes support the weights A and P by means of the cords MA and NP; it is required to find the forces of the weights to move the wheel. Draw the straight line KOL through the centre O, so as to meet the cords perpendicularly at K and L; and with centre O and radius OL, which is the greater of OK and OL, describe a circle meeting the cord MA at D; and draw the straight line OD, and let AC be drawn parallel to it and DC perpendicular to it. Since it makes no difference whether points K, L, and D of the cords are attached or not attached to the plane of the wheel, the weights will have the same effect whether they are suspended from the points K and L or from D and L. And if now the total force of the weight A is represented by line AD, it will be resolved into forces [i.e. components] AC and CD, of which AC, drawing spoke OD directly from the centre, has no effect in moving the wheel, while the other force DC, drawing spoke DO

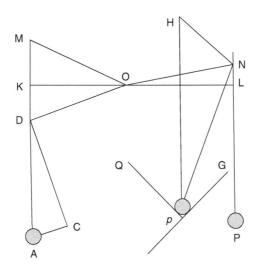

Figure 4.2

93

perpendicularly, has the same effect as if it were drawing spoke OL (equal to OD) perpendicularly; that is, it has the same effect as the weight P, provided that the weight P is to the weight A as the force DC is to the force DA; that is (because triangles ADC and DOK are similar), as OK to OD or OL. Therefore, the weights A and P, which are inversely as the spokes OK and OL (which are in a straight line), will be equipollent and thus will stand in equilibrium, which is a very well-known property of the balance, the lever, and the wheel and axle. But if either weight is greater than in this ratio, its force to move the wheel will be so much the greater.

But if the weight p, equal to the weight P, is partly suspended by the cord Np and partly lies on the oblique plane pG, draw pH perpendicular to the plane of the horizon and NH perpendicular to the plane pG; then if the force of the weight p tending downwards is represented by the line pH, it can be resolved into the forces [i.e. components] pN and HN. If there were some plane pQ perpendicular to the cord pN and cutting the other plane pG in a line parallel to the horizon, and the weight p were only lying on these planes pQ and pG, the weight p would press these planes perpendicularly with the forces pN and HN – plane pQ, that is, with force pN and plane pG with force HN. Therefore, if the plane pQ is removed, so that the weight stretches the cord, then – since the cord, in sustaining the weight, now takes the place of the plane which has been removed – the cord will be stretched by the same force pN with which the plane was formerly pressed. Thus the tension of this oblique cord will be to the tension of the other, and perpendicular, cord PN as pN to pH. Therefore, if the weight p is to the weight A in a ratio that is compounded of the inverse ratio of the least distances of their respective cords pN and AM from the centre of the wheel and the direct ratio of pH to pN, the weights will have the same power to move the wheel and so will sustain each other, as anyone can test.

Now, the weight p, lying on those two oblique planes, has the role of a wedge between the inner surfaces of a body that has been split open; and hence the forces of a wedge and hammer can be determined, because the force with which the weight p presses the plane pQ is to the force with which weight p is impelled along the line pH towards the planes, whether by its own gravity or by the blow of a hammer, as pN is to pH, and because the force with which p presses plane pQ is to the force by which it presses the other plane pG as pN to NH. Furthermore, the force of a screw can also be determined by a similar resolution of forces, inasmuch as it is a wedge impelled by a lever. Therefore, this corollary can be used very extensively, and the variety of its applications clearly shows its truth, since the whole of mechanics – demonstrated in different ways by those who have written on this subject – depends on what has just now been said. For from this are easily derived the forces of machines, which are generally composed of wheels, drums, pulleys, levers, stretched strings, and weights, ascending directly or obliquely, and the other mechanical powers, as well as the forces of tendons to move the bones of animals.

Corollary 3

The quantity of motion, which is determined by adding the motions made in one direction and subtracting the motions made in the opposite direction, is not changed by the action of bodies on one another.

For an action and the reaction opposite to it are equal by law 3, and thus by law 2 the changes which they produce in motions are equal and in opposite directions. Therefore, if motions are in the same direction, whatever is added to the motion of the first body [literally, the fleeing body] will be subtracted from the motion of the second body [literally, the pursuing body] in such a way that the sum remains the same as before. But if the bodies meet head-on, the quantity subtracted from each of the motions will be the same, and thus the difference of the motions made in opposite directions will remain the same.

For example, suppose a spherical body A is three times as large as a spherical body B and has two parts of velocity, and let B follow A in the same straight line with ten parts of velocity; then the motion of A is to the motion of B as six to ten. Suppose that their motions are of six parts and ten parts respectively; the sum will be sixteen parts. When the bodies collide, therefore, if body A gains three or four or five parts of motion, body B will lose just as many parts of motion and thus after reflection body A will continue with nine or ten or eleven parts of motion and B with seven or six or five parts of motion, the sum being always, as originally, sixteen parts of motion. Suppose body A gains nine or ten or eleven or twelve parts of motion and so moves forwards with fifteen or sixteen or seventeen or eighteen parts of motion after meeting body B; then body B, by losing as many parts of motion as A gains, will either move forwards with one part, having lost nine parts of motion, or will be at rest, having lost its forward motion of ten parts, or will move backwards with one part of motion, having lost its motion and (if I may say so) one part more, or will move backwards with two parts of motion because a forward motion of twelve parts has been subtracted. And thus the sums, $15 + 1$ or $16 + 0$, of the motions in the same direction and the differences, $17 - 1$ and $18 - 2$, of the motions in opposite directions will always be sixteen parts of motion, just as before the bodies met and were reflected. And since the motions with which the bodies will continue to move after reflection are known, the velocity of each will be found, on the supposition that it is to the velocity before reflection as the motion after reflection is to the motion before reflection. For example, in the last case, where the motion of body A was six parts before reflection and eighteen parts afterwards, and its velocity was two parts before reflection, its velocity will be found to be six parts after reflection on the basis of the following statement: as six parts of motion before reflection is to eighteen parts of motion afterwards, so two parts of velocity before reflection is to six parts of velocity afterwards.

But if bodies that either are not spherical or are moving in different straight lines strike against each other obliquely and it is required to find their motions after reflection, the position of the plane by which the colliding bodies are touched at the point of collision must be determined; then (by corollary 2) the motion of each body must be resolved into two motions, one perpendicular to this plane and the other parallel to it. Because the bodies act upon each other along a line perpendicular to this plane, the parallel motions [i.e. components] must be kept the same after reflection; and equal changes in opposite directions must be attributed to the perpendicular motions in such a way that the sum of the motions in the same direction and the difference of the motions in opposite directions remain the same as before the bodies came together. The circular motions of bodies about their own centres also generally arise from reflections of this sort. But I do not consider such cases in what follows, and it would be too tedious to demonstrate everything relating to this subject.

Corollary 4

The common centre of gravity of two or more bodies does not change its state whether of motion or of rest as a result of the actions of the bodies upon one another, and therefore the common centre of gravity of all bodies acting upon one another (excluding external actions and impediments) either is at rest or moves uniformly straight forward.

For if two points move forwards with uniform motion in straight lines, and the distance between them is divided in a given ratio, the dividing point either is at rest or moves forwards uniformly in a straight line. This is demonstrated below in lemma 23 and its corollary for the case in which the motions of the points take place in the same plane, and it can be demonstrated by the same reasoning for the case in which those motions do not take place in the same plane. Therefore, if any number of bodies move uniformly in straight lines, the common centre of gravity of any two either is at rest or moves forwards uniformly in a straight line, because any line joining these bodies through their centres – which move forwards uniformly in straight lines – is divided by this common centre in a given ratio. Similarly, the common centre of gravity of these two bodies and any third body either is at rest or moves forwards uniformly in a straight line, because the distance between the common centre of the two bodies and the centre of the third body is divided in a given ratio by the common centre of the three. In the same way, the common centre of these three and of any fourth body either is at rest or moves forwards uniformly in a straight line, because that common centre divides in a given ratio the distance between the common centre of the three and the centre of the fourth body, and so on without end. Therefore, in a system of bodies in which the bodies are entirely free of actions upon one another and of all other actions impressed upon them externally, and in which each body accordingly moves uniformly in its individual straight line, the common centre of gravity of them all either is at rest or moves uniformly straight forward.

Further, in a system of two bodies acting on each other, since the distances of their centres from the common centre of gravity are inversely as the bodies, the relative motions of these bodies, whether of approaching that centre or of receding from it, will be equal. Accordingly, as a result of equal changes in opposite directions in the motions of these bodies, and consequently as a result of the actions of the bodies on each other, that centre is neither accelerated nor retarded nor does it undergo any change in its state of motion or of rest. In a system of several bodies, the common centre of gravity of any two acting upon each other does not in any way change its state as a result of that action, and the common centre of gravity of the rest of the bodies (with which that action has nothing to do) is not affected by that action; the distance between these two centres is divided by the common centre of gravity of all the bodies into parts inversely proportional to the total sums of the bodies whose centres they are, and (since those two centres maintain their state of moving or of being at rest) the common centre of all maintains its state also – for all these reasons it is obvious that this common centre of all never changes its state with respect to motion and rest as a result of the actions of two bodies upon each other. Moreover, in such a system all the actions of bodies upon one another either occur between two bodies or are compounded of such actions between two bodies and therefore never introduce any change in the state of motion or of rest of the common centre of all. Thus, since that centre either is at rest or moves forwards uniformly in some straight line, when the bodies do not act upon one another, that centre will, notwithstanding the actions of the bodies upon one another, continue either to be always at rest or to move always uniformly straight forwards, unless it is driven from this state by forces impressed on the system from outside. Therefore, the law is the same for a system of several bodies as for a single body with respect to perseverance in a state of motion or of rest. For the progressive motion, whether of a single body or of a system of bodies, should always be reckoned by the motion of the centre of gravity.

Corollary 5

When bodies are enclosed in a given space, their motions in relation to one another are the same whether the space is at rest or whether it is moving uniformly straight forward without circular motion.

For in either case the differences of the motions tending in the same direction and the sums of those tending in opposite directions are the same at the beginning (by hypothesis), and from these sums or differences there arise the collisions and impulses [literally, impetuses] with which the bodies strike one another. Therefore, by law 2, the effects of the collisions will be equal in both cases, and thus the motions with respect to one another in the one case will remain equal to the motions with respect to one another in the other case. This is proved clearly by experience: on a ship, all the motions are the same with respect to one another whether the ship is at rest or is moving uniformly straight forwards.

Corollary 6

If bodies are moving in any way whatsoever with respect to one another and are urged by equal accelerative forces along parallel lines, they will all continue to move with respect to one another in the same way as they would if they were not acted on by those forces.

For those forces, by acting equally (in proportion to the quantities of the bodies to be moved) and along parallel lines, will (by law 2) move all the bodies equally (with respect to velocity), and so will never change their positions and motions with respect to one another.

Scholium

The principles I have set forth are accepted by mathematicians and confirmed by experiments of many kinds. By means of the first two laws and the first two corollaries Galileo found that the descent of heavy bodies is in the squared ratio of the time and that the motion of projectiles occurs in a parabola, as experiment confirms, except insofar as these motions are somewhat retarded by the resistance of the air. When a body falls, uniform gravity, by acting equally in individual equal particles of time, impresses equal forces upon that body and generates equal velocities; and in the total time it impresses a total force and generates a total velocity proportional to the time. And the spaces described in proportional times are as the velocities and the times jointly, that is, in the squared ratio of the times. And when a body is projected upwards, uniform gravity impresses forces and takes away velocities proportional to the times; and the times of ascending to the greatest heights are as the velocities to be taken away, and these heights are as the velocities and the times jointly, or as the squares of the velocities. And when a body is projected along any straight line, its motion arising from the projection is compounded with the motion arising from gravity.

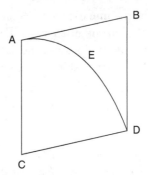

Figure 4.3

For example, let body A by the motion of projection alone describe the straight line AB in a given time, and by the motion of falling alone describe the vertical distance AC in the same time; then complete the parallelogram ABDC, and by the compounded motion the body will be found in place D at the end of the time; and the curved line AED which the body will describe will be a parabola which the straight line AB touches at A and whose ordinate BD is as AB.[2]

What has been demonstrated concerning the times of oscillating pendulums depends on the same first two laws and first two corollaries, and this is supported by daily experience with clocks. From the same laws and corollaries and law 3, Sir Christopher Wren, Dr John Wallis, and Mr Christiaan Huygens, easily the foremost geometers of the previous generation, independently found the rules of the collisions and reflections of hard bodies, and communicated them to the Royal Society at nearly the same time, entirely agreeing with one another (as to these rules); and Wallis was indeed the first to publish what had been found, followed by Wren and Huygens. But Wren additionally proved the truth of these rules before the Royal Society by means of an experiment with pendulums, which the eminent Mariotte soon after thought worthy to be made the subject of a whole book.[8]

---

[8] See "A Summary Account of the General Laws of Motion by Dr. John Wallis, and Dr. Christopher Wren," *Philosophical Transactions* 3 (1668), 864–8, and "A Summary Account of the Laws of Motion, Communicated by Mr. Christian Hugens in a Letter to the R. Society," *Philosophical Transactions* 4 (1669), 925–8. Edmé Mariotte wrote *Traité de la Percussion, ou Chocq des Corps dans lequel les Principales Regles du Mouvement* (Paris, 1673), which went into several editions.

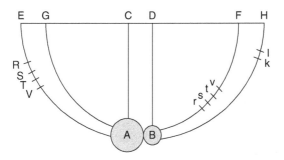

Figure 4.4

However, if this experiment is to agree precisely with the theories, account must be taken of both the resistance of the air and the elastic force of the colliding bodies. Let the spherical bodies A and B be suspended from centres C and D by parallel and equal cords AC and BD.

With these centres and with those distances as radii describe semicircles EAF and GBH bisected by radii CA and DB. Take away body B, and let body A be brought to any point R of the arc EAF and be let go from there, and let it return after one oscillation to point V. RV is the retardation arising from the resistance of the air. Let ST be a fourth of RV and be located in the middle so that RS and TV are equal and RS is to ST as 3 to 2. Then ST will closely approximate the retardation in the descent from S to A. Restore body B to its original place. Let body A fall from point S, and its velocity at the place of reflection A, without sensible error, will be as great as if it had fallen in a vacuum from place T. Therefore let this velocity be represented by the chord of the arc TA. For it is a proposition very well known to geometers that the velocity of a pendulum in its lowest point is as the chord of the arc that it has described in falling. After reflection let body A arrive at place s, and body B at place k. Take away body B and find place v such that if body A is let go from this place and after one oscillation returns to place r, st will be a fourth of rv and be located in the middle, so that rs and tv are equal; and let the chord of the arc tA represent the velocity that body A had in place A immediately after reflection. For t will be that true and correct place to which body A must have ascended if there had been no resistance of the air. By a similar method the place k, to which body B ascends, will have to be corrected, and the place l, to which that body must have ascended in a vacuum, will have to be found. In this manner it is possible to make all our experiments, just as if we were in a vacuum. Finally body A will have to be multiplied (so to speak) by the chord of the arc TA, which represents its velocity, in order to get its motion in place A immediately before reflection, and then by the chord of the arc tA in order to get its motion in place A immediately after reflection. And thus body B will have to be multiplied by the chord of the arc B*l* in order to get its motion immediately after reflection. And by a similar method, when two bodies are let go simultaneously from different places, the motions of both will have to be found before as well as after reflection, and then finally the motions will have to be compared with each other in order to determine the effects of the reflection.

On making a test in this way with ten-foot pendulums, using unequal as well as equal bodies, and making the bodies come together from very large distances apart, say of eight or twelve or sixteen feet, I always found – within an error of less than three inches in the measurements – that when the bodies met each other directly, the changes of motions made in the bodies in opposite directions were equal, and consequently that the action and reaction were always equal. For example, if body A collided with body B, which was at rest, with nine parts of motion and, losing seven parts, proceeded after reflection with two, body B rebounded with those seven parts. If the bodies met head-on, A with twelve parts of motion and B with six, and A rebounded with two, B rebounded with eight, fourteen parts being subtracted from each. Subtract twelve parts from the motion of A and nothing will remain; subtract another two parts, and a motion of two parts in the opposite direction will be produced; and so, subtracting fourteen parts from the six parts of the motion of body B, eight parts will be produced in the opposite direction. But if the bodies moved in the same direction, A more quickly with fourteen parts and B more slowly with five parts, and after reflection A moved with five parts, then B moved with fourteen, nine parts having been transferred from A to B. And so in all other cases. As a result of the meeting and collision of bodies, the quantity of motion – determined by adding the motions in the same direction and subtracting the motions in opposite directions – was never changed. I would attribute the error of an inch or two in the measurements to the difficulty of doing everything with sufficient accuracy. It was difficult both to release the pendulums simultaneously in such a way that the bodies would impinge upon each other in the lowest place AB, and to note the places s and k to which the bodies ascended after colliding. But also, with respect to the pendulous bodies themselves, errors were introduced by the unequal density of the parts and by irregularities of texture arising from other causes.

Further, lest anyone object that the rule which this experiment was designed to prove presupposes that bodies are either absolutely hard or at least perfectly elastic and thus of a kind which do not occur naturally, I add that the experiments just described work equally well with soft bodies and with hard ones, since surely they do not in any way depend on the condition of hardness. For if this rule is to be tested in bodies that are not perfectly hard, it will only be necessary to decrease the reflection in a fixed proportion to the quantity of elastic force. In the theory of Wren and Huygens, absolutely hard bodies rebound from each other with the velocity with which they have collided. This will be affirmed with more certainty of perfectly elastic bodies. In imperfectly elastic bodies the velocity of rebounding must be decreased together with the elastic force, because that force (except when the parts of the bodies are damaged as a result of collision, or experience some sort of extension such as would be caused by a hammer blow) is fixed and determinate (as far as I can tell) and makes the bodies rebound from each other with a relative velocity that is in a given ratio to the relative velocity with which they collide. I have tested this as follows with tightly wound balls of wool strongly compressed. First, releasing the pendulums and measuring their reflection, I found the quantity of their elastic force; then from this force I determined what the reflections would be in other cases of their collision, and the experiments which were made agreed with the computations. The balls always rebounded from each other with a relative velocity that was to the relative velocity of their colliding as 5 to 9, more or less. Steel balls rebounded with nearly the same velocity and cork balls with a slightly smaller velocity, while with glass balls the proportion was roughly 15 to 16. And in this manner the third law of motion – insofar as it relates to impacts and reflections – is proved by this theory, which plainly agrees with experiments.

I demonstrate the third law of motion for attractions briefly as follows.[9] Suppose that between any two bodies A and B that attract each other any

---

[9] Cf. the discussion in Newton's letter to Cotes, in this volume (pp. 160–62).

obstacle is interposed so as to impede their coming together. If one body A is more attracted towards the other body B than that other body B is attracted towards the first body A, then the obstacle will be more strongly pressed by body A than by body B and accordingly will not remain in equilibrium. The stronger pressure will prevail and will make the system of the two bodies and the obstacle move straight forwards in the direction from A towards B and, in empty space, go on indefinitely with a motion that is always accelerated, which is absurd and contrary to the first law of motion. For according to the first law, the system will have to persevere in its state of resting or of moving uniformly straight forwards, and accordingly the bodies will urge the obstacle equally and on that account will be equally attracted to each other. I have tested this with a lodestone and iron. If these are placed in separate vessels that touch each other and float side by side in still water, neither one will drive the other forwards, but because of the equality of the attraction in both directions they will sustain their mutual endeavours towards each other, and at last, having attained equilibrium, they will be at rest.

In the same way gravity is mutual between the earth and its parts. Let the earth FI be cut by any plane EG into two parts EGF and EGI; then their weights towards each other will be equal. For if the greater part EGI is cut into two parts EGKH and HKI by another plane HK parallel to the first plane EG, in such a way that HKI is equal to the part EFG that has been cut off earlier, it is manifest that the middle part EGKH will not preponderate towards either of the outer parts but will, so to speak, be suspended in equilibrium between both and will be at rest. Moreover, the outer part HKI will press upon the middle part with all its weight and will urge it towards the other outer part EGF, and therefore the force by which EGI, the sum of the parts HKI and EGKH, tends towards the third part EGF is equal to the weight of the part HKI, that is, equal to the weight of the third part EGF. And therefore the weights of the two parts EGI and EGF towards each other are equal, as I set out to demonstrate. And if these weights were not equal, the whole earth, floating in an aether free of resistance, would yield to the greater weight and in receding from it would go off indefinitely.

As bodies are equipollent in collisions and reflections if their velocities are inversely as their inherent forces [i.e. forces of inertia], so in the motions of machines those agents [i.e. acting bodies] whose velocities

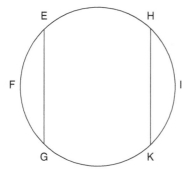

Figure 4.5

(reckoned in the direction of their forces) are inversely as their inherent forces are equipollent and sustain one another by their contrary endeavours. Thus weights are equipollent in moving the arms of a balance if during oscillation of the balance they are inversely as their velocities upwards and downwards; that is, weights which move straight up and down are equipollent if they are inversely as the distances between the axis of the balance and the points from which they are suspended; but if such weights are interfered with by oblique planes or other obstacles that are introduced and thus ascend or descend obliquely, they are equipollent if they are inversely as the ascents and descents insofar as these are reckoned with respect to a perpendicular, and this is so because the direction of gravity is downwards. Similarly, in a pulley or combination of pulleys, the weight will be sustained by the force of the hand pulling the rope vertically, which is to the weight (ascending either straight up or obliquely) as the velocity of the perpendicular ascent to the velocity of the hand pulling the rope. In clocks and similar devices, which are constructed out of engaged gears, the contrary forces that promote and hinder the motion of the gears will sustain each other if they are inversely as the velocities of the parts of the gears upon which they are impressed. The force of a screw to press a body is to the force of a hand turning the handle as the circular velocity of the handle, in the part where it is urged by the hand, is to the progressive velocity of the screw towards the pressed body. The forces by which a wedge presses the two parts of the wood that it splits are to the force of the hammer upon the wedge as the progress of the wedge (in the direction of the force impressed upon it by the hammer) is to the velocity with which the parts of the wood yield to the wedge along lines perpendicular to the faces of the wedge. And the case is the same for all machines.

The effectiveness and usefulness of all machines or devices consist wholly in our being able to increase the force by decreasing the velocity, and vice versa; in this way the problem is solved in the case of any working machine or device: 'To move a given weight by a given force' or to overcome any other given resistance by a given force. For if machines are constructed in such a way that the velocities of the agent [or acting body] and the resistant [or resisting body] are inversely as the forces, the agent will sustain the resistance and, if there is a greater disparity of velocities, will overcome that resistance. Of course the disparity of the velocities may be so great that it can also overcome all the resistance which generally arises from the friction of contiguous bodies sliding over one another, from the cohesion of continuous bodies that are to be separated from one another, or from the weights of bodies to be raised; and if all this resistance is overcome, the remaining force will produce an acceleration of motion proportional to itself, partly in the parts of the machine, partly in the resisting body.

But my purpose here is not to write a treatise on mechanics. By these examples I wished only to show the wide range and the certainty of the third law of motion. For if the action of an agent is reckoned by its force and velocity jointly, and if, similarly, the reaction of a resistant is reckoned jointly by the velocities of its individual parts and the forces of resistance arising from their friction, cohesion, weight, and acceleration, the action and reaction will always be equal to each other in all examples of using devices or machines. And to the extent to which the action is propagated through the machine and ultimately impressed upon each resisting body, its ultimate direction will always be opposite to the direction of the reaction.

Book 1: The Motions of Bodies

Book 1: Section II

Scholium

By these propositions we are directed to the analogy between centripetal forces and the central bodies towards which those forces tend. For it is reasonable that forces directed towards bodies depend on the nature and the quantity of matter of such bodies, as happens in the case of magnetic bodies. And whenever cases of this sort occur, the attractions of the bodies must be reckoned by assigning proper forces to their individual particles and then taking the sums of these forces.

I use the word 'attraction' here in a general sense for any endeavour whatever of bodies to approach one another, whether that endeavour occurs as a result of the action of the bodies either drawn towards one another or acting on one another by means of spirits emitted or whether it arises from the action of aether or of air or of any medium whatsoever – whether corporeal or incorporeal – in any way impelling towards one another the bodies floating therein. I use the word 'impulse' in the same general sense, considering in this treatise not the species of forces and their physical qualities but their quantities and mathematical proportions, as I have explained in the definitions.

Mathematics requires an investigation of those quantities of forces and their proportions that follow from any conditions that may be supposed. Then, coming down to physics, these proportions must be compared with the phenomena, so that it may be found out which conditions [or laws] of forces apply to each kind of attracting bodies. And then, finally, it will be possible to argue more securely concerning the physical species, physical causes, and physical proportions of these forces. Let us see, therefore, what the forces are by which spherical bodies, consisting of particles that attract in the way already set forth, must act upon one another, and what sorts of motions result from such forces.

Book 3: The System of the World

Rules for the Study of Natural Philosophy

Rule 1

No more causes of natural things should be admitted than are both true and sufficient to explain their phenomena.

As the philosophers say: Nature does nothing in vain, and more causes are in vain when fewer suffice. For nature is simple and does not indulge in the luxury of superfluous causes.

Rule 2

Therefore, the causes assigned to natural effects of the same kind must be, so far as possible, the same.

Examples are the cause of respiration in man and beast, or of the falling of stones in Europe and America, or of the light of a kitchen fire and the sun, or of the reflection of light on our earth and the planets.

Rule 3

Those qualities of bodies that cannot be intended and remitted [i.e. increased and diminished] and that belong to all bodies on which experiments can be made should be taken as qualities of all bodies universally.

For the qualities of bodies can be known only through experiments; and therefore qualities that square with experiments universally are to be regarded as universal qualities; and qualities that cannot be diminished cannot be taken away from bodies. Certainly idle fancies ought not to be fabricated recklessly against the evidence of experiments, nor should we depart from the analogy of nature, since nature is always simple and ever consonant with itself. The extension of bodies is known to us only through our senses, and yet there are bodies beyond the range of these senses; but because extension is found in all sensible bodies, it is ascribed to all bodies universally. We know by experience that some bodies are hard. Moreover, because the hardness of the whole arises from the hardness of its parts, we justly infer from this not only the hardness of the undivided particles of bodies that are accessible to our senses, but also of all other bodies. That all bodies are impenetrable we gather not by reason but by our senses. We find those bodies that we handle to be impenetrable, and hence we conclude that impenetrability is a property of all bodies universally. That all bodies are movable and persevere in motion or in rest by means of certain forces (which we call forces of inertia) we infer from finding these properties in the bodies that we have seen. The extension, hardness, impenetrability, mobility, and force of inertia of the whole arise from the extension, hardness, impenetrability, mobility, and force of inertia of each of the parts; and thus we conclude that every one of the least parts of all bodies is extended, hard, impenetrable, movable, and endowed with a force of inertia. And this is the foundation of all natural philosophy. Further, from phenomena we know that the divided, contiguous parts of bodies can be separated from one another, and from mathematics it is certain that the undivided parts can be distinguished into smaller parts by our reason. But it is uncertain whether those parts which have been distinguished in this way and not yet divided can actually be divided and separated from one another by the forces of nature. But if it were established by even a single experiment that in the breaking of a hard and solid body, any undivided particle underwent division, we should conclude by the force of this third rule not only that divided parts are separable but also that undivided parts can be divided indefinitely.

Finally, if it is universally established by experiments and astronomical observations that all bodies on or near the earth gravitate [literally, are heavy] towards the earth, and do so in proportion to the quantity of matter in each body, and that the moon gravitates [is heavy] towards the earth in proportion to the quantity of its matter, and that our sea in turn gravitates [is heavy] towards the moon, and that all planets gravitate [are heavy] towards one another, and that there is a similar gravity [heaviness] of comets towards the sun, it will have to be concluded by this third rule that all bodies gravitate towards one another. Indeed, the argument from phenomena will be even stronger for universal gravity than for the impenetrability of bodies, for which, of course, we have not a single experiment, and not even an observation, in the case of the heavenly bodies. Yet I am by no means affirming that gravity is essential to bodies. By inherent force I mean only the force of inertia. This is immutable. Gravity is diminished as bodies recede from the earth.

Rule 4

In experimental philosophy, propositions gathered from phenomena by induction should be considered either exactly or very nearly true notwithstanding any contrary hypotheses, until yet other phenomena make such propositions either more exact or liable to exceptions.

This rule should be followed so that arguments based on induction may not be nullified by hypotheses.

General Scholium

The hypothesis of vortices is beset with many difficulties. If, by a radius drawn to the sun, each and every planet is to describe areas proportional to the time, the periodic times of the parts of the vortex must be as the squares of the distances from the sun. If the periodic times of the planets are to be as the $\frac{3}{2}$ powers of the distances from the sun, the periodic times of the parts of the vortex must be as the $\frac{3}{2}$ powers of the distances. If the smaller vortices revolving about Saturn, Jupiter, and the other planets are to be preserved and are to float without agitation in the vortex of the sun, the periodic times of the parts of the solar vortex must be the same. The axial revolutions [i.e. rotations] of the sun and planets, which would have to agree with the motions of their vortices, differ from all these proportions. The motions of comets are extremely regular, observe the same laws as the motions of planets, and cannot be explained by vortices. Comets go with very eccentric motions into all parts of the heavens, which cannot happen unless vortices are eliminated.[10]

The only resistance which projectiles encounter in our air is from the air. With the air removed, as it is in Boyle's vacuum, resistance ceases, since a tenuous feather and solid gold fall with equal velocity in such a vacuum. And the case is the same for the celestial spaces, which are above the atmosphere of the earth. All bodies must move very freely in these spaces, and therefore planets and comets must revolve continually in orbits given in kind and in position, according to the laws set forth above. They will indeed persevere in their orbits by the laws of gravity, but they certainly could not originally have acquired the regular position of the orbits by these laws.

The six primary planets revolve about the sun in circles concentric with the sun, with the same direction of motion, and very nearly in the same plane. Ten moons revolve about the earth, Jupiter, and Saturn in concentric circles, with the same direction of motion, very nearly in the planes of the orbits of the planets. And all these regular motions do not have their origin in mechanical causes, since comets go freely in very eccentric orbits and into all parts of the heavens. And with this kind of motion the comets pass very swiftly and very easily through the orbits of the planets; and in their aphelia, where they are slower and spend a longer time, they are at the greatest possible distance from one another, so as to attract one another as little as possible.

---

[10] Cf. again Newton's 1693 letter to Leibniz, in this volume.

This most elegant system of the sun, planets, and comets could not have arisen without the design and dominion of an intelligent and powerful being. And if the fixed stars are the centres of similar systems, they will all be constructed according to a similar design and subject to the dominion of *One*, especially since the light of the fixed stars is of the same nature as the light of the sun, and all the systems send light into all the others. And so that the systems of the fixed stars will not fall upon one another as a result of their gravity, he has placed them at immense distances from one another.

He rules all things, not as the world soul but as the lord of all. And because of his dominion he is called Lord God *Pantokrator*.[11] For 'god' is a relative word and has reference to servants, and godhood is the lordship of God, not over his own body as is supposed by those for whom God is the world soul, but over servants. The supreme God is an eternal, infinite, and absolutely perfect being; but a being, however perfect, without dominion is not the Lord God. For we do say my God, your God, the God of Israel, the God of Gods, and Lord of Lords, but we do not say my eternal one, your eternal one, the eternal one of Israel, the eternal one of the gods; we do not say my infinite one, or my perfect one. These designations [i.e. eternal, infinite, perfect] do not have reference to servants. The word 'god' is used far and wide[12] to mean 'lord', but every lord is not a god. The lordship of a spiritual being constitutes a god, a true lordship constitutes a true god, a supreme lordship a supreme god, an imaginary lordship an imaginary god. And from true lordship it follows that the true God is living, intelligent, and powerful; from the other perfections, that he is supreme, or supremely perfect. He is eternal and infinite, omnipotent and omniscient, that is, he endures from eternity to eternity, and he is present from infinity to infinity; he rules all things, and he knows all things that happen or can happen. He is not eternity and infinity, but eternal and infinite; he is not duration and space, but he endures and is present. He endures always

---

[11] These endnotes are Newton's. The first, labeled "a" in the third edition of the *Principia*, is as follows: That is, universal ruler. The second and third, labeled "b" and "c," are included in English translation here (translated by me).

[12] Pocock derives the Latin word *Deus* from the Arabic *du* (and in the oblique case *di*) which signifies "lord." And in this sense princes are called gods: Psalms 82:6 and John 10:35. And Moses is called a god to his brother Aaron, and a god to King Pharaoh (Exodus 4:16 and 7:1). And in the same sense, the souls of dead princes were formerly called gods by the heathens, but falsely so, because of their lack of dominion.

and is present everywhere, and by existing always and everywhere he constitutes duration and space. Since each and every particle of space is *always*, and each and every indivisible moment of duration is *everywhere*, certainly the maker and lord of all things will not be *never* or *nowhere*.

Every sentient soul, at different times and in different organs of senses and motions, is the same indivisible person. There are parts that are successive in duration and coexistent in space, but neither of these exist in the person of man or in his thinking principle, and much less in the thinking substance of God. Every man, insofar as he is a thing that has senses, is one and the same man throughout his lifetime in each and every organ of his senses. God is one and the same God always and everywhere. He is omnipresent not only *virtually* but also *substantially*; for action requires substance. In him[13] all things are contained and move, but he does not act on them nor they on him.

It is agreed that the supreme God necessarily exists, and by the same necessity he is *always* and *everywhere*. It follows that all of him is like himself: he is all eye, all ear, all brain, all arm, all force of sensing, of understanding, and of acting, but in a way not at all human, in a way not at all corporeal, in a way utterly unknown to us. As a blind man has no idea of colours, so we have no idea of the ways in which the most wise God senses and understands all things. He totally lacks any body and corporeal shape, and so he cannot be seen or heard or touched, nor ought he to be worshiped in the form of something corporeal. We have ideas of his attributes, but we certainly do not know what is the substance of any thing. We see only the shapes and colours of bodies, we hear only their sounds, we touch only their external surfaces, we smell only their odours, and we taste their flavours. But there is no direct sense and there are no indirect reflected actions by which we know innermost substances; much less do we have an idea of the substance of God. We know him only by his properties and attributes and by the wisest and best construction of

---

[13] This was the opinion of the Ancients, so Pythagoras in Cicero, *De Natura Deorum*, book 1, Thales, Anaxogoras, Virgil, *Georg.*, book 4, v. 221, and *Æneid*, book 6, v. 726; Philo, *Allegory*, at the beginning of book 1. Aratus in his *Phænom*, at the beginning. So also the sacred writers, as St. Paul, Acts 17:27, 28. St. John's Gospel 14:2. Moses in Deuteronomy 4:39 and 10:14. David, Psalms 139:7, 8, 9. Solomon 1 Kings 8:27. Job 22:12, 13, 14. Jeremiah 23:23, 24. The idolaters supposed the sun, the moon and the stars, human souls, and other parts of the world to be parts of the supreme God and therefore to be worshipped, but falsely.

things and their final causes, and we admire him because of his perfections; but we venerate and worship him because of his dominion. For we worship him as servants, and a god without dominion, providence, and final causes is nothing other than fate and nature. No variation of things arises from blind metaphysical necessity, which must be the same always and everywhere. All the diversity of created things, each in its place and time, could only have arisen from the ideas and the will of a necessarily existing being. But God is said allegorically to see, hear, speak, laugh, love, hate, desire, give, receive, be angry, fight, build, form, construct. For all discourse about God is derived through a certain similitude from things human, which while not perfect is nevertheless a similitude of some kind. This concludes the discussion of God, and to treat of God from phenomena is certainly a part of natural philosophy.

Thus far I have explained the phenomena of the heavens and of our sea by the force of gravity, but I have not yet assigned a cause to gravity. Indeed, this force arises from some cause that penetrates as far as the centres of the sun and planets without any diminution of its power to act, and that acts not in proportion to the quantity of the *surfaces* of the particles on which it acts (as mechanical causes are wont to do) but in proportion to the quantity of *solid* matter, and whose action is extended everywhere to immense distances, always decreasing as the squares of the distances. Gravity towards the sun is compounded of the gravities towards the individual particles of the sun, and at increasing distances from the sun decreases exactly as the squares of the distances as far out as the orbit of Saturn, as is manifest from the fact that the aphelia of the planets are at rest, and even as far as the farthest aphelia of the comets, provided that those aphelia are at rest. I have not as yet been able to deduce from phenomena the reason for these properties of gravity, and I do not feign hypotheses. For whatever is not deduced from the phenomena must be called a hypothesis; and hypotheses, whether metaphysical or physical, or based on occult qualities, or mechanical, have no place in experimental philosophy. In this experimental philosophy, propositions are deduced from the phenomena and are made general by induction. The impenetrability, mobility, and impetus of bodies, and the laws of motion and the law of gravity have been found by this method. And it is enough that gravity really exists and acts according to the laws that we have set forth and is sufficient to explain all the motions of the heavenly bodies and of our sea.

A few things could now be added concerning a certain very subtle spirit pervading gross bodies and lying hidden in them; by its force and actions, the particles of bodies attract one another at very small distances and cohere when they become contiguous; and electrical [i.e. electrified] bodies act at greater distances, repelling as well as attracting neighbouring corpuscles; and light is emitted, reflected, refracted, inflected, and heats bodies; and all sensation is excited, and the limbs of animals move at command of the will, namely, by the vibrations of this spirit being propagated through the solid fibres of the nerves from the external organs of the senses to the brain and from the brain into the muscles. But these things cannot be explained in a few words; furthermore, there is not a sufficient number of experiments to determine and demonstrate accurately the laws governing the actions of this spirit.

Chapter V
"An Account of the System of the World"[1]

i Scripture abused to prove the immoveableness of the globe of the earth

In determining the true system of the world the main question is whether the earth do rest or be moved. For deciding this some bring texts of scripture, but in my opinion misinterpreted, the scriptures speaking not in the language of astronomers (as they think) but in that of the common people to whom they were written. So where 'tis said that[2] God hath made the round world so fast that it cannot be moved, the prophet intended not to teach mathematicians the spherical figure and immoveableness of the whole earth and sea in the heavens but to tell the vulgar in their own dialect that God had made the great continent of Asia, Europe and Africa so fast upon its foundations in the great ocean that it cannot be moved therein after the manner of a floating island. For this continent was the whole habitable world anciently known and by the ancient eastern nations was accounted[3] round or circular, as was also the[4] sea encompassing it. And this earth and sea they accounted flat as if the sun, moon and stars ascended out of the ocean at their rising and went down into it again at their setting.

---

[1] Newton's spelling and punctuation have been modernized – e.g., so that "Jerusalem" and "Job" are spelled with a "j" rather than an "i" – but quotations and paraphrases from scriptural texts have not been. Abbreviations have been altered in a few cases. Throughout this text, we reproduce Newton's notes; we do not reproduce any elements of the text that were crossed out, including notes. Newton's notes are reproduced here as endnotes.

This continent is the world or earth usually mentioned in scripture and there described to be[5] broad and to have[6] end or[7] borders, that is circular ones, whose centre some placed in Egypt others at Delphos, others at Jerusalem. And this world the prophets consider as established in the ocean upon sure and immoveable foundations at the first creation. The heavens were of old and the earth standing out of the water and in the water (that is in the midst of the ocean like an island) by the word of God (2 Pet. 3.5.). Thou Lord in the beginning hast laid the foundations of the earth and the heavens are the work of thine hands (Psalms 102.25, Proverbs 8.29). Where wast thou when I laid the foundations of the earth. Declare if thou hast understanding who hath laid the measures thereof or who hath stretched the line over it. Whereupon are the foundations thereof fixed or who hath laid the corner stone thereof, when the stars of the morning praised me together, etc. (Job 38.4). The earth is the Lord's and all that therein is the compass of the world and they that dwell therein. For he hath founded it upon the seas and established it upon the floods (Psalms 24.1, 2 and 136.6). Thou hast laid the foundation of the round world (Psalms 89.12). When he set a circle upon the face of the deep (that is, formed it circular about the earth) – when he gave to the sea his decree that the waters should not pass his commandment, when he appointed the foundations of the earth, then was I by him (Proverbs 8.27, 29). He laid the foundations of the earth that it never should move at any time: Thou encompassed it with the deep like as with a garment (Psalms 104.5). So then the round world spoken of in scriptures is such a world as hath foundations and is founded in the waters and by consequence 'tis not the whole globe of the earth and sea but only the habitable dry land. For the whole globe hath no foundations, but this habitable world is founded in the seas. And since this world by reason of the firmness of its foundations is said in scripture to be immoveable this immoveableness cannot be of the whole globe together, but only of its parts one amongst another and signifies nothing more than that those parts are firmly compacted together so that the dry land or continent of Europe, Asia and Africa cannot be moved upon the main body of the globe on which it is founded. For this immoveableness of the earth is opposite to that it's motion spoken of in Job. He removeth the mountains and they feel not when he overthroweth them in his wrath: He removeth the earth out of her place that the pillars thereof do shake (Job 9.6).

ii Mathematics abused to prove the globe of the earth immoveable

There is another sort of arguments against the motion of the whole earth taken from our senses, as if the earth could not be moved without our being many ways sensible of its motion. But this way of arguing proceeds from want of skill and judgement in mathematical things, and therefore is insisted upon only by the common people and such mathematicians as understand not so much as the principles of mechanics. Were the earth moved unevenly by jogs such motion would be easily perceived, but an even motion such as the earth's is supposed, ought to be imperceptible. For any system of bodies the motions of the bodies one amongst anot [her] are the same whether the system rest or be [moved] on uniformly, as is mathematically demonstrable. So the motions of all things in a ship are found the same whether the ship rest or be under sail. In both cases things fall perpendicularly down by the mast and projectiles fly alike towards all quarters. Nor can a blinded mariner tell whether the ship move fast or slow or not at all. And there is the same reason of the system of the earth, sea and air with the things therein. We cannot tell by our senses whether they all rest or move on evenly together.

iii Accurate skill in geometry and mechanics requisite to decide the question

Such arguments as these being insufficient to determine the question, 'tis fit we should lay aside these and the like vulgar prejudices and have recourse to some strict and proper way of reasoning. Now the question being about motion is a mathematical one and therefore requires skill in mathematics to decide it. And seeing it is more difficult to argue demonstratively about magnitude and motion together than about magnitude alone, there is greater skill required here than in pure geometry so that none but able mathematicians may pretend to be competent judges of this matter. The great difficulty of this part of mathematics seems to be the reason that the ancients made but little progress in it. In this last age since the revival and advancement of these studies, some able mathematicians such as Galileo and Huygens have carried it on further than the ancients did. Mister Newton to advance it far enough for his purpose has spent the two first of his three books [in the *Principia*] in demonstrating new propositions about force and motion before he begins to consider the system of the world. Then in his third book he teaches that system from the propositions demonstrated in the two first. The design of this paper is to give you an account of this system and refer you to the demonstrations thereof to the book itself or to the judgement of such mathematicians as have perused it ... [end of manuscript].

Notes

2 Psalms 93.2 and 96.10.
3 Strabo Geog. 1. 1. p. 2, 4.
4 Proverbs 8.27. Job 9.8.
5 Job 38.18. Psalms 50.1.
6 Job 28.24 and 37.3. Psalms 46.9 and 72.8.
7 Psalms 74.17.

Chapter VI
Correspondence with Richard Bentley [1691–3]

Paper of directions given by Newton to Bentley respecting the books to be read before endeavoring to read and understand the *Principia*

c. July 1691

Next after Euclid's *Elements* the elements of the Conic sections are to be understood. And for this end you may read either the first part of the *Elementa Curvarum* of John De Witt, or De la Hire's late treatise of the conic sections, or Dr Barrow's epitome of Apollonius.

For algebra read first Barthin's introduction and then peruse such problems as you will find scattered up & down in the commentaries on Descartes's *Geometry* and other algebraical writings of Francis Schooten. I do not mean that you should read over all those commentaries, but only the solutions of such problems as you will here & there meet with. You may meet with De Witt's *Elementa curvarum* & Bartholin's introduction bound up together with Descartes's *Geometry* and Schooten's commentaries.

For astronomy read first the short account of the Copernican system in the end of Gassendi's *Astronomy* & then so much of Mercator's *Astronomy* as concerns the same system & the new discoveries made in the heavens by telescopes in the appendix.

These are sufficient for understanding my book: but if you can procure Huygens's *Horologium oscillatorium*, the perusal of that will make you much more ready.

At the first perusal of my book it's enough if you understand the propositions with some of the demonstrations which are easier than the rest. For when you understand the easier they will afterwards give you light into the harder. When you have read the first 60 pages, pass on to the 3rd book & when you see the design of that you may turn back to such propositions as you shall have a desire to know, or peruse the whole in order if you think fit.

'Directions from Mr Newton by his own hand'

Cambridge, 10 December 1692

To the Reverend Dr Richard Bentley, at the Bishop of Worcester's House in Parkstreet, Westminster.

SIR,

When I wrote my treatise about our system,[1] I had an eye upon such principles as might work with considering men, for the belief of a deity, and nothing can rejoice me more than to find it useful for that purpose. But if I have done the public any service this way, it is due to nothing but industry and patient thought.

As to your first query, it seems to me that if the matter of our sun and planets, and all the matter of the universe, were evenly scattered throughout all the heavens, and every particle had an innate gravity towards all the rest, and the whole space, throughout which this matter was scattered, was but finite; the matter on the outside of this space would by its gravity tend towards all the matter on the inside, and by consequence fall down into the middle of the whole space, and there compose one great spherical mass. But if the matter was evenly dispersed throughout an infinite space, it would never convene into one mass, but some of it would convene into one mass and some into another, so as to make an infinite number of great masses, scattered at great distances from one to another throughout all that infinite space. And thus might the sun and fixed stars be formed, supposing the matter were of a lucid nature. But how the matter should divide itself into two sorts, and that part of it, which is fit to compose a shining body, should fall down into one mass and make a sun, and the rest,

---

[1] That is, the *Principia*.

which is fit to compose an opaque body, should coalesce, not into one great body, like the shining matter, but into many little ones or if the sun at first were an opaque body like the planets, or the planets lucid bodies like the sun, how it alone should be changed into a shining body, while all they continue opaque, or all they be changed into opaque ones, while it remains unchanged, I do not think explicable by mere natural causes, but am forced to ascribe it to the counsel and contrivance of a voluntary agent.

The same power, whether natural or supernatural, which placed the sun in the centre of the six primary planets, placed Saturn in the centre of the orbits of its five secondary planets, and Jupiter in the centre of its four secondary planets, and the earth in the centre of the moon's orbit; and therefore had this cause been a blind one, without contrivance or design, the sun would have been a body of the same kind with Saturn, Jupiter, and the earth, that is, without light and heat. Why there is one body in our system qualified to give light and heat to all the rest, I know no reason, but because the author of the system thought it convenient; and why there is but one body of this kind I know no reason, but because one was sufficient to warm and enlighten all the rest. For the Cartesian hypothesis of suns losing their light, and then turning into comets, and comets into planets, can have no place in my system, and is plainly erroneous; because it is certain that as often as they appear to us, they descend into the system of our planets, lower than the orbit of Jupiter, and sometimes lower than the orbits of Venus and Mercury, and yet never stay here, but always return from the sun with the same degrees of motion by which they approached it.

To your second query, I answer, that the motions which the planets now have could not spring from any natural cause alone, but were impressed by an intelligent agent. For since comets descend into the region of our planets, and here move all manner of ways, going sometimes the same way with the planets, sometimes the contrary way, and sometimes in cross ways, in planes inclined to the plane of the ecliptic, and at all kinds of angles, it is plain that there is no natural cause which could determine all the planets, both primary and secondary, to move the same way and in the same plane, without any considerable variation. This must have been the effect of counsel. Nor is there any natural cause which could give the planets those just degrees of velocity, in proportion to their distances from the sun, and other central bodies, which were requisite to make them move in such concentric orbits about those bodies. Had the planets been as swift as comets, in proportion to their distances from the sun (as they would have been, had their motion been caused by their gravity, whereby the matter, at the first formation of the planets, might fall from the remote regions towards the sun), they would not move in concentric orbits, but in such eccentric ones as the comets move in. Were all the planets as swift as Mercury, or as slow as Saturn or its satellites; or were their several velocities otherwise much greater or less than they are, as they might have been had they arose from any other cause than their gravities; or had the distances from the centres about which they move been greater or less than they are with the same velocities; or had the quantity of matter in the sun, or in Saturn, Jupiter, and the earth, and by consequence their gravitating power, been greater or less than it is; the primary planets could not have revolved about the sun, nor the secondary ones about Saturn, Jupiter, and the earth, in concentric circles as they do, but would have moved in hyperbolas, or parabolas, or in ellipses very eccentric. To make this system, therefore, with all its motions, required a cause which understood, and compared together, the quantities of matter in the several bodies of the sun and planets, and the gravitating powers resulting from thence; the several distances of the primary planets from the sun, and of the secondary ones from Saturn, Jupiter, and the earth; and the velocities with which these planets could revolve about those quantities of matter in the central bodies; and to compare and adjust all these things together, in so great a variety of bodies, argues that cause to be not blind and fortuitous, but very well skilled in mechanics and geometry.

To your third query, I answer, that it may be represented that the sun may, by heating those planets most which are nearest to it, cause them to be better concocted, and more condensed by concoction. But when I consider that our earth is much more heated in its bowels below the upper crust by subterraneous fermentations of mineral bodies than by the sun, I see not why the interior parts of Jupiter and Saturn might not be as much heated, concocted, and coagulated by those fermentations as our earth is and therefore this various density should have some other cause than the various distances of the planets from the sun. And I am confirmed in this opinion by considering that the planets Jupiter and Saturn, as they are rarer than the rest, so they are vastly greater, and contain a far greater quantity of matter, and have many satellites about them; which qualifications surely arose not from their being placed at so great a distance from the sun, but were rather the cause why the creator placed them at that great distance. For by their gravitating powers they disturb one another's motions very sensibly, as I find by some late observations of Mr Flamsteed,[2] and had they been placed much nearer to the sun and to one another, they would by the same powers have caused a considerable disturbance in the whole system.

To your fourth query, I answer, that in the hypothesis of vortices, the inclination of the axis of the earth might, in my opinion, be ascribed to the situation of the earth's vortex before it was absorbed by the neighbouring vortices, and the earth turned from a sun to a comet; but this inclination ought to decrease constantly in compliance with the motion of the earth's vortex, whose axis is much less inclined to the ecliptic, as appears by the motion of the moon carried about therein. If the sun by its rays could carry about the planets, yet I do not see how it could thereby effect their diurnal motions.

Lastly, I see nothing extraordinary in the inclination of the earth's axis for proving a deity, unless you will urge it as a contrivance for winter and summer, and for making the earth habitable towards the poles; and that the diurnal rotations of the sun and planets, as they could hardly arise from any cause purely mechanical, so by being determined all the same way with the annual and menstrual motions, they seem to make up that harmony in the system, which, as I explained above, was the effect of choice rather than chance.

There is yet another argument for a deity, which I take to be a very strong one, but till the principles on which it is grounded are better received, I think it more advisable to let it sleep.

I am,
Your most humble Servant to command,
Is. Newton

---

[2] John Flamsteed was an astronomer working in Greenwich whose observational data proved important for Newton's work in the *Principia*, and with whom Newton corresponded (and fought) frequently.

Cambridge, 17 January 1693

For Mr Bentley, at the Palace at Worcester.

Sir,

I agree with you, that if matter evenly diffused through a finite space, not spherical, should fall into a solid mass, this mass would affect the figure of the whole space, provided it were not soft, like the old chaos, but so hard and solid from the beginning that the weight of its protuberant parts could not make it yield to their pressure. Yet by earthquakes loosening the parts of this solid, the protuberances might sometimes sink a little by their weight, and thereby the mass might, by degrees, approach a spherical figure.

The reason why matter evenly scattered through a finite space would convene in the midst, you conceive the same with me; but that there should be a central particle, so accurately placed in the middle, as to be always equally attracted on all sides, and thereby continue without motion, seems to me a supposition fully as hard as to make the sharpest needle land upright on its point upon a looking glass. For if the very mathematical centre of the central particle be not accurately in the very mathematical centre of the attractive power of the whole mass, the particle will not be attracted equally on all sides. And much harder it is to suppose that all the particles in an infinite space should be so accurately poised one among another, as to stand still in a perfect equilibrium. For I reckon this as hard as to make not one needle only, but an infinite number of them (so many as there are particles in an infinite space) stand accurately poised upon their points. Yet I grant it possible, at least by a divine power; and if they were once to be placed, I agree with you that they would continue in that posture without motion forever, unless put into new motion by the same power. When therefore I said that matter evenly spread through all space would convene by its gravity into one or more great masses, I understand it of matter not resting in an accurate poise.

But you argue, in the next paragraph of your letter, that every particle of matter in an infinite space has an infinite quantity of matter on all sides, and by consequence an infinite attraction every way, and therefore must rest in equilibrium, because all infinites are equal. Yet you suspect a paralogism[3] in this argument; and I conceive the paralogism lies in the position, that all infinites are equal. The generality of mankind consider infinites no other ways than indefinitely; and in this sense, they say all infinites are equal; though they would speak more truly if they should say, they are neither equal nor unequal, nor have any certain difference or proportion one to another. In this sense, therefore, no conclusions can be drawn from them about the equality, proportions, or differences of things, and they that attempt to do it usually fall into paralogisms. So when men argue against the infinite divisibility of magnitude, by saying that if an inch may be divided into an infinite number of parts, the sum of those parts will be an inch; and if a foot may be divided into an infinite number of parts, the sum of those parts must be a foot, and therefore since all infinites are equal, those sums must be equal, that is, an inch equal to a foot.

The falseness of the conclusion shows an error in the premises, and the error lies in the position, that all infinites are equal. There is therefore another way of considering infinites used by mathematicians, and that is, under certain definite restrictions and limitations, whereby infinites are determined to have certain differences or proportions to one another. Thus Dr Wallis considers them in his *Arithmetica Infinitorium*,[4] where by the various proportions of infinite sums, he gathers the various proportions of infinite magnitudes: which way of arguing is generally allowed by mathematicians, and yet would not be good were all infinites equal. According to the same way of considering infinites, a mathematician would tell you, that though there be an infinite number of infinitely little parts in an inch, yet there is twelve times that number of such parts in a foot, that is, the infinite number of those parts in a foot is not equal to, but twelve times bigger than, the infinite number of them in an inch. And so a mathematician will tell you, that if a body stood in equilibrium between any two equal and contrary attracting infinite forces; and if to either of these forces you add any new finite attracting force, that new force, how little whatsoever, will destroy their equilibrium, and put the body into the same motion into which it would put it were those two contrary equal forces but finite, or even

---

[3] An error in reasoning.
[4] Newton refers here to John Wallis, *The Arithmetic of Infinites*, or *Arithmetica Infinitorum, sive Nova Methodus Inquirendi in Curvilineorum Quadraturam* (Oxford, 1656).

none at all; so that in this case the two equal infinites by the addition of a finite to either of them, become unequal in our ways of reckoning. And after these ways we must reckon if from the considerations of infinites we would always draw true conclusions.

To the last part of your letter, I answer, first, that if the earth (without the moon) were placed anywhere with its centre in the *Orbis Magnus* [the earth's solar orbit], and stood still there without any gravitation or projection, and there at once were infused into it both a gravitating energy towards the sun and a transverse impulse of a just quantity, moving it directly in a tangent to the *Orbis Magnus*, the compounds of this attraction and projection would, according to my notion, cause a circular revolution of the earth about the sun. But the transverse impulse must be a just quantity, for if it be too big or too little, it will cause the earth to move in some other line. Secondly, I do not know any power in nature which could cause this transverse motion without the divine arm. Blondel tells us somewhere in his book of bombs,[5] that Plato affirms that the motion of the planets is such, as if they had all of them been created by God in some region very remote from our system, and let fall from thence towards the sun, and so soon as they arrived at their several orbits, their motion of falling turned aside into a transverse one. And this is true, supposing the gravitating power of the sun was double at that moment of time in which they all arrive at their several orbits; but then the divine power is here required in a double respect, namely, to turn the descending motions of the falling planets into a side motion, and at the same time to double the attractive power of the sun. So then gravity may put the planets into motion, but without the divine power it could never put them into such a circulating motion as they have about the sun; and therefore, for this, as well as other reasons, I am compelled to ascribe the frame of this system to an intelligent agent.

You sometimes speak of gravity as essential and inherent to matter. Pray do not ascribe that notion to me; for the cause of gravity is what I do not pretend to know, and therefore would take more time to consider of it. I fear what I have said of infinites, will seem obscure to you; but it is enough if you understand, that infinites when considered absolutely

---

[5] The reference is to Francois Blondel, *L'Art de Jetter les Bombes* (Paris, 1683).

without any restriction or limitation, are neither equal nor unequal, nor have any certain proportion one to another, and therefore the principle that all infinites are equal, is a precarious one.

Sir, I am,
Your most humble Servant,
Is. Newton

Cambridge, 11 February 1693

To Mr BENTLEY, at the Palace at Worcester.

SIR,

The hypothesis of deriving the frame of the world by mechanical principles from matter evenly spread through the heavens, being inconsistent with my system, I had considered it very little before your letters put me upon it, and therefore trouble you with a line or two more about it, if this comes not too late for your use.

In my former [letter] I represented that the diurnal rotations of the planets could not be derived from gravity, but required a divine arm to impress them. And though gravity might give the planets a motion of descent towards the sun, either directly or with some little obliquity, yet the transverse motions by which they revolve in their several orbits required the divine arm to impress them according to the tangents of their orbits. I would now add, that the hypothesis of matter's being at first evenly spread through the heavens is, in my opinion, inconsistent with the hypothesis of innate gravity, without a supernatural power to reconcile them, and therefore it infers [i.e. implies] a deity. For if there be innate gravity, it is impossible now for the matter of the earth and all the planets and stars to fly up from them, and become evenly spread throughout all the heavens, without a supernatural power, and certainly that which can never be hereafter without a supernatural power, could never be heretofore without the same powers. You queried, whether matter evenly spread throughout a finite space, of some other figure than spherical, would not in falling down towards a central body cause that body to be of the same figure with the whole space, and I answered, yes. But in my answer it is to be supposed that the matter descends directly downwards to that body, and that that body has no diurnal rotation.

This, Sir, is all I would add to my former letters.
I am, Your most humble Servant,
Is. Newton

Bentley to Newton

18 February 1693

Honoured Sir,

Understanding that the publication of my sermons might be delayed a while without any damage to the bookseller, I have kept them in my hands, & shall keep them a little longer. And, though there were yet several matters in them, about which I would have purchased your opinion at no small rate, nevertheless I had not presumed any further to interrupt your worthy design with questions from a stranger. But your unexpected and voluntary favour by the last post doth encourage me to request you, that you would run over this abstract and thread of my first unpublished sermon; & to acquaint me with what you find in it that is not conformable to truth & your hypothesis. My mind would be very much at ease, if I have that satisfaction, before the discourses are out of my power.

Proved, in the 6 sermon, that the present system of the world cannot have been eternal. So that matter being eternal (according to the atheists) all was once a chaos, that is, all matter was evenly or near upon evenly diffused in the mundane spaces.

I proceed therefore in this 7th to show, that matter in such a chaos could never naturally convene into this or a like system. To which end we must consider some systematical phenomena of the present world. And:

(1) all bodies around our earth gravitate, even the lightest comparatively, & in their natural elements.

(2) Gravity or the weight of bodies is proportional to the quantity of matter, at equal distances from the centre.

(3) Gravity is not peculiar to terrestrial bodies, but common to all the planets and the Sun. Nay the whole bodies of Sun and planets

mutually gravitate towards one another; and in a word 'all bodies gravitate towards all. This universal gravitation or attraction is the τὸ φαινόμενον or matter of fact, for the demonstration of which I must refer you to ... Indeed as to the cause and origin of this gravity he was pleased to determine nothing. But you will perceive in the sequel of this discourse, that it is above all mechanism or power of inanimate matter, & must proceed from a higher principle and a divine energy & impression.' {I have written these words at large, that you may see if I am tender enough, how I engage your name in this matter.}

(4) Now if gravity be proportional to the quantity of matter, there is a necessity of admitting a vacuum.

(5) And to estimate what proportion the void space in our system may bear to the solid Mass. Refined gold (though even that be porous, because dissoluble in ☿ and aqua regia, and the *tantum non* impossibility that the figures of its corpuscles should be adapted for total contact) is to common water as 19 to 1, and water to common air as 850 to 1, so that gold is to air as 16150 to 1, so that the void space in the texture of common air is 16150 times as big, as the solid mass. And because air hath an elastic endeavour to expand itself, and the space it occupies, being reciprocally as its compression, the higher it is, 'tis the less compressed and more rarefied, and at the height of a few miles it has some million parts of void space to one of real body. And at the height of 1 terrestrial semidiameter: (as ... hath calculated) 'tis so very tenuous, that a sphere of our common air (already 16150 parts nothing) expanded to the thinness of that region would more than take up the whole orb of Saturn, which is many million millions of times bigger than all the globe of the earth: and yet higher above that, the rarefaction gradually increases *in immensum*. So that the whole concave of the firmament, except the Sun, planets, and atmospheres, may be considered as a mere void.

(6) *Esto hypothesis;* that every fixed star is as a sun; so that the proportion of void space to matter that is found in our Sun's vortex will near upon hold in the rest of the mundane space.

{I know what Kepler says, *Epitome Astronomia* p. 36, therefore query, if this hypothesis may pass.} Allow then that the globe of the earth is entirely solid and dense, and that all the matter of our Sun, planets, atmospheres, and aether is about 50000 times as much as the bulk of the earth. Astronomers will bear us witness that we are liberal enough. Now the *Orbis Magnus* (7000 terrestrial diameters wide) is 343,000,000,000 times as big as the whole earth and therefore is 6860000 times as big as all the matter of our system. But by the doctrine of the parallaxis, we cannot well allow less (in the Copernican hypothesis) than 100000 diameters of the *Orbis Magnus*: for the diameter of the firmament. So that the whole concave of the firmament is (in the 3 plic. prop.) 1000,000,000,000,000 times as big as the sphere of the *Orbis Magnus*, and therefore (multiplying this by 6860000) it is 6,860,000,000,000,000,000,000 times as big as all the matter of our system. So that if all that matter was evenly dispersed in the concave of the firmament, every corpuscle would have a sphere of void space around it 68600 ... times bigger than its own dimensions: and the diameter of the sphere would be above 19,000,000 times longer than the diameter of the corpuscle (supposing the corpuscle to be spherical). And further, because of the equal spheres of other corpuscles about that corpuscle, the void space about every corpuscle becomes twice as wide as it was, having a diameter compounded of the diameter of its own sphere and the 2 semidiameters of the spheres of the 2 next corpuscles opposite, so that every atom has a void space about it 8+68600 ... times as big as the atom, and would be distant 19,000,000 times its own length (if spherical) from any other corpuscle. And by the same supposition of equal diffusion in the whole surface of the void sphere about every atom (whose diam. is 38,000,000 times as long as the diameter of the atoms) there can be no more than 12 atoms, placed at equal distances from the central one and from each other (like the centre and angles of an icosahedron.) So that lastly, every atom is not only so many million millions of times distant from any other atom, but if it should be moved and impelled (without attraction or gravitation) to the length of that distance, it is many more million millions odds to a unit, that it doth not hit & strike upon one of those 12 atoms. But the proportion of this void to matter within our firmament, may hold in all the other mundane spaces beyond it. {The measure of the *Orbis Magnus* – 7000 terrestrial diameters – and of the firmament – 100000 diameters of the *Orbis Magnus* – I take from Andreas Tacquet, being round numbers. If you substitute better instead of them, the calculation may be soon altered.}

I am aware, that half of the diameter of the firmament should be allowed for the radii of the several vortices of the next fixed stars, so that the space of our Sun's vortex should be diminished, as 8 to 1. But because the semi-radius of the firmament may be immensely greater than we supposed it, we think that abatement not worth considering.

(1) Now the design of all this is to show, which (if the premises be granted) is evident at first sight, that in the supposition of such a chaos, no quantity of common motion (without attraction) could ever cause those straggling atoms to convene into great masses & move, as they do in our system, a circular motion being impossible to be produced naturally, unless there be either a gravitation or want of room.

(2) And as for gravitation, 'tis impossible that that should either be coeternal & essential to matter, or ever acquired by it. Not essential and coeternal to matter; for then even our system would have been eternal (if gravity could form it) against our atheist's supposition & what we have proved in our last. For let them assign any given time, that matter convened from a chaos into our system, they must affirm that before the given time matter gravitated eternally without convening, which is absurd. {Sir, I make account, that your courteous suggestion by your last, that a chaos is inconsistent with the hypothesis of innate gravity, is included in this paragraph of mine.} And again, 'tis unconceivable, that inanimate brute matter should (without a divine impression) operate upon & affect other matter without mutual contact: as it must, if gravitation be essential and inherent in it.

(3) But then if gravitation cannot be essential to matter, neither could it ever be acquired by matter. This is self evident if gravitation be true attraction. And if it be not true attraction,

matter could never convene from a chaos into a system like ours (paragraph I). Nay even now, since the forming of our system, gravitation is inexplicable otherwise than by attraction. 'Tis not magnetism, as you have shown. 'Tis not the effect of vortical motion; because it is proportional to the quantity of matter, for if the earth was hollow, there would be no less weight of bodies in the air (according to vortices) than if it was solid to the centre; there would be no less pressure towards the Sun, if the whole space of the Sun were a mere void, than if a dense body. Again, a vortical motion, without gravitation antecedent to it, supposes and requires either an absolute full, or at least a dense texture of the aethereal matter; contrary to what is proved before, & what appears from the motions of comets: and besides, as you have shown, it contradicts the phenomena of the slower motion of planets *in Apheliis quam Periheliis* [in the aphelion rather than the perihelion], and the sesquilateral [one and a half times] proportion of the periodical motions to their orbits. In a word: if gravity be not attraction, it must be caused by impulse and contact; but that can never solve universal attraction, in all situations, lateral as well as descending &c according to the phenomena of your hypothesis.

{Sir, to my conceptions, universal gravitation according to your doctrine is so impossible to be solved mechanically, that I was much surprised to see you warn me what I ascribed to you, for you pretended not to know the cause of it. As to innate gravity, you perceive that it is wholly against my purpose and argumentation. If I used that word, it was only for brevity's sake. But I must needs desire your judgement of what is here delivered to that purpose. I looked a little into Huygens's *de la Pesanteur*, when it newly came out; and I well remember, that it cannot be reconciled to your doctrine, and Varignon's book I read, which, besides that it cannot explain universal gravity, is confuted by the most vulgar phenomena. He makes long filets of *Materia subtilis* [subtle matter] reach from the top of the earth's vortex to the earth: all bodies descend that are in the lower half, because the superior part of the filets are the longer: all ascend in the higher half for the contrary reason. But in the middle of them there is a considerable space of equilibrium, indifferent both to ascent & descent, which he calls *espace de repos:* and in that the Moon moves in a circle without ascending or descending. Very well. Therefore in the filets of the Sun's vortex, all the space between Mercury & Saturn is an *espace de repose*, a small distance for the equilibrium; so much longer than the whole half of the filets from Mercury to the body of the Sun.}

(4) But though we could suppose gravitation essential to matter, or rather supervene into matter while it was diffused in a chaos; yet it could never naturally constitute a system like ours.

(i) For if matter be finite, and seeing extension is not matter, the sum of the mundane matter must consist of separate parts divided and disterminated [divided or bounded] by vacuum; but such parts cannot be positively infinite, any more than there can be an actually and positively infinite arithmetical Sum, which is a contradiction in terms. It may be said, that all bodies have infinite puncta, so that there are infinite sums. Indeed at that rate all numbers are infinite, as containing infinite fractions: even fractions themselves are infinite. But such puncta are not quanta, so that the case is different *toto genere*. Can a positive sum contain infinite ones, twos, or infinite *given* fractions? Can it have infinite quota and quanta as the atoms we speak of are? I say then if matter be finite it must be in a finite space: but then, by universal gravity, in an even diffusion all matter would convene in one mass in the middle of the space and if never so unevenly diffused, all would convene still into one mass, though not in the middle of the mundane space, but in the centre of the common gravity.

(ii) Nay though we suppose it once constituted, even then, even now all would convene together, in a finite system. I grant that if the whole world was but one Sun and all the rest planets moving about it, they would not convene. But in several fixed stars, that have no motion about each other; they with their systems of planets would all convene in the common centre of mundane gravity; if the present world was not sustained by a divine power.

{Sir, in a finite world where there are *outward* fixed stars, this seems plainly necessary. But in the supposition of an infinite space, let me ask your opinion. I acquiesce to your authority, that in matter diffused in an infinite space, 'tis as hard to keep those infinite particles fixed at an equilibrium, as poise infinite needles on their points upon an infinite speculum. Instead of particles, let me assume fixed stars or great fixed masses of opaque matter; is it not as hard, that such infinite masses in an infinite space should maintain an equilibrium, and not convene together? So that though our system was infinite, it could not be preserved but by the power of God.}

> (iii) Moreover, in such a chaos, though gravity should supervene to matter, the planets could never acquire their transverse motions about the Sun, etc. If they were formed in the same orbits they now move in, they could never begin to move circularly; the aethereal matter could not impress it, for that is too thin, & is indifferent to east or west, as appears from comets. Nor could gravity act in a descent. We therefore suppose the planets to be formed in some higher regions, and first descend towards the Sun, whereby they would acquire their velocities. But then they would have continued their descent to the Sun, unless a divine power gave them that transverse motion, against that vast impetus that such great bodies must fall with. So that on all accounts there's a necessity of introducing a God.

{As to what you cite from Blondel, I have read the same in Honoré Fabri's *Astronomia physica*, and Galileo's system, pp. 10 and 17: who adds that by the velocity of Saturn one may compute at what distance from the Sun it was formed, according to the degrees of acceleration, found out by himself, of the progression of odd numbers (but he must surely have erred, not knowing what you have since shown, that the velocity of descent as well as weight of bodies decreases as the square of the distance increases) and that there is that proportion of the distances and velocities of all the planets *quam proxime*, as if they all dropped from the same height. (But you seem to reject this, saying, that the gravitation of the sun must be doubled, at the very moment they reach their orbits.) I confess I could make no use of the passage of Galileo & Fabri; because I could not calculate: so that I said no more, but in general, as above; & that rather; because I knew that there must be some given heights, from whence each of them descending might acquire their present velocities. But I own, that if I could understand that thing, it would not be only ornamental to the discourse, but a great improvement of the argument for a divine power. For I think it more impossible that they should be all formed naturally at the same, than at various distances: and 'tis the miracle of all miracles, if they were naturally formed at such intervals of time, as all of them to arrive at their respective orbits at the very same moment. Which is necessary, if I rightly conceive your meaning about doubling the Sun's attraction. For if Mercury fell first, and when it reached its orbit, the Sun's attraction was doubled. That continuing doubled, the descents of the succeeding planets would be proportionably accelerated. Which would disturb the supposed proportion betwixt Mercury's velocity and theirs.

Honoured Sir. This is the content of the former sermon: the latter is an argument of a divine goodness from the meliority [superiority] in our system, above what was necessary to be in natural causality. I hope I shall have no need to give you more trouble in that: but Sir, while I am writing this, I have received a letter from my bookseller calling away for the Press. Let me but beg of you by the next post some brief hints what you approve of and what not. For I have resolved to expect your answer let him be never so clamorous. Sir, I heartily ask your pardon for giving you the trouble of this; which I must increase likewise by another piece of boldness in desiring your good leave to present you with my eight poor discourses; when these two last are made public.[6]

Sir I am your most obliged & Humble Servant
R. BENTLEY.

Newton to Bentley

Cambridge, 25 February 1692/3

For Mr BENTLEY, at the Palace at Worcester.

SIR,

Because you desire speed, I will answer your letter with what brevity I can. In the six positions you lay down in the beginning of your letter,

---

[6] Bentley gave a total of eight lectures while serving as the first Boyle lecturer.

I agree with you. Your assuming the *Orbis Magnus* 7,000 diameters of the earth wide, implies the sun's horizontal parallax to be half a minute. Flamsteed and Cassini[7] have of late observed it to be about 10", and thus the *Orbis Magnus* must be 21,000 or in a rounder number 20,000 diameters of the earth wide. Either computation I think will do well, and I think it not worthwhile to alter your numbers.

In the next part of your letter you lay down four other positions, founded upon the six first. The first of these four seems very evident, supposing you take attraction so generally as by it to understand any force by which distant bodies endeavour to come together without mechanical impulse. The second seems not so clear; for it may be said, that there might be other systems of worlds before the present ones, and others before those, and so on to all past eternity, and by consequence that gravity may be coeternal to matter, and have the same effect from all eternity as at present, unless you have somewhere proved that old systems cannot gradually pass into new ones, or that this system had not its original from the exhaling matter of former decaying systems, but from a chaos of matter evenly dispersed throughout all space; for something of this kind, I think, you say was the subject of your sixth sermon; and the growth of new systems out of old ones, without the mediation of a divine power, seems to me apparently absurd.

The last clause of the second position I like very well. It is inconceivable that inanimate brute matter should, without the mediation of something else, which is not material, operate upon and affect other matter without mutual contact, as it must be, if gravitation in the sense of Epicurus, be essential and inherent in it. And this is one reason why I desired you would not ascribe innate gravity to me. That gravity should be innate, inherent, and essential to matter, so that one body may act upon another at a distance through a vacuum without the mediation of anything else, by and through which their action and force may be conveyed from one to another, is to me so great an absurdity, that I believe no man who has in philosophical matters a competent faculty of thinking can ever fall into it. Gravity must be caused by an agent acting constantly according to certain laws; but whether this agent be material or immaterial, I have left to the consideration of my readers.

---

[7] See the note on p. 124 about Flamsteed; Jean-Dominique Cassini presented important astronomical data including, among other things, observations of Jupiter and Saturn.

Your fourth assertion, that the world could not be formed by innate gravity alone, you confirm by three arguments. But in your first argument you seem to make a *petitio principii*;[8] for whereas many ancient philosophers and others, as well theists as atheists, have all allowed that there may be worlds and parcels of matter innumerable or infinite, you deny this by representing it as absurd as that there should be positively an infinite arithmetical sum or number, which is a contradiction in terms; but you do not prove it as absurd. Neither do you prove that what men mean by an infinite sum or number is a contradiction in nature, for a contradiction in terms implies no more than an impropriety of speech. Those things which men understand by improper and contradictious phrases may be sometimes really in nature without any contradiction at all. A silver inkhorn, a paper lantern, an iron whetstone, [are] absurd phrases, that the things signified thereby are really in nature. If any man should say that a number and a sum, to speak properly, is that which may be numbered and summed, but things infinite are numberless, or as we usually speak, innumerable and sumless, or insummable, and therefore ought not to be called a number or sum, he will speak properly enough, and your argument against him will, I fear, lose its force. And that if any man shall take the words number and sum in a larger sense, so as to understand thereby things which in the proper way of speaking are numberless and sumless (as you seem to do when you allow an infinite number of points in a line), I could readily allow him the use of the contradictious phrases of innumerable number, or sumless sum, without inferring from thence any absurdity in the thing he means by those phrases. However, if by this, or any other argument, you have proved the finiteness of the universe, it follows, that all matter would fall down from the outsides, and convene in the middle. That the matter in falling might concrete into many round masses, like the bodies of the planets, and these by attracting one another might acquire an obliquity of descent, by means of which they might fall, not upon the great central body, but upon the side of it, and fetch a compass about, and then ascend again by the same steps and degrees of motion and velocity with which they descended before, much after the manner that the comets revolve about

---

[8] A begging of the question at issue.

the sun; but a circular motion in concentric orbits about the sun they could never acquire by gravity alone.

And though all the matter were divided at first into several systems, and every system by a divine power constituted like ours: that would the outside systems descend towards the middlemost so that this frame of things could not always subsist without a divine power to conserve it, which is the second argument; and to your third I fully assent.

As for the passage of Plato, there is no common place from whence all the planets being let fall, and descending with uniform and equal gravities (as Galileo supposes), would at their arrival to their several orbits acquire their several velocities, with which they now revolve in them. If we suppose the gravity of all the planets towards the sun to be of such a quantity as it really is, and that the motions of the planets are turned upwards, every planet will ascend to twice its height from the sun. Saturn will ascend till it be twice as high from the sun as it is at present, and no higher; Jupiter will ascend as high again as at present, that is, a little above the orbit of Saturn. Mercury will ascend to twice its present height, that is, to the orbit of Venus; and so of the rest. And then by falling down again from the places to which they ascended, they will arrive again at their several orbits with the same velocities they had at first, and with which they now revolve. But if so soon as their motions by which they revolve are turned upwards, the gravitating power of the sun, by which their ascent is perpetually retarded, be diminished by one half, they will now ascend perpetually, and all of them at all equal distances from the sun will be equally swift. Mercury when it arrives at the orbit of Venus, will be as swift as Venus; and it and Venus, when they arrive at the orbit of the earth, will be as swift as the earth; and so of the rest. If they begin all of them to ascend at once, and ascend in the same line, they will constantly in ascending become nearer and nearer together, and their motions will constantly approach to an equality, and become at length slower than any motion assignable. Suppose therefore that they ascended till they were almost contiguous, and their motions inconsiderably little, and that all their motions were at the same moment of time turned back again, or which comes almost to the same thing, that they were only deprived of their motions, and let fall at that time, they would all at once arrive at their several orbits, each with the velocity it had at first; and if their motions were then turned sideways, and at the same time the gravitating power of the sun doubled, that it might be strong enough to retain them in their orbits, they would revolve in them as before their ascent. But if the gravitating power of the sun was not doubled, they would go away from their orbits into the highest heavens in parabolical lines. These things follow from my *Mathematical Principles of Natural Philosophy*, Book 1, Propositions 33, 34, 36, 37.

I thank you very kindly for your designed present, and rest
Your most humble Servant to command,
Is. Newton

Chapter VII
Correspondence with G. W. Leibniz [1693/1712]

Leibniz to Newton

Hanover, 7 March 1692/3

To the celebrated Isaac Newton:
Gottfried Wilhelm Leibniz sends cordial greetings

How great I think the debt owed to you, by our knowledge of mathematics and of all nature, I have acknowledged in public also when occasion offered. You had given an astonishing development to geometry by your series; but when you published your work, the *Principia*, you showed that even what is not subject to the received analysis is an open book to you. I too have tried by the application of convenient symbols, which exhibit differences and sums, to submit that geometry which I call 'transcendent' in some sense to analysis, and the attempt did not go badly. But to put the last touches I am still looking for something big from you, first how best problems which seek lines from a given property of their tangents, may be reduced to squarings, and next how the squarings themselves – and this is what I would like very much to see – may be reduced to the rectifications of curves, simpler in all cases than the measurings of surfaces or volumes.

But above all I would wish that, perfected in geometrical problems, you would continue, as you have begun, to handle nature in mathematical terms; and in this field you have by yourself with very few companions gained an immense return for your labour. You have made the astonishing discovery that Kepler's ellipses result simply from the conception of attraction or gravitation and passage in a planet. And yet I would incline to believe that all these are caused or regulated by the motion of a fluid medium, on the analogy of gravity and magnetism as we know it here.[1] Yet this solution would not at all detract from the value and truth of your discovery. I do not doubt that you have weighed what Christiaan Huygens, that other supreme mathematician, has remarked in the appendix to his book about the cause of light and gravity.[2] I would like your opinion in reply: for it is by the friendly collaboration of you eminent specialists in this field that the truth can best be unearthed.

Now, as you also have thrown most light on precisely the science of dioptrics by explaining unexpected phenomena of colours, I would like your opinion about Huygens's explanation of light, assuredly a most brilliant one since the law of sines works out so happily.[3] Huygens indicated to me that you had informed him of some new phenomena of colours. I would like it very much if the system of the so-called fixed colours could be deduced from apparent colours, or else that the method of producing them by refractions could be demonstrated so that some whole surface should display a definite colour.

In catalogues of books published in England I several times came across books on mathematics by Newton. But I was in doubt whether they were by you, as I hope, or by another of the same name.[4]

My fellow countryman Heinson[5] on his return assured me of your friendly feelings towards me. But of my veneration for you not only he can testify, but Stepney too, once your fellow resident in the same College, now his Britannic Majesty's ambassador to the Imperial Court, lately to his Serene Highness the Elector of Brandenburg.[6]

---

[1] Leibniz here signals his desire to defend a vortex theory of gravity, the vortex being the "fluid medium" he mentions. His primary response to the theory of gravity outlined in the *Principia*, the *Tentamen* of 1689, outlines his vortex theory in detail. The *Tentamen* is available in English translation and in a critical edition by Meli, *Equivalence and Priority*.

[2] In 1690, Huygens's *Treatise on Light and Discourse on the Cause of Gravity* appeared in one volume in French from a publisher in Leiden; Newton had this edition in his library.

[3] In his *Treatise on Light*, Huygens deduces the laws of reflection and refraction from a principle he introduces in discussing the process of wave propagation.

[4] They were not in fact by Newton, but rather by John Newton (1622–78).

[5] He refers to Johann Theodor Heinson, who had been elected to the Royal Society as a fellow in 1692.

[6] George Stepney was a fellow of Trinity College, Cambridge in 1687.

I write this rather that you should understand my devotion to you, a devotion that has lost nothing by the silence of so many years,[7] than that with empty, and worse than empty, letters I should interrupt the devoted studies by which you increase the patrimony of mankind. Farewell.

Newton to Leibniz

Cambridge, 16 October 1693

To the celebrated Gottfried Wilhelm Leibniz:
Isaac Newton sends greetings

As I did not reply at once on receipt of your letter, it slipped from my hands and was long mislaid among my papers, and I could not lay hands on it until yesterday. This vexed me since I value your friendship very highly and have for many years considered you as one of the leading geometers of this century, as I have also acknowledged on every occasion that offered. For although I do my best to avoid philosophical and mathematical correspondences, I was however afraid that our friendship might be diminished by silence, and at the very moment too when our friend Wallis has inserted into his imminent new edition of his *History of Algebra*[8] some new points from letters which I once wrote to you by the hand of Mr Oldenburg,[9] and so has given me a handle to write to you on that question also. For he asked me to reveal a certain double method which I had there concealed by transposed letters. And so I have been compelled to expound as briefly as possible my method of fluxions which I had concealed by this sentence: *given an equation involving any number of fluent quantities to find the fluxions, and conversely.* I hope indeed that I have written nothing to displease you, and if there is anything that you think deserves censure, please let me know of it by letter, since I value friends more highly than mathematical discoveries.

The reduction of squarings to the straightenings of curves which you seem to want I discovered in this form: let the abscissa of any curve be x,

---

[7] The last letter was written on 12 July 1677.

[8] John Wallis's *A Treatise on Algebra, both Historical and Practical* (1685) appeared in a Latin edition as *De Algebra Tractatus: Historicus et Practicus* in 1693 from an Oxford publisher.

[9] Newton wrote a letter on 24 October 1676, a portion of which he had Oldenburg send to Leibniz.

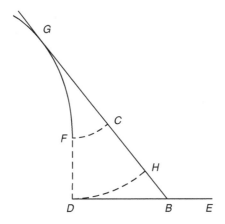

Figure 7.1

its ordinate y, and its area az, supposing that a is a given quantity; let x flow uniformly; and let its fluxion $x = a$, and let y be the fluxion of y. From a given point D in the right line DE given in position, mark off $DB = x$, and let an indefinite line BCG be drawn on the condition that the cosine of the angle DBG is to the radius as the fluxion y is to the fluxion $x = a$, and let a curve FG be found which the straight line BG always touches. For this is always possible to be done geometrically where the relation of the fluxions x and y is geometrical.

Let G be the point of contact; and where the point B coincides with point D, let point G coincide with point F. In the tangent BG let GC be taken equal to the curve GF, and CH equal to the straight line FD; then BH will equal z; and when it is found the desired area az is reached.

Huygens is a master, and his remarks on my discoveries are brilliant.[10] The parallax of the sun is less than I had concluded it to be; and it would seem [in his view] the motion of sounds is perhaps more rectilinear. But some very fine matter seems to fill the heavens. For since celestial motions are more regular than if they arose from vortices and observe other laws, so much so that vortices contribute not to the

---

[10] This refers to Huygens's *Treatise on Light*, which Leibniz mentions in his letter to Newton above (see n. 2 above).

regulation but the disturbance of the motions of planets and comets; and since all phenomena of the heavens and of the sea follow precisely, so far as I am aware, from nothing but gravity acting in accordance with the laws described by me; and since nature is very simple, I have myself concluded that all other causes are to be rejected and that the heavens are to be stripped as far as may be of all matter, lest the motions of planets and comets be hindered or rendered irregular. But if, meanwhile, someone explains gravity along with all its laws by the action of some subtle matter, and shows that the motion of planets and comets will not be disturbed by this matter, I shall be far from objecting. As for the phenomena of colours, the so-called apparent colours as well as the fixed, I conceive myself to have discovered the surest explanation, but I refrain from publishing books for fear that disputes and controversies may be raised against me by ignoramuses.[11] The Newton whose works meet your eye in the catalogues of published books is someone else. My aim in these pages has been to give proof that I am your most sincere friend and that I value your friendship very highly. Farewell.

Leibniz to Hartsoeker published in *Memoirs of Literature*

Hanover, 10 February 1711

You speak, sir, as if you knew not what I mean by *conspiring motions*; and ask, whether what I call so, be not the same thing with rest? I answer, it is not. For rest does not tend to make or preserve the cohesion of the parts that are at rest; and though two bodies remain one by another, they make no effort to continue to remain together, whether they touch one another, or not: but when there is a *conspiring motion* in their parts, which is disturbed by a separation, some strength is required to overcome that obstacle. Nor is it necessary that in the *conspiring motions* the parts should not change their distance. They may very well change it, provided that spontaneous change be quite another thing than a violent change, which would occasion a separation, and disturb those motions: and the parts of bodies resist a separation, not because they have a tendency to be divided; for in such a case they would resist still, if they

---

[11] Newton is presumably referring here to his discussion of colors in his optical papers from the 1670s. The "book" he wrote on this and related topics, the *Opticks*, was not published until 1704.

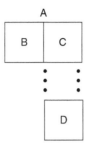

Figure 7.2

were altogether at rest, which is contrary to what I maintain; but because they have a considerable motion, which must be disturbed by a separation. If those parts tend to a separation of themselves, they help anyone who would separate them; but when they do not help him, it does not follow that they make an opposition, and some positive cause is requisite for that.

I own that some force is requisite to expel a body from its place, or to make it go faster than it would do of itself; but if the body D tends to drive the body C from its place, the resistance of the body C, which lessens the swiftness of the body D, has nothing in it; from whence it may be inferred that the body B, though nothing tends to drive it out, ought to accompany the body C, whether the interval between B and C be great or small, or none at all. We must therefore suppose, in order to produce that union between B and C, or their going along together, some other reasons than rest, or the situation of the one by the other; but because it ought to proceed from the mechanism, I can find it nowhere but in the *conspiring motion*, common to some parts of the bodies B and C, which conveys some parts from the one into the other by a kind of circulation, and which must be disturbed by the separation of the bodies.

To say that the *conspiring motions* are a fiction, is the same as to say, that every motion is a fiction. For, sir, how will you make a motion unless there be some relation among the motions of the parts? The very nature of fluids in agitation leads them to those motions that are most fitting.

You say your atoms have no parts; and you think it strange that I should suppose one may conceive that an atom A has two parts B and C. But are you not obliged to own, that one may conceive that an atom D goes against the atom A, without going directly against the part B; and in such a manner that it would carry C along with it, and leave B, if A was not an atom, or a solid body? There is therefore some reason to affirm, that the pretended atom is not without parts. You must assign the causes of its *atomity*,[12] if I may so speak, that is, why D cannot carry C along with it, without carrying B at the same time; and you must find a strong glue to make one of those parts stick to the other, if you are not willing to have recourse to the *conspiring motion*.

If you allege only the will of God for it, you have recourse to a miracle, and even to a perpetual miracle; for the will of God works through a miracle, whenever we are not able to account for that will and its effects from the nature of the objects. For example, if anyone should say, it is God's will that a planet should move round in its orbit, without any other cause of its motion, I maintain, that it would be a perpetual miracle: for by the nature of things, the planet going round tends to remove from its orbit through the tangent, if nothing hinders it; and God must continually prevent it, if no natural cause does it. The same ought to be said of your atoms; for the body C will be naturally carried away by the body D, and the body B will not follow, if nothing hinders such a separation; and if you look out for the reason of it in the will of God, you must suppose a miracle.

It may be said in a very good sense that everything is a continued miracle, that is, worthy of admiration: but it seems to me that the example of a planet which goes round and preserves its motion in its orbit without any other help but that of God, being compared with a planet kept in its orbit by the matter which constantly drives it towards the sun, plainly shows what difference there is between reasonable natural miracles, and those that are properly so called, or supernatural; or rather between a reasonable explication, and a fiction invented to support an ill-grounded opinion. Such is the method of those who say, after Mr De Roberval's Aristarchus, that all bodies attract one another by a law of nature, which God made in the beginning of things.[13] For alleging nothing else to obtain such an effect, and admitting nothing that was made by God whereby it may appear how he attains to that end, they have recourse to a miracle, that is, to a supernatural thing, which continues forever, when the question is to find out a natural cause.

---

[12] Leibniz coins a term here, but perhaps his meaning is plain.
[13] See Giles Persone de Roberval, *Aristarchi Samii De Mundi Systemate, Partibus, et Motibus eiusdem Libellus* (Paris, 1644).

You are in the right, sir, when you say we ought frequently to acknowledge our ignorance, and that it is a wiser method than to run into nonsense, by pretending to account for those things, which we do not understand. But to own that we know not the causes of some effects, is a different thing from affirming that there are some things of which no reason can be given, which is contrary to the first principles of reasoning: it is just as if somebody had denied the axiom, which Archimedes made use of in his book *de Aequiponderantibus*,[14] viz., that a balance, when everything is equal on both sides, remains in an *equilibrium*, under pretence that things are not sufficiently understood, and that perhaps the balance undergoes some alteration without any reason for it.

Thus the ancients and the moderns, who own that gravity is an *occult quality*, are in the right, if they mean by it that there is a certain mechanism unknown to them, whereby all bodies tend towards the centre of the earth. But if they mean that the thing is performed without any mechanism by a simple *primitive quality*, or by a law of God, who produces that effect without using any intelligible means, it is an unreasonable occult quality, and so very occult, that it is impossible it should ever be clear, though an angel, or God himself, should undertake to explain it.

The same ought to be said of *hardness*. If anyone acknowledges that the mechanism, which occasions hardness, is unknown to him, he is in the right; but if he pretends that hardness proceeds from any other cause than mechanism, and if he has recourse to a primitive hardness, as the assertors of atoms do, he recurs to a quality that is so occult, that it can never be made clear; that is, to a thing both unreasonable and contrary to the first principles of reasoning, since he owns that there are some natural things that have no natural cause.

Those are also guilty of the same fault who admit an indifference of *equilibrium*, as if the will could be determined, when all things are equal on both sides both inwardly and outwardly. Such a case never happens: there is always a greater inclination on one side than on the other; and the will is always inclined by some reason, or disposition, without being necessitated; and I dare say that many faults committed in arguing

---

[14] Leibniz may have had this edition of Archimedes in mind: *Archimedous Panta Sozomena = Archimedis Opera quae Extant: Novis Demonstrationibus Commentariisque Illustrata*, ed. David Rivault Flurance (Paris, 1615).

proceed from not duly observing this great principle, *that nothing happens without a sufficient season for it*. A principle, the force and consequences whereof have not been sufficiently considered by Descartes, and many other great men. That principle is sufficient to destroy the *vacuum*, the atoms, and the occult qualities of some philosophers, and even the first element of Descartes, with his globes, and many other fictions.

Thus, sir, you see why God could not create atoms, that is, bodies hard by their own nature, bodies of a primitive and insuperable hardness not to be accounted for; as he could not create planets that should move round of themselves, without any cause that should prevent their removing through the tangent: for a miracle at least must keep the planet in, and prevent the separation of the parts of the hard body, if a mechanical or intelligible cause does not do it. Granting the possibility of atoms, and the impossibility of a *vacuum*, I don't see why we should be forced to have recourse to a first element, that is, to a matter altogether fluid. Why may we not suppose space to be filled up with a matter that has different degrees of fluidity and tenacity, as I believe it is the nature of all matter?

Nor do I see why hard bodies should necessarily receive all their motion from fluid bodies, especially from a mass altogether fluid, or from our first element. For all matter being equally susceptible of motion, and equally incapable of producing it in itself, the most solid bodies may receive it, as well as those that are most fluid. Nay, it might be said, that the motion communicated to some few hard bodies may serve to account for the motion of many fluid bodies; and consequently, that it is anterior in order. For a solid body, thrown into a fluid, puts it into motion and produces a kind of circulation necessary to fill up the place which otherwise would remain empty behind the solid body; and that circulation forms a kind of vortex that has some affinity with that which we conceive round the lodestone [i.e. magnet].

It ought not to be said, that the universe is like an animal endued with life and intelligence: for then one might be apt to believe that God is the soul of that animal; whereas he is *intelligentia supramundana*, and the cause of the world: and if the universe was unlimited, it would be a collection of animals and other beings, but it could not be a single animal.

Your first element is not more susceptible of life and intelligence than any other bulk of matter; and since it is not organized, it is not fit it should have any perception, which must always answer the actions of organs, if you will have nature to act orderly and coherently.

You say, sir, that it is impossible for us to apprehend how a substance comes to have life and perception: and you are in the right, when the question is about particulars and the beginning of things. But perhaps you will own that the thing is more intelligible in my system of the *pre-established harmony*, by conceiving that our spiritual substances do naturally represent what happens in that part of matter to which they are united.

I have sufficiently answered those who objected to me that such a system was inconsistent with *free will*; for God knowing what men's minds would freely choose in time, adapted their bodies to it beforehand. Mr Jaquelot, who raised such an objection against me by word of mouth, was satisfied with my answer, as he owned in his book against Mr Bayle: nay, he has cleared it with an elegant comparison. I have answered Father Lami's objection in the same manner; and my answer has been inserted in the *Journal des Sçavans*. When Mr Bernoulli was Professor at Groningen, he maintained some theses, wherein he vindicated my opinion concerning the *pre-established harmony*.[15]

To conclude, the imperfections observable in the universe are like the dissonances of an excellent piece of music, which contribute to render it more perfect, in the opinion of the best judges. And therefore it cannot be said that when God created the world he made an imperfect machine. It is true, there are some machines in this world, that have not always, and from the beginning, [had] all the perfection that they are capable of.

I return you many thanks, sir, for your good wishes about the beginning of the New Year; and I wish you may long contribute to the improvement of the sciences, being with great zeal,

SIR,
Your most humble, and most obedient servant,
Leibniz

---

[15] See M. Jaquelot, *Entretiens de Maxime et de Themiste, ou, Reponse à l'Examen de la Theologie de Mr. Bayle* (Rotterdam, 1707); Pierre Bayle's most famous work is the *Dictionnaire Historique et Critique* (Rotterdam, 1697). Bayle and Leibniz were famous interlocutors. Due to François Lami's criticisms of Leibniz's conception of the pre-established harmony, Leibniz wrote a draft of a reply to Lami in 1702. Leibniz also corresponded in the fall of 1698 with the mathematician Johann Bernoulli.

Newton to the editor of the *Memoirs of Literature* [unpublished]

London, c. May 1712

Sir

In your weekly paper dated 5 May 1712 I meet with two letters, one written by Mr Leibniz to Mr Hartsoeker, the other by Mr Hartsoeker to Mr Leibniz in answer to the former. And in the letter of Mr Leibniz I meet with some things reflecting upon the English; I hope you will do them the justice to publish this vindication as you have printed the reflection. He writes thus: 'It may be said in a very good sense that everything is a continual miracle, that is, worthy of admiration, but it seems to me that the example of a planet which goes round and preserves it[s] motion in its orbit without any other help but that of God, being compared with a planet kept in its orbit by that matter which constantly drives it towards the sun, plainly shows what difference there is between reasonable natural miracles and those that are properly so called or supernatural; or rather between a reasonable explication, and a fiction invented to support an ill-grounded opinion. Such is the method of those who say, after Mr de Roberval's Aristarchus,[16] that all bodies attract one another by a law of nature which God made in the beginning of things. For alleging nothing else to obtain such an effect and admitting nothing that was made by God whereby it may appear how he attains to that end, they have recourse to a miracle, that is, to a supernatural thing, which continues forever, when the question is to find out a natural cause.'[17] Thus far Mr Leibniz. I know not what just occasion there was for this reflection in a discourse foreign to this matter, but it's plain this was intended against some in England and I hope to make it as plain that it was undeserved. For the true state of the case is this. It has been proved by some that all bodies upon the surface of the earth gravitate towards the earth in proportion to the quantity of matter in each of them; that the moon tends towards the earth and all the planets towards one another by the same law; and that by this tendency

---

[16] See n. 14 above.

[17] Each of Newton's paraphrases of Leibniz's original letter is very nearly exact; they have not been altered to correspond exactly to Leibniz's text, except in the case of the phrase "reasonable natural miracles," which I have altered both in the original and in Newton's quotation to match Leibniz's original French.

all their motions are performed. These things have been proved by mathematical demonstrations grounded upon experiments and the phenomena of nature: and Mr Leibniz himself cannot deny that they have been proved. But he objects that because *they allege nothing else to obtain such an effect* (he means a tendency of all bodies towards one another) *besides a law of nature which God made in the beginning of things and admit nothing that was made by God* (he means no vortices) *whereby it may appear how God attains to that end, they have recourse to a miracle, and that is, to a supernatural thing which continues for ever, when the question is to find out a natural cause.* Because they do not explain gravity by a mechanical hypothesis, he charges them with making it a super-natural thing, a miracle and a fiction invented to support an ill-grounded opinion and compares their method of philosophy to that of Mr de Roberval's Aristarchus, which is all one as to call it romantic [i.e. fictional]. They show that there is a universal gravity and that all the phenomena of the heavens are the effect of it and with the cause of gravity they meddle not but leave it to be found out by them that can explain it, whether mechanically or otherwise. And doth it deserve to be scouted with the language of a supernatural thing, a miracle, a fiction invented to support an ill-grounded opinion, and a method of philosophy after Mr Roberval's romance?

But Mr Leibniz goes on. 'The ancients and the moderns, who own that gravity is an occult quality, are in the right, if they mean by it that there is a certain mechanism unknown to them whereby all bodies tend towards the centre of the earth. But if they mean that the thing is performed without any mechanism by a simple primitive quality or by a law of God who produces that effect without using any intelligible means, it is an unreasonable and occult quality, and so very occult that it is impossible that it should ever be done though an angel or God himself should undertake to explain it.' The same ought to be said of hardness. So then gravity and hardness must go for unreasonable occult qualities unless they can be explained mechanically. And why may not the same be said of the *vis inertiae* [force of inertia] and the extension, the duration and mobility of bodies, and yet no man ever attempted to explain these qualities mechanically, or took them for miracles or supernatural things or fictions or occult qualities. They are the natural, real, reasonable, manifest qualities of all bodies seated in them by the will of God from the beginning of the creation and perfectly incapable of being explained mechanically, and so may be the hardness of primitive particles of bodies. And therefore if any man should say that bodies attract one another by a power whose cause is unknown to us, or by a power seated in the frame of nature by the will of God, or by a power seated in a substance in which bodies move and float without resistance and which has therefore no *vis inertiae* but acts by other laws than those that are mechanical: I know not why he should be said to introduce miracles and occult qualities and fictions into the world. For Mr Leibniz himself will scarce say that thinking is mechanical as it must be if to explain it otherwise be to make a miracle, an occult quality, and a fiction.

But he goes on and tells us that God *could not create planets that* should move round of themselves without any cause that should prevent their removing through the tangent. For a miracle at least must keep *the planet in*. But certainly God could create planets that should move round of themselves without any other cause than gravity that should prevent their removing through the tangent. For gravity without a miracle may keep the planets in. And to understand this without knowing the cause of gravity, is as good a progress in philosophy as to understand the frame of a clock and the dependence of the wheels upon one another without knowing the cause of the gravity of the weight which moves the machine is in the philosophy of clockwork; or the understanding of the frame of the bones and muscles and their connection in the body of an animal and how the bones are moved by the contracting or dilating of the muscles without knowing how the muscles are contracted or dilated by the power of the mind, is [in] the philosophy of animal motion.

Chapter VIII
Correspondence with Roger Cotes [1713]

Cotes to Bentley

10 March 1713

Sir,

I received what you wrote to me in Sir Isaac's letter. I will set about the index in a day or two. As to the preface I should be glad to know from Sir Isaac with what view he thinks proper to have it written. You know the Book has been received abroad with some disadvantage, and the cause of it may easily be guessed at. The *Commercium Epistolicum*[1] lately published by order of the Royal Society gives such indubitable proof of Mr Leibniz's want of candour that I shall not scruple in the least to speak out the full truth of the matter if it be thought convenient. There are some pieces of his looking this way, which deserve a censure, as his *Tentamen de Motuum Coelestium causis*. If Sir Isaac is willing that something of this nature may be done, I should be very glad if, whilst I am making the index, he would be pleased to consider of it and put down a few notes of what he thinks most material to be insisted on. This I say upon supposition that I write the preface myself. But I think it will be much more advisable that you or he or both of you should write it whilst you are in town. You may depend upon it that I will own it, and defend it as well as I can, if hereafter there be occasion.

---

[1] See chapter IX of this volume.

I am, Sir,
Your most obliged
and humble Servant
ROGER COTES

Bentley to Cotes

12 March 1713
At Sir Isaac Newton's

Dear Sir,

I communicated your letter to Sir Isaac, who happened to make me a visit this morning, and we appointed to meet this evening at his house and there to write you an answer. For the close of your letter, which proposes a preface to be drawn up here, and to be fathered by you, we will impute it to your modesty; but you must not press it further, but go about it yourself. For the subject of the preface, you know it must be to give an account, first of the work itself, secondly of the improvements of the new edition; and then you have Sir Isaac's consent to add what you think proper about the controversy of the first invention. You yourself are full master of it, and want no hints to be given you: however when it is drawn up, you shall have his and my judgement, to suggest any thing that may improve it. 'Tis both our opinions, to spare the *Name* of M. Leibniz, and abstain from all words or epithets of reproach: for else, that will be the reply (not that it's untrue) but that it's rude and uncivil. Sir Isaac presents his service to you.

I am
Yours,
R. BENTLEY

Cotes to Newton

18 March 1713

Sir.

I have received Dr Bentley's letter in answer to that which I wrote to him concerning the preface. I am very well satisfied with the directions there given, and have accordingly been considering of the matter. I think it will be proper besides the account of the book and its improvements to add something more particularly concerning the manner of philosophizing made use of and wherein it differs from that of Descartes and others. I mean in first demonstrating the principles it employs. This I would not only assert but make evident by a short deduction of the principle of gravity from the phenomena of nature, in a popular way, that it may be understood by ordinary readers and may serve at the same time as a specimen to them of the method of the whole book. That you may the better understand what I aim at, I think to proceed in some such manner.

'Tis one of the primary laws of nature, that all bodies preserve in their state, etc. Hence it follows that bodies which are moved in curve lines and continually hindered from going on along the tangents to those curve lines must incessantly be acted upon by some force sufficient for that purpose. The planets ('tis matter of fact) revolve in curve lines. Therefore, etc.

Again, 'tis mathematically demonstrated that *Corpus omne, quod movetur, etc., proposition 2, book 1* and *Corpus omne, quod radio, etc. proposition 3, book 1*.[2] Now 'tis confessed by all astronomers, that the primary planets about the Sun and the secondary about their respective primaries do describe areas proportional to the times. Therefore the force by which they are continually diverted from the tangents of their orbits is directed and tends towards their central bodies. Which force (from what cause whatever it proceeds) may therefore not improperly be called centripetal in respect of the revolving body and attractive in respect of the central.

Furthermore, 'tis mathematically demonstrated that {corollary 6, proposition 4, book 1} and {corollary 1, proposition 4, book 1}. But

[2] Proposition two of book 1 reads (*Principia*, 446): "Every body that moves [*Corpus omne quod, cum movetur*] in some curved line described in a plane and, by a radius drawn to a point, either unmoving or moving uniformly forward with a rectilinear motion, describes areas around that point proportional to the times, is urged by a centripetal force tending toward that same point." In the definitions, which appear before Book 1, Newton defines a "centripetal" force as follows: "Centripetal force is the force by which bodies are drawn from all sides, are impelled, or in any way tend, toward some point as to a center" (Definition five, *Principia*, 405). Proposition three of book 1 reads (*Principia*, 448): "Every body that, by a radius [*Corpus omne quod, radio ad*] drawn to the center of a second body moving in any way whatever, describes about that center areas that are proportional to the times is urged by a force compounded of the centripetal force tending toward that second body and of the whole accelerative force by which that second body is urged."

'tis agreed on by astronomers, that etc. or etc. Therefore the centripetal forces of the primary planets revolving about the Sun and of the secondary planets revolving about their primary ones, are in a duplicate proportion, etc.

In this manner I would proceed to the 4th proposition of book 3 and then to the 5th. But in the first corollary of the 5th I meet with a difficulty, it lies in these words *Et cum attractio omnis mutua sit* [and since every attraction is mutual].[3] I am persuaded they are then true when the attraction may properly be so called, otherwise they may be false. You will understand my meaning by an example. Suppose two globes *A* and *B* placed at a distance from each other upon a table, and that whilst *A* remains at rest *B* is moved towards it by an invisible hand.
A bystander who observes this motion but not the cause of it, will say that *B* does certainly tend to the centre of *A*, and thereupon he may call the force of the invisible hand the centripetal force of *B*, or the attraction of *A* since the effect appears the same as if it did truly proceed from a proper and real attraction of *A*. But then I think he cannot by virtue of the axiom {Attractio omnis mutua est [attraction is always mutual]} conclude contrary to his sense and observation, that the globe *A* does also move towards the globe *B* and will meet it at the common centre of gravity of both bodies. This is what stops me in the train of reasoning by which as I said I would make out in a popular way the 7th proposition of book 3. I shall be glad to have your resolution of the difficulty, for such I take it to be. If it appears so to you also; I think it should be obviated in the last sheet of your book which is not yet printed off, or by an addendum to be printed with the errata table. For 'till this objection be cleared I would not undertake to answer anyone who should assert you do *Hypothesim fingere* [feign hypotheses]. I think you seem tacitly to make this supposition that the attractive force resides in the central body.

After this specimen I think it will be proper to add some things by which your book may be cleared from some prejudices which have been industriously laid against it. As that it deserts mechanical causes, is built upon miracles and recurs to occult qualities. That you may not

---

[3] The first corollary to proposition five of book 3 (*Principia*, 806) reads: "Therefore, there is gravity toward all planets universally. For no one doubts that Venus, Mercury, and the rest [of the planets] are bodies of the same kind as Jupiter and Saturn. And since, by the third law of motion, every attraction is mutual, Jupiter will gravitate toward all its satellites, Saturn toward its satellites, and the earth will gravitate toward the moon, and the sun toward all the primary planets."

think it unnecessary to answer such objections you may be pleased to consult a weekly paper called *Memoirs of Literature* sold by Ann Baldwin. In the 18th number of the second volume of those papers, which was published May 5th, 1712, you will find a very extraordinary letter of Mr Leibniz to Mr Hartsoeker which will confirm what I have said.[4] I do not propose to mention Mr Leibniz's name, it were better to neglect him; but the objections I think may very well be answered and even retorted upon the maintainers of vortices.

After I have spoke of your book it will come in my way to mention the improvements of geometry upon which it is built, and there I must mention the time when these improvements were first made and by whom they were made. I intend to say nothing of Mr Leibniz but desire you will give me leave to appeal to the *Commercium Epistolicum* to vouch what I shall say of yourself, and to insert into my preface the very words of the judgement of the [Royal] Society (page 120, *Commercium Epistolicum*) that foreigners may more generally be acquainted with the true state of the case.

I am Sir,
Your most Humble Servant.
ROGER COTES

Newton to Cotes

London, 28 March 1713

Sir

I had your [letter] of Feb 18th, and the difficulty you mention which lies in these words 'And since, by the third law of motion, every attraction is mutual' is removed by considering that as in geometry the word 'hypothesis' is not taken in so large a sense as to include the axioms and postulates, so in experimental philosophy it is not to be taken in so large a sense as to include the first principles or axioms which I call the laws of motion. These principles are deduced from phenomena and made general by induction: which is the highest evidence that a proposition can have in this philosophy. And the word 'hypothesis' is

---

[4] See chapter VII of this volume.

here used by me to signify only such a proposition as is not a phenomenon nor deduced from any phenomena but assumed or supposed
without any experimental proof. Now the mutual and mutually equal
attraction of bodies is a branch of the third law of motion and how this
branch is deduced from phenomena you may see in the end of the
corollaries of the laws of motion, page 22.[5] If a body attracts another
body contiguous to it and is not mutually attracted by the other: the
attracted body will drive the other before it and both will go away
together with an accelerated motion *in infinitum*, as it were by a self-
moving principle, contrary to the first law of motion, whereas there is no
such phenomenon in all nature.

At the end of the last paragraph but two now ready to be printed off
I desire you to add after the words 'and a God without dominion,
providence, and final causes is nothing other than fate and nature' these
words: 'This concludes the discussion of God, and to treat of God from
phenomena is certainly a part of natural philosophy.'

And for preventing exceptions against the use of the word 'hypothesis'
I desire you to conclude the next paragraph in this manner: 'For whatever
is not deduced from the phenomena must be called a hypothesis; and
hypotheses, whether metaphysical or physical, or based on occult
qualities, or mechanical, have no place in experimental philosophy. In this
experimental philosophy, propositions are deduced from the phenomena
and are made general by induction. The impenetrability, mobility, and
impetus of bodies, and the laws of motion and the law of gravity have been
found by this method. And it is enough that gravity really exists and acts
according to the laws that we have set forth and is sufficient to explain all
the motions of the heavenly bodies and of our sea.'[6]

I have not time to finish this letter but intend to write to you again on
Tuesday.
I am, your most humble Servant
Is. NEWTON
For the Reverend Mr Roger Cotes
Professor of Astronomy, at his Chamber in Trinity College in
Cambridge.

---

[5] See p. 104 in this volume.
[6] In all three cases, Newton gives the passages and additions in Latin.

Newton to Cotes

Unsent Draft: Circa March 1713

Sir

I like your design of adding something more particularly concerning the manner of philosophizing made use of in the *Principia* and wherein it differs from the method of others, viz. by deducing things mathematically from principles derived from phenomena by induction. These principles are the three laws of motion. And these laws in being deduced from phenomena by induction and backed with reason and the three general rules of philosophizing are distinguished from hypotheses and considered as axioms. Upon these are founded all the propositions in the first and second book. And these propositions are in the third book applied to the motions of the heavenly bodies.

And first because the planets move in curve lines, it follows from the first axiom or law of nature that they are incessantly acted upon by some force which continually diverts them from a rectilinear course.

Again from propositions 2 and 3 [of] Book 1, it follows that this force is directed towards the central bodies about which the planets move.

And by proposition 6, corollary 4 of Book 1, and proposition 45, corollary 1 of Book 1, that this force in receding from the central body decreases in a duplicate proportion of the distance. Etc.

And when you come at the difficulty you mention in the first corollary of the fifth proposition of the third book, which lies in these words 'And since, by the third law of motion, every attraction is mutual': the objection you mention may be proposed and answered in this manner. (1) That it is but an hypothesis not founded upon any one observation. (2) That it is attended with the absurd consequence described [on] page 22, namely that a body attracted by another body without mutually attracting it would go to the other body and drive it away before it with an accelerated motion *in infinitum*, contrary to the first law of motion. And such an absurd hypothesis, which would disturb all nature, is not to be admitted in opposition to the first and third laws of motion which are grounded upon phenomena. For that all attraction is mutual and mutually equal follows from both those laws. One may suppose that bodies may by an unknown power be perpetually accelerated and so reject the first law of motion. One may suppose that God can create a penetrable body and so reject the impenetrability of matter. But to admit of such hypotheses in opposition to rational propositions founded upon phenomena by induction is to destroy all arguments taken from phenomena by induction and all principles founded upon such arguments. And therefore as I regard not hypotheses in explaining the phenomena of nature, so I regard them not in opposition to arguments founded upon phenomena by induction or to principles settled upon such arguments. In arguing for any principle or proposition from phenomena by induction, hypotheses are not to be considered. The argument holds good till some phenomenon can be produced against it. This argument holds good by the third rule of philosophizing. And if we break that rule, we cannot affirm any one general law of nature: we cannot so much as affirm that all matter is impenetrable. Experimental philosophy reduces phenomena to general rules and looks upon the rules to be general when they hold generally in phenomena. It is not enough to object that a contrary phenomenon may happen but to make a legitimate objection, a contrary phenomenon must be actually produced. Hypothetical philosophy consists in imaginary explications of things and imaginary arguments for or against such explications, or against the arguments of experimental philosophers founded upon induction. The first sort of philosophy is followed by me, the latter too much by Descartes, Leibniz, and some others. And according to the first sort of philosophy the three laws of motion are proposed as general principles of philosophy though founded upon phenomena by no better argument than that of induction without exception of any one phenomenon. For the impenetrability of matter is grounded upon no better an argument. And the mutual equality of attraction (which is a branch of the third law of motion) is backed by this further argument, that is, if the attraction between two bodies was not mutual and mutually equal they would not stay *in rerum natura* [in the natural world]. The body which is most strongly attracted would go to the other and press upon it, and by the excess of its pressure both would go away together with a motion accelerated *in infinitum*. If a great mountain upon either pole of the earth gravitated towards the rest of the earth more than the rest of the earth gravitated towards the mountain, the weight of the mountain would drive the earth from the plane of the ecliptic and cause it, so soon as it could extricate itself from the system of the sun and planets, to go away *in infinitum* with a motion perpetually accelerated. Thus the objection which you mention is not only an hypothesis and on that account to be excluded [from] experimental philosophy, but also introduces a principle of self-motion into bodies which would disturb the whole frame of nature, and in the general opinion of mankind is as remote from the nature of matter as impenetrability [read: penetrability] is reckoned to be. Experimental philosophy argues only from phenomena, draws general conclusions from the consent of phenomena, and looks upon the conclusion as general when the consent is general without exception, though the generality cannot be demonstrated a priori. In mathematics all propositions not demonstrated mathematically are hypotheses, but some are admitted as principles under the name of axioms or postulates without being called hypotheses. So in experimental philosophy it's proper to distinguish propositions into principles, propositions, and hypotheses, calling those propositions which are deduced from phenomena by proper arguments and made general by induction (the best way of arguing in philosophy for a general proposition) and those hypotheses which are not deduced from phenomena by proper arguments. But if any man will take the word 'hypothesis' in a larger sense, he may extend it, if he pleases, to the impenetrability of matter, the laws of motion, and the axioms of geometers. For it is not worth the while to dispute about the signification of a word.

What has been said, doth not hinder the body B from being moved by an invisible hand towards the resting body A: [ends].

Newton to Cotes

31 March 1713

Sir

On Saturday last I wrote to you, representing that experimental philosophy proceeds only upon phenomena and deduces general propositions from them only by induction. And such is the proof of mutual attraction. And the arguments for the impenetrability, mobility and force of all bodies and for the laws of motion are no better. And he that in experimental philosophy would except against any of these must draw his objection from some experiment or phenomenon and not from a mere hypothesis, if the induction be of any force.

In the same letter, I sent you also an addition to the last paragraph but two and an emendation to the last paragraph but one in the paper now to be printed off in the end of the book.

I hear that Mr Bernoulli has sent a paper of 40 pages to be published in the *Acta Leipsica* relating to what I have written upon the curve lines described by projectiles in resisting mediums. And therein he partly makes observations upon what I have written and partly improves it. To prevent being blamed by him or others for any disingenuity in not acknowledging my oversights or slips in the first edition I believe it will not be amiss to print next after the old Praefatio ad Lectorem [preface to the reader], the following account of this new edition.

In this second edition of the *Principles*, many emendations have been made throughout. In book 1, section 2, the finding of forces by which bodies could revolve in given orbits has been made easier and has been enlarged. In book 2, section 7, the theory of resisting fluids is more accurately investigated and confirmed by new experiments. In book 3, the theory of the moon and the precession of the equinoxes are deduced more fully from their principles, and the theory of comets is confirmed by more examples of their orbits, calculated with greater accuracy.

28 March 1713   *I.N.*[7]

If you write any further Preface, I must not see it. For I find that I shall be examined about it. The cuts for the comet of 1680 and 1681 are printed off [and] will be sent to Dr Bentley this week by the carrier. I am

Your most humble servant
ISAAC NEWTON

Cotes to Samuel Clarke

25 June 1713

   Sir

I received your very kind letter, I return you my thanks for your corrections of the preface, and particularly for your advice in relation to that place where I seemed to assert gravity to be essential to bodies. I am

---

[7] In the letter, this paragraph is written in Latin; it became the author's preface to the second edition of the *Principia*. See *Philosophiae Naturalis Principia Mathematica*, ed. I. B. Cohen and Aleandre Koyré, with Anne Whitman (Cambridge, MA: Harvard University Press, 1972), vol. I, 18.

fully of your mind that it would have furnished matter for cavilling, and therefore I struck it out immediately upon Dr Cannon's mentioning your objection to me, and so it never was printed. [The impression of the whole book was] finished about a week ago.

My design in that passage was not to assert gravity to be essential to matter, but rather to assert that we are ignorant of the essential properties of matter and that in respect of our knowledge gravity might possibly lay as fair a claim to that title as the other properties which I mentioned. For I understand by essential properties such properties without which no others belonging to the same substance can exist: and I would not undertake to prove that it were impossible for any of the other properties of bodies to exist without even extension.

Be pleased to present my humble service to Sir Isaac when you see him next, and let him know that the book is finished.

I am Sir
Your much Obliged Friend
and Humble Servant
R C

Bentley to Newton

30 JUNE 1713

Dear Sir

At last your book is happily brought forth; and I thank you anew that you did me the honour to be its conveyer to the world. You will receive by the carrier, according to your order, 6 copies; but pray be so free as to command what more you shall want. We have no binders here, that either work well or quick; so you must accept of them in quires. I gave Roger [Cotes] a dozen, who presents one to Drs Clark and Whiston. This I tell you, that you may not give double. And on that account I tell you, that I have sent one to the Treasurer, Lord Trevor, and Bishop of Ely. We thought it was properest for you to present Dr Halley: so you will not forget him. I have sent (though at great abatement) 200 already to France and Holland: the edition in England to the last buyer is 15*s* in quires: and we shall take care to keep it up so, for the honour of the book. I can think of nothing more at present, but shall expect your commands, if you have any thing to order me. I am with all respect and esteem

Your affectionate
humble Servant
RI: Bentley

Chapter IX
An Account of the Book Entitled
Commercium Epistolicum [1715]

The philosophy which Mr Newton in his *Principles* and *Opticks* has pursued is experimental; and it is not the business of experimental philosophy to teach the causes of things any further than they can be proved by experiments. We are not to fill this philosophy with opinions which cannot be proved by phenomena. In this philosophy hypotheses have no place, unless as conjectures or questions proposed to be examined by experiments. For this reason, Mr Newton in his *Opticks* distinguished those things which were made certain by experiments from those things which remained uncertain, and which he therefore proposed in the end of his *Opticks* in the form of queries. For this reason, in the preface to his *Principles*, when he had mentioned the motions of the planets, comets, moon and sea as deduced in this book from gravity, he added: 'If only we could derive the other phenomena of nature from mechanical principles by the same kind of reasoning! For many things lead me to have a suspicion that all phenomena may depend on certain forces by which the particles of bodies, by causes not yet known, either are impelled towards one another and cohere in regular figures, or are repelled from one another and recede. Since these forces are unknown, philosophers have hitherto made trial of nature in vain.' And in the end of this book in the second edition, he said that for want of a sufficient number of experiments, he forbore to describe the laws of the actions of the spirit or agent by which this attraction is performed. And for the same reason he is silent about the cause of gravity, there occurring no experiments or phenomena by which he might prove what was the cause thereof. And this he hath abundantly declared in his *Principles*, near the beginning thereof, in these words: 'I am not now considering the physical causes and sites of forces' [definition 8]. And a little after: 'Moreover, I use interchangeably and indiscriminately words signifying attraction, impulse, or any sort of propensity towards a centre, considering these forces not from a physical but only from a mathematical point of view. Therefore, let the reader beware of thinking that by words of this kind I am anywhere defining a species or mode of action or a physical cause or reason, or that I am attributing forces in a true and physical sense to centres (which are mathematical points) if I happen to say that centres attract or that centres have forces.' And in the end of his *Opticks*: 'How these attractions [viz. gravitational, magnetic, & electrical] may be performed, I do not here consider. What I call attraction may be performed by impulse, or by some other means unknown to me. I use 'attraction' here to signify only in general any force by which bodies tend towards one another, whatsoever be the cause. For we must learn from the phenomena of nature what bodies attract one another, and what are the laws and properties of the attraction, before we enquire the cause by which the attraction is performed.' And a little after he mentions the same attractions as forces which by phenomena appear to have a being in nature, though their causes be not yet known; and distinguishes them from the occult qualities which are supposed to flow from the specific forms of things. And in the Scholium at the end of his *Principles*, after he had mentioned the properties of gravity, he added: 'I have not as yet been able to deduce from phenomena the reason for these properties of gravity, and I do not feign hypotheses. For whatever is not deduced from the phenomena must be called a hypothesis; and hypotheses, whether metaphysical or physical, or based on occult qualities, have no place in experimental philosophy ... And it is enough that gravity really exists and acts according to the laws that we have set forth and is sufficient to explain all the motions of the heavenly bodies and of our sea.' And after all this, one would wonder that Mr Newton should be reflected upon for not explaining the causes of gravity and other attractions by hypotheses; as if it were a crime to content himself with certainties and let uncertainties alone. And yet the editors of the *Acta Eruditorum*: (a) have told the world that Mr Newton denies that the cause of gravity is mechanical, and that if the spirit or agent by which electrical attraction is performed be not the aether or subtle matter of Descartes, it is less valuable than an hypothesis, and perhaps may be the hylarchic principle of Dr Henry More;[1] and Mr Leibniz: (b) hath accused him of making gravity a natural or essential property of bodies, and an occult quality and miracle. And by this sort of raillery they are persuading the Germans that Mr Newton wants judgement, and was not able to invent the infinitesimal method [the calculus].

It must be allowed that these two gentlemen differ very much in philosophy. The one proceeds upon the evidence arising from experiments and phenomena, and stops where such evidence is wanting; the other is taken up with hypotheses, and propounds them, not to be examined by experiments, but to be believed without examination. The one for want of experiments to decide the question doth not affirm whether the cause of gravity be mechanical or not mechanical: the other that it is a perpetual miracle if it be not mechanical. The one (by way of enquiry) attributes it to the power of the creator that the least particles of matter are hard: the other attributes the hardness of matter to conspiring motions, and calls it a perpetual miracle if the cause of this hardness be other than mechanical. The one doth not affirm that animal motion in man is purely mechanical: the other teaches that it is purely mechanical, the soul or mind (according to the hypothesis of a pre-established harmony) never acting upon the body so as to alter or influence its motions. The one teaches that God (the God in whom we live and move and have our being)[2] is omnipresent, but not as a soul of the world: the other that he is not the soul of the world, but INTELLIGENTIA SUPRAMUNDANA, an intelligence above the bounds of the world; whence it seems to follow that he cannot do any thing within the bounds of the world, unless by an incredible miracle. The one teaches that philosophers are to argue from phenomena and experiments to the causes thereof, and thence to the causes of those causes, and so on till we come to the first cause: the other that all the actions of the first cause are miracles, and all the laws impressed on nature by the will of God are

---

[1] Henry More was an important Cambridge Platonist whose work influenced Newton while he was a student at Trinity College in the 1660s. The "hylarchic" principle is said to be a type of non-material agent that would somehow control material bodies.
[2] Newton quotes here a passage from Acts (17:28) that was often cited in this period.

perpetual miracles and occult qualities, and therefore not to be considered in philosophy. But must the constant and universal laws of nature, if derived from the power of God or the action of a cause not yet known to us, be called miracles and occult qualities, that is to say, wonders and absurdities? Must all the arguments for a God taken from the phenomena of nature be exploded by new hard names? And must experimental philosophy be exploded as miraculous and absurd because it asserts nothing more than can be proved by experiments, and we cannot yet prove by experiments that all the phenomena in nature can be solved by mere mechanical causes? Certainly these things deserve to be better considered.

Chapter X
Queries to the *Opticks* [1721]

Query 21

Is not this medium[1] much rarer within the dense bodies of the Sun, stars, planets and comets, than in the empty celestial spaces between them? And in passing from them to great distances, does it not grow denser and denser perpetually, and thereby cause the gravity of those great bodies towards one another, and of their parts towards the bodies; every body endeavouring to go from the denser parts of the medium towards the rarer? For if this medium be rarer within the Sun's body than at its surface, and rarer there than at the hundredth part of an inch from its body, and rarer there than at the fiftieth part of an inch from its body, and rarer there than at the orbit of *Saturn*; I see no reason why the increase of density should stop anywhere, and not rather be continued through all distances from the Sun to *Saturn*, and beyond. And though this increase of density may at great distances be exceeding slow, yet if the elastic force of this medium be exceeding great, it may suffice to impel bodies from the denser parts of the medium towards the rarer, with all that power which we call gravity. And that the elastic force of this medium is exceeding great, may be gathered from the swiftness of its vibrations. Sounds move about 1140 *English* feet in a second minute of time, and in seven or eight minutes of time they move about one hundred *English* miles. Light moves from the Sun to us in about seven

---

[1] Newton introduced an "aethereal" medium in query 18.

or eight minutes of time, which distance is about 70000000 *English* miles, supposing the horizontal parallax of the Sun to be about 12". And the vibrations or pulses of this medium, that they may cause the alternate fits of easy transmission and easy reflection, must be swifter than light, and by consequence above 700000 times swifter than sounds. And therefore the elastic force of this medium, in proportion to its density, must be above 700000 x 700000 (that is, above 490000000000) times greater than the elastic force of the air is in proportion to its density. For the velocities of the pulses of elastic mediums are in a sub-duplicate *ratio* of the elasticities and the rarities of the mediums taken together.

As attraction is stronger in small magnets than in great ones in proportion to their bulk, and gravity is greater in the surfaces of small planets than in those of great ones in proportion to their bulk, and small bodies are agitated much more by electric attraction than great ones; so the smallness of the rays of light may contribute very much to the power of the agent by which they are refracted. And so if anyone should suppose that *aether* (like our air) may contain particles which endeavour to recede from one another (for I do not know what this *aether* is) and that its particles are exceedingly smaller than those of air, or even than those of light: the exceeding smallness of its particles may contribute to the greatness of the force by which those particles may recede from one another, and thereby make that medium exceedingly more rare and elastic than air, and by consequence exceedingly less able to resist the motions of projectiles, and exceedingly more able to press upon gross bodies, by endeavouring to expand it self.

Query 28

Are not all hypotheses erroneous, in which light is supposed to consist in pression or motion, propagated through a fluid medium?[2] For in all these hypotheses the phenomena of light have been hitherto explained by supposing that they arise from new modifications of the rays; which is an erroneous supposition. If light consisted only in pression propagated without actual motion, it would not be able to agitate and heat the bodies which refract and reflect it. If it consisted in motion propagated to all

---

[2] Newton returns here to a principal theme of his debate with Robert Hooke about the nature of light in 1672 – see chapter 1 and the Introduction (pp. xiv–xviii) above.

distances in an instant, it would require an infinite force every moment, in every shining particle, to generate that motion. And if it consisted in pression or motion, propagated either in an instant or in time, it would bend into the shadow. For pression or motion cannot be propagated in a fluid in right lines, beyond an obstacle which stops part of the motion, but will bend and spread every way into the quiescent medium which lies beyond the obstacle. Gravity tends downwards, but the pressure of water arising from gravity tends every way with equal force, and is propagated as readily, and with as much force sideways as downwards, and through crooked passages as through straight ones. The waves on the surface of stagnating water, passing by the sides of a broad obstacle which stops part of them, bend afterwards and dilate themselves gradually into the quiet water behind the obstacle. The waves, pulses or vibrations of the air, wherein sounds consist, bend manifestly, though not so much as the waves of water. For a bell or a cannon may be heard beyond a hill which intercepts the sight of the sounding body, and sounds are propagated as readily through crooked pipes as through straight ones. But light is never known to follow crooked passages, nor to bend into the shadow. For the fixed stars by the interposition of any of the planets cease to be seen. And so do the parts of the Sun by the interposition of the Moon, Mercury or Venus. The rays which pass very near to the edges of any body, are bent a little by the action of the body, as we showed above; but this bending is not towards but from the shadow, and is performed only in the passage of the ray by the body, and at a very small distance from it. So soon as the ray is past the body, it goes right on.

To explain the unusual refraction of island crystal by pression or motion propagated, has not hitherto been attempted (to my knowledge) except by *Huygens*, who for that end supposed two several vibrating mediums within that crystal. But when he tried the refractions in two successive pieces of that crystal, and found them such as is mentioned above; he confessed himself at a loss for explaining them. For pressions or motions, propagated from a shining body through a uniform medium, must be on all sides alike; whereas by those experiments it appears, that the rays of light have different properties in their different aides. He suspected that the pulses of *aether* in passing through the first crystal might receive certain new modifications, which might determine them to be propagated in this or that medium within the second crystal, according to the position of that crystal. But what modifications those might be he could not say, nor think of any thing satisfactory in that point.[3] And if he had known that the unusual refraction depends not on new modifications, but on the original and unchangeable dispositions of the rays, he would have found it as difficult to explain how those dispositions which he supposed to be impressed on the rays by the first crystal, could be in them before their incidence on that crystal, and in general, how all rays emitted by shining bodies, can have those dispositions in them from the beginning. To me, at least, this seems inexplicable, if light be nothing else than pression or motion propagated through *aether*.

And it is as difficult to explain by these hypotheses, how rays can be alternately in fits of easy reflection and easy transmission; unless perhaps one might suppose that there are in all space two aethereal vibrating mediums, and that the vibrations of one of them constitute light, and the vibrations of the other are swifter, and as often as they overtake the vibrations of the first, put them into those fits. But how two *aethers* can be diffused through all space, one of which acts upon the other, and by consequence is reacted upon, without retarding, shattering, dispersing and confounding one another's motions, is inconceivable. And against filling the heavens with fluid mediums, unless they be exceeding rare, a great objection arises from the regular and very lasting motions of the planets and comets in all manner of courses through the heavens. For thence it is manifest, that the heavens are void of all sensible resistance, and by consequence of all sensible matter.[4]

For the resisting power of fluid mediums arises partly from the attrition of the parts of the medium, and partly from the *vis inertiae* [force of inertia] of the matter. That part of the resistance of a spherical body which arises from the attrition of the parts of the medium is very nearly as the diameter, or at the most, as the *factum* [factor] of the diameter, and the velocity of the spherical body together. And that part of the resistance which arises from the *vis inertiae* of the matter, is as the square of that *factum*. And by this difference the two sorts of resistance may be distinguished from one another in any medium; and these being distinguished,

---

[3] Newton quotes from Huygens, "Mais pour dire comment cela se fait, je n'ay rien trove jusqu' ici qui me satisfasse" (c.5, p. 91). That is, "But for saying how this is done, I have never found anything that satisfies me." This is my translation.

[4] Newton also discusses this issue in his letter to Leibniz of 1693 (p. 145 above) and in the General Scholium to the *Principia* (p. 110 above).

it will be found that almost all the resistance of bodies of a competent magnitude moving in air, water, quicksilver, and such like fluids with a competent velocity, arises from the *vis inertiae* of the parts of the fluid.

Now that part of the resisting power of any medium which arises from the tenacity, friction, or attrition of the parts of the medium, may be diminished by dividing the matter into smaller parts, and making the parts more smooth and slippery: but that part of the resistance which arises from the *vis inertiae* is proportional to the density of the matter, and cannot be diminished by dividing the matter into smaller parts, nor by any other means than by decreasing the density of the medium. And for these reasons the density of fluid mediums is very nearly proportional to their resistance. Liquors [i.e. liquids] which differ not much in density, as water, spirit of wine, spirit of turpentine, hot oil, differ not much in resistance. Water is thirteen or fourteen times lighter than quicksilver, and by consequence thirteen or fourteen times rarer, and its resistance is less than that of quicksilver in the same proportion, or thereabouts, as I have found by experiments made with pendulums. The open air in which we breathe is eight or nine hundred times lighter than water, and by consequence eight or nine hundred times rarer, and accordingly its resistance is less than that of water in the same proportion, or thereabouts; as I have also found by experiments made with pendulums. And in thinner air the resistance is still less, and at length, by rarefying the air becomes insensible. For small feathers falling in the open air meet with great resistance, but in a tall glass well emptied of air, they fall as fast as lead or gold, as I have seen tried several times. Whence the resistance seems still to decrease in proportion to the density of the fluid. For I do not find by any experiments that bodies moving in quicksilver, water, or air, meet with any other sensible resistance than what arises from the density and tenacity of those sensible fluids, as they would do if the pores of those fluids, and all other spaces, were filled with a dense and subtle fluid. Now if the resistance in a vessel well emptied of air was but a hundred times less than in the open air, it would be about a million times less than in quicksilver [mercury]. But it seems to be much less in such a vessel, and still much less in the heavens, at the height of three or four hundred miles from the earth, or above. For Mr Boyle has showed that air may be rarefied above ten thousand times in vessels of glass; and the heavens are much emptier of air than any *vacuum* we can make below. For since the air is compressed by the weight of the incumbent atmosphere, and the density of air is proportional to the force compressing it, it follows by computation that at the height of about seven and a half English miles from the earth, the air is four times rarer than at the surface of the earth; and at the height of 15 miles it is sixteen times rarer than that at the surface of the earth; and at the height of 22½, 30, or 38 miles, it is respectively 64, 256, or 1024 times rarer, or thereabouts; and at the height of 76, 152, 228 miles, it is about 1,000,000, 1,000,000,000,000, or 1,000,000,000,000,000,000 times rarer; and so on.

Heat promotes fluidity very much by diminishing the tenacity of bodies. It makes many bodies fluid which are not fluid in cold, and increases the fluidity of tenacious liquids, as of oil, balsam, and honey, and thereby decreases their resistance. But it decreases not the resistance of water considerably, as it would do if any considerable part of the resistance of water arose from the attrition or tenacity of its parts. And therefore the resistance of water arises principally and almost entirely from the *vis inertiae* of its matter; and by consequence, if the heavens were as dense as water, they would not have much less resistance than water; if as dense as quicksilver, they would not have much less resistance than quicksilver; if absolutely dense, or full of matter without any vacuum, let the matter be never so subtle and fluid, they would have a greater resistance than quicksilver. A solid globe in such a medium would lose above half its motion in moving three times the length of its diameter, and a globe not solid (such as are the planets) would be retarded sooner. And therefore to make way for the regular and lasting motions of the planets and comets, it's necessary to empty the heavens of all matter, except perhaps some very thin vapours, steams, or effluvia [discharges], arising from the atmospheres of the earth, planets, and comets, and from such an exceedingly rare aethereal medium as we described above. A dense fluid can be of no use for explaining the phenomena of nature, the motions of the planets and comets being better explained without it. It serves only to disturb and retard the motions of those great bodies, and make the frame of nature languish: and in the pores of bodies, it serves only to stop the vibrating motions of their parts, wherein their heat and activity consists.[5] And as it is of no use, and

---

[5] Cf. Newton's letter to Leibniz of 1693 on p. 144 of this volume.

hinders the operations of nature, and makes her languish, so there is no evidence for its existence, and therefore it ought to be rejected. And if it be rejected, the hypotheses that light consists in pression [pressure] or motion, propagated through such a medium, are rejected with it.

And for rejecting such a medium, we have the authority of those the oldest and most celebrated philosophers of Greece and Phoenicia, who made a *vacuum*, and atoms, and the gravity of atoms, the first principles of their philosophy; tacitly attributing gravity to some other cause than dense matter. Later philosophers banish the consideration of such a cause out of natural philosophy, feigning hypotheses for explaining all things mechanically, and referring other causes to metaphysics: whereas the main business of natural philosophy is to argue from phenomena without feigning hypotheses, and to deduce causes from effects, till we come to the very first cause, which certainly is not mechanical; and not only to unfold the mechanism of the world, but chiefly to resolve these and such like questions.

What is there in places almost empty of matter, and whence is it that the sun and planets gravitate towards one another, without dense matter between them? Whence is it that nature doth nothing in vain; and whence arises all that order and beauty which we see in the world? To what end are comets, and whence is it that planets move all one and the same way in orbits concentric, while comets move all manner of ways in orbits very eccentric; and what hinders the fixed stars from falling upon one another? How came the bodies of animals to be contrived with so much art, and for what ends were their several parts? Was the eye contrived without skill in optics, and the ear without knowledge of sounds? How do the motions of the body follow from the will, and whence is the instinct in animals? Is not the sensory of animals that place to which the sensitive substance is present, and into which the sensible species of things are carried through the nerves and brain, that there they may be perceived by their immediate presence to that substance? And these things being rightly dispatched, does it not appear from phenomena that there is a being incorporeal, living, intelligent, omnipresent, who in infinite space, as it were in his sensory,[6] sees the things

---

[6] This phrase, which did not appear with the qualification "as it were" in some copies of the *Opticks*, was the centerpiece of a controversy between the Newtonians (especially Samuel Clarke) and Leibniz. See Alexandre Koyré and I. Bernard Cohen, "The Case of the Missing *Tanquam*," *Isis* 52, 555–66.

themselves intimately, and thoroughly perceives them, and comprehends them wholly by their immediate presence to himself: of which things the images only carried through the organs of sense into our little sensoriums, are there seen and beheld by that which in us perceives and thinks. And though every true step made in this philosophy brings us not immediately to the knowledge of the first cause, yet it brings us nearer to it, and on that account is to be highly valued.

Query 29

Are not the rays of light very small bodies emitted from shining substances? For such bodies will pass through uniform mediums in right lines without bending into the shadow, which is the nature of the rays of light. They will also be capable of several properties, and be able to conserve their properties unchanged in passing through several mediums, which is another condition of the rays of light. Pellucid substances act upon the rays of light at a distance in refracting, reflecting, and inflecting them, and the rays mutually agitate the parts of those substances at a distance for heating them; and this action and reaction at a distance very much resembles an attractive force between bodies. If refraction be performed by attraction of the rays, the sines of incidence must be to the sines of refraction in a given proportion, as we showed in our *Principles of Philosophy*: and this rule is true by experience. The rays of light in going out of glass into a *vacuum*, are bent towards the glass; and if they fall too obliquely on the *vacuum*, they are bent backwards into the glass, and totally reflected; and this reflection cannot be ascribed to the resistance of an absolute *vacuum*, but must be caused by the power of the glass attracting the rays at their going out of it into the *vacuum*, and bringing them back. For if the farther surface of the glass be moistened with water or clear oil, or liquid and clear honey, the rays which would otherwise be reflected will go into the water, oil, or honey; and therefore are not reflected before they arrive at the farther surface of the glass, and begin to go out of it. If they go out of it into the water, oil, or honey, they go on, because the attraction of the glass is almost balanced and rendered ineffectual by the contrary attraction of the liquor. But if they go out of it into a *vacuum* which has no attraction to balance that of the glass, the attraction of the glass either bends and refracts them, or brings them back and reflects them. And this is still more evident by laying together two prisms of glass, or two object glasses of very long telescopes, the one plane, the other a little convex, and so compressing them that they do not fully touch, nor are too far asunder. For the light which falls upon the farther surface of the first glass where the interval between the glasses is not above the ten hundred thousandth part of an inch, will go through that surface, and through the air or *vacuum* between the glasses, and enter into the second glass, as was explained in the first, fourth, and eighth observations of the first part of the second book. But, if the second glass be taken away, the light which goes out of the second surface of the first glass into the air or *vacuum*, will not go on forwards, but turns back into the first glass, and is reflected; and therefore it is drawn back by the power of the first glass, there being nothing else to turn it back. Nothing more is requisite for producing all the variety of colours, and degrees of refrangibility, than that the rays of light be bodies of different sizes, the least of which may take violet the weakest and darkest of the colours, and be more easily diverted by refracting surfaces from the right course; and the rest as they are bigger and bigger, may make the stronger and more lucid colours, blue, green, yellow, and red, and be more and more difficultly diverted. Nothing more is requisite for putting the rays of light into fits of easy reflection and easy transmission, than that they be small bodies which by their attractive powers, or some other force, stir up vibrations in what they act upon, which vibrations being swifter than the rays, overtake them successively, and agitate them so as by turns to increase and decrease their velocities, and thereby put them into those fits. And lastly, the unusual refraction of island crystal looks very much as if it were performed by some kind of attractive virtue lodged in certain sides both of the rays and of the particles of the crystal. For were it not for some kind of disposition or virtue lodged in some sides of the particles of the crystal, and not in their other sides, and which inclines and bends the rays towards the coast of unusual refraction, the rays which fall perpendicularly on the crystal, would not be refracted towards that coast rather than towards any other coast, both at their incidence and at their emergence, so as to emerge perpendicularly by a contrary situation of the coast of unusual refraction at the second surface; the crystal acting upon the rays after they have passed through it, and are emerging into the air; or, if you please, into a *vacuum*. And since the crystal by this disposition or virtue does not act upon the rays, unless when one of their sides of unusual refraction looks towards that coast, this argues a virtue or disposition in those sides of the rays, which answers to, and sympathizes with, that virtue of disposition of the crystal, as the poles of two magnets answer to one another. And as magnetism may be intended and remitted, and is found only in the magnet and in iron: so this virtue of refracting the perpendicular rays is greater in island crystal, less in crystal of the rock, and is not yet found in other bodies. I do not say that this virtue is magnetic: it seems to be of another kind. I only say, that whatever it be, it's difficult to conceive how the rays of light, unless they be bodies, can have a permanent virtue in two of their sides which is not in their other sides, and this without any regard to their position to the space or medium through which they pass.

What I mean in this question by a *vacuum*, and by the attractions of the rays of light towards glass or crystal, may be understood by what was said in the 18th, 19th and 20th questions.

Query 30

Are not gross bodies and light convertible into one another, and may not bodies receive much of their activity from the particles of light which enter their composition? For all fixed bodies being heated emit light so long as they continue sufficiently hot, and light mutually stops in bodies as often as its rays strike upon their parts, as we showed above. I know no body less apt to shine than water; and yet water by frequent distillations changes into fixed earth, as Mr Boyle has tried; and then this earth being enabled to endure a sufficient heat, shines by heat like other bodies.

The changing of bodies into light, and light into bodies, is very conformable to the course of nature, which seems delighted with transmutations. Water, which is a very fluid tasteless salt, changes by heat into vapour, which is a sort of air, and by cold into ice, which is a hard, pellucid, brittle, fusible stone; and this stone returns into water by heat, and vapour returns into water by cold. Earth by heat becomes fire, and by cold returns into earth. Dense bodies by fermentation rarefy into several sorts of air, and this air by fermentation, and sometimes without it, returns into dense bodies. Mercury appears sometimes in the form of a fluid metal, sometimes in the form of a hard brittle metal, sometimes in the form of a corrosive pellucid salt called sublimate, sometimes in the form of a tasteless, pellucid, volatile white earth, called *mercurius dulcis*;

or in that of a red opaque volatile earth, called cinnabar;[7] or in that of a red or white precipitate, or in that of a fluid salt; and in distillation it turns into vapour, and being agitated in a vacuum, it shines like fire. And after all these changes it returns again into its first form of mercury. Eggs grow from insensible magnitudes, and change into animals; tadpoles into frogs; and worms into flies. All birds, beasts, and fishes, insects, trees and other vegetables, with their several parts, grow out of water and watery tinctures and salts, and by putrefaction [decomposition] return again into watery substances. And water standing a few days in the open air, yields a tincture, which (like that of malt) by standing longer yields a sediment and a spirit, but before putrefaction is fit nourishment for animals and vegetables. And among such various and strange transmutations, why may not nature change bodies into light, and light into bodies?

Query 31

Have not the small particles of bodies certain powers, virtues, or forces, by which they act at a distance, not only upon the rays of light for reflecting, refracting, and inflecting them, but also upon one another for producing a great part of the phenomena of nature? For it's well known, that bodies act one upon another by the attractions of gravity, magnetism, and electricity; and these instances show the tenor and course of nature, and make it not improbable but that there may be more attractive powers than these. Nature is very consonant and conformable to herself. How these attractions may be performed, I do not here consider. What I call attraction may be performed by impulse, or by some other means unknown to me. I use that word here to signify only in general any force by which bodies tend towards one another, whatsoever be the cause. For we must learn from the phenomena of nature what bodies attract one another, and what are the laws and properties of the attraction, before we enquire the cause by which the attraction is performed. The attractions of gravity, magnetism, and electricity, reach to very sensible distances, and so have been observed by vulgar eyes, and there may be others which reach to so small distances as hitherto escape

---

[7] Sublimate is mercuric chloride ($HgCl_2$), *mercurius dulcis* is mercurous chloride (Hg_2Cl_2), and cinnabar is mercury sulfide (HgS).

observation; and perhaps electrical attraction may reach to such small distances, even without being excited by friction.

[...]

The parts of all homogeneal hard bodies which fully touch one another, stick together very strongly. And for explaining how this may be, some have invented hooked atoms, which is begging the question; and others tell us that bodies are glued together by rest, that is, by an occult quality, or rather by nothing; and others, that they stick together by conspiring motions, that is, by relative rest amongst themselves. I [would] rather infer from their cohesion that their particles attract one another by some force, which in immediate contact is exceeding strong, at small distances performs the chymical operations above mentioned, and reaches not far from the particles with any sensible effect.

All bodies seem to be composed of hard particles: for otherwise fluids would not congeal; as water, oils, vinegar, and spirit or oil of vitriol [sulphuric acid] do by freezing; mercury by fumes of lead; spirit of nitre and mercury, by dissolving the mercury and evaporating the flegm [liquid obtained by distillation]; spirit of wine and spirit of urine, by deflegming and mixing them; and spirit of urine and spirit of salt, by subliming them together to make sal-armoniac [ammonium chloride]. Even the rays of light seem to be hard bodies; for otherwise they would not retain different properties in their different sides. And therefore hardness may be reckoned the property of all uncompounded matter. At least, this seems to be as evident as the universal impenetrability of matter. For all bodies, so far as experience reaches, are either hard, or may be hardened; and we have no other evidence of universal impenetrability, besides a large experience without an experimental exception.[8] Now if compound bodies are so very hard as we find some of them to be, and yet are very porous, and consist of parts which are only laid together, the simple particles which are void of pores, and were never yet divided, must be much harder. For such hard particles being heaped up together, can scarce touch one another in more than a few points, and therefore must be separable by much less force than is

---

[8] This is a paraphrase of one part of the third rule in the Rules for Philosophy (*regulae philoso-phandi*) (this volume p. 109).

requisite to break a solid particle, whose parts touch in all the space between them, without any pores or interstices to weaken their cohesion. And how such very hard particles which are only laid together and touch only in a few points, can stick together, and that so firmly as they do, without the assistance of something which causes them to be attracted or pressed towards one another, is very difficult to conceive.

[. . .]

Now the smallest particles of matter may cohere by the strongest attractions, and compose bigger particles of weaker virtue; and many of these may cohere and compose bigger particles whose virtue is still weaker, and so on for diverse successions, until the progression end in the biggest particles on which the operations in chymistry, and the colours of natural bodies, depend and which by cohering compose bodies of a sensible magnitude. If the body is compact, and bends or yields inward to pression without any sliding of its parts, it is hard and elastic, returning to its figure with a force rising from the mutual attraction of its parts. If the parts slide upon one another, the body is malleable or soft. If they slip easily, and are of a fit size to be agitated by heat, and the heat is big enough to keep them in agitation, the body is fluid; and if it be apt to stick to things, it is humid; and the drops of every fluid affect a round figure by the mutual attraction of their parts, as the globe of the earth and sea affects a round figure by the mutual attraction of its parts by gravity.

Since metals dissolved in acids attract but a small quantity of the acid, their attractive force can reach but to a small distance from them. And as in algebra, where affirmative quantities vanish and cease, there negative ones begin; so in mechanics, where attraction ceases, there a repulsive virtue ought to succeed. And that there is such a virtue, seems to follow from the reflections and inflections [bending] of the rays of light. For the rays are repelled by bodies in both these cases, without the immediate contact of the reflecting or inflecting body. It seems also to follow from the emission of light; the ray so soon as it is shaken off from a shining body by the vibrating motion of the parts of the body, and gets beyond the reach of attraction, being driven away with exceeding great velocity. For that force which is sufficient to turn it back in reflection, may be sufficient to emit it. It seems also to follow from the production of air and vapour. The particles when they are shaken off from bodies by heat or fermentation, so soon as they are beyond the reach of the attraction of the body, recede from it, and also from one another with great strength, and keep at a distance, so as sometimes to take up above a million of times more space than they did before in the form of a dense body. Which vast contraction and expansion seems unintelligible, by feigning the particles of air to be springy and ramous [branching], or rolled up like hoops, or by any other means than a repulsive power. The particles of fluids which do not cohere too strongly, and are of such a smallness as renders them most susceptible of those agitations which keep liquors in a fluor [liquids in a fluid state], are most easily separated and rarefied into vapour, and in the language of the chymists, they are volatile, rarefying with an easy heat, and condensing with cold. But those which are grosser, and so less susceptible of agitation, or cohere by a stronger attraction, are not separated without a stronger heat, or perhaps not without fermentation. And these last are the bodies which chymists call fixed [non-volatile], and being rarefied by fermentation, become true permanent air; those particles receding from one another with the greatest force, and being most difficultly brought together, which upon contact cohere most strongly. And because the particles of permanent air are grosser, and arise from denser substances than those of vapours, thence it is that true air is more ponderous than vapour, and that a moist atmosphere is lighter than a dry one, quantity for quantity. From the same repelling power it seems to be that flies walk upon the water without wetting their feet; and that the object glasses of long telescopes lie upon one another without touching; and that dry powders are difficultly made to touch one another so as to stick together, unless by melting them, or wetting them with water, which by exhaling may bring them together; and that two polished marbles, which by immediate contact stick together, are difficultly brought so close together as to stick.

And thus nature will be very conformable to herself and very simple, performing all the great motions of the heavenly bodies by the attraction of gravity which intercedes those bodies, and almost all the small ones of their particles by some other attractive and repelling powers which intercede the particles. The *vis inertiae* is a passive principle by which bodies persist in their motion or rest, receive motion in proportion to the force impressing it, and resist as much as they are resisted. By this principle alone there never could have been any motion in the world.

Some other principle was necessary for putting bodies into motion; and now [that] they are in motion, some other principle is necessary for conserving the motion. For from the various composition of two motions, it is very certain that there is not always the same quantity of motion in the world. For if two globes joined by a slender rod revolve about their common centre of gravity with an uniform motion, while that centre moves on uniformly in a right line drawn in the plane of their circular motion, the sum of the motions of the two globes, as often as the globes are in the right line described by their common centre of gravity, will be bigger than the sum of their motions, when they are in a line perpendicular to that right line. By this instance it appears that motion may be got or lost. But by reason of the tenacity of fluids, and attrition of their parts, and the weakness of elasticity in solids, motion is much more apt to be lost than got, and is always upon the decay. For bodies which are either absolutely hard, or so soft as to be void of elasticity, will not rebound from one another. Impenetrability makes them only stop. If two equal bodies meet directly in a vacuum, they will by the laws of motion stop where they meet and lose all their motion, and remain in rest, unless they be elastic and receive new motion from their spring. If they have so much elasticity as suffices to make them rebound with a quarter, or half, or three quarters of the force with which they come together, they will lose three quarters, or half, or a quarter of their motion. And this may be tried, by letting two equal pendulums fall against one another from equal heights. If the pendulums be of lead or soft clay, they will lose all or almost all their motions: if of elastic bodies, they will lose all but what they recover from their elasticity. If it be said that they can lose no motion but what they communicate to other bodies, the consequence is that in a vacuum they can lose no motion, but when they meet they must go on and penetrate one another's dimensions. If three equal round vessels be filled, the one with water, the other with oil, the third with molten pitch [a residue of tar], and the liquors be stirred about alike to give them a vortical [rotating] motion; the pitch by its tenacity will lose its motion quickly, the oil being less tenacious will keep it longer, and the water being less tenacious will keep it longest, but yet will lose it in a short time. Whence it is easy to understand, that if many contiguous vortices of molten pitch were each of them as large as those which some suppose to revolve about the sun and fixed stars, yet these and all their parts would, by their tenacity and stiffness, communicate their motion to one another till they all rested among themselves. Vortices of oil or water, or some fluider matter, might continue longer in motion; but unless the matter were void of all tenacity and attrition of parts, and communication of motion (which is not to be supposed), the motion would constantly decay. Seeing therefore the variety of motion which we find in the world is always decreasing, there is a necessity of conserving and recruiting it by active principles, such as are the cause of gravity, by which planets and comets keep their motions in their orbits, and bodies acquire great motion in falling; and the cause of fermentation, by which the heart and blood of animals are kept in perpetual motion and heat; the inward parts of the earth are constantly warmed, and in some places grow very hot; bodies burn and shine, mountains take fire, the caverns of the earth are blown up, and the sun continues violently hot and lucid, and warms all things by its light. For we meet with very little motion in the world, besides what is owing to these active principles. And if it were not for these principles, the bodies of the earth, planets, comets, sun, and all things in them, would grow cold and freeze, and become inactive masses; and all putrefaction, generation, vegetation, and life would cease, and the planets and comets would not remain in their orbits.

All these things being considered, it seems probable to me, that God in the beginning formed matter in solid, massy, hard, impenetrable, moveable particles, of such sizes and figures, and with such other properties, and in such proportion to space, as most conduced to the end for which he formed them; and that these primitive particles being solids, are incomparably harder than any porous bodies compounded of them; even so very hard, as never to wear or break in pieces: no ordinary power being able to divide what God himself made one in the first creation. While the particles continue entire, they may compose bodies of one and the same nature and texture in all ages: but should they wear away, or break in pieces, the nature of things depending on them, would be changed. Water and earth, composed of old worn particles and fragments of particles, would not be of the same nature and texture now, with water and earth composed of entire particles in the beginning. And therefore, that nature may be lasting, the changes of corporeal things are to be placed only in the various separations and new associations and motions of these permanent particles; compound bodies being apt to break, not in the midst of solid particles, but where those particles are laid together, and only touch in a few points.

It seems to me farther, that these particles have not only a *vis inertiae*, accompanied with such passive laws of motion as naturally result from that force, but also that they are moved by certain active principles, such as is that of gravity, and that which causes fermentation, and the cohesion of bodies. These principles I consider, not as occult qualities, supposed to result from the specific forms of things, but as general laws of nature, by which the things themselves are formed; their truth appearing to us by phenomena, though their causes be not yet discovered. For these are manifest qualities, and their causes only are occult. And the Aristotelians gave the name of occult qualities, not to manifest qualities, but to such qualities only as they supposed to lie hid in bodies, and to be the unknown causes of manifest effects: such as would be the causes of gravity, and of magnetic and electric attractions, and of fermentations, if we should suppose that these forces or actions arose from qualities unknown to us, and incapable of being discovered and made manifest. Such occult qualities put a stop to the improvement of natural philosophy, and therefore of late years have been rejected. To tell us that every species of things is endowed with an occult specific quality by which it acts and produces manifest effects, is to tell us nothing: but to derive two or three general principles of motion from phenomena, and afterwards to tell us how the properties and actions of all corporeal things follow from those manifest principles, would be a very great step in philosophy, though the causes of those principles were not yet discovered: and therefore I scruple not to propose the principles of motion above mentioned, they being of very general extent, and leave their causes to be found out.

Now by the help of these principles, all material things seem to have been composed of the hard and solid particles above mentioned, variously associated in the first creation by the counsel of an intelligent agent. For it became him who created them to set them in order. And if he did so, it's unphilosophical to seek for any other origin of the world, or to pretend that it might arise out of a chaos by the mere laws of nature; though being once formed, it may continue by those laws for many ages. For while comets move in very eccentric orbits in all manner of positions, blind fate could never make all the planets move one and the same way in orbits concentric, some inconsiderable irregularities excepted, which may have risen from the mutual actions of comets and planets upon one another, and which will be apt to increase, till this system wants a reformation. Such a wonderful uniformity in the planetary system must be allowed the effect of choice. And so must the uniformity in the bodies of animals, they having generally a right and a left side shaped alike, and on either side of their bodies two legs behind, and either two arms, or two legs, or two wings before upon their shoulders, and between their shoulders a neck running down into a backbone, and a head upon it; and in the head two ears, two eyes, a nose, a mouth, and a tongue, alike situated. Also the first contrivance of those very artificial parts of animals, the eyes, ears, brain, muscles, heart, lungs, midriff, glands, larynx, hands, wings, swimming bladders, natural spectacles, and other organs of sense and motion; and the instinct of brutes and insects, can be the effect of nothing else than the wisdom and skill of a powerful ever-living agent, who being in all places, is more able by his will to move the bodies within his boundless uniform sensorium,[9] and thereby to form and reform the parts of the universe, than we are by our will to move the parts of our own bodies. And yet we are not to consider the world as the body of God, or the several parts thereof, as the parts of God. He is a uniform being, void of any members or parts, and they are his creatures subordinate to him, and subservient to his will; and he is no more the soul of them, than the soul of man is the soul of the species of things carried through the organs of sense into the place of its sensation, where it perceives them by means of its immediate presence, without the intervention of any third thing. The organs of sense are not for enabling the soul to perceive the species of things in its sensorium, but only for conveying them thither; and God has no need of such organs, he being everywhere present to the things themselves. And since space is divisible *in infinitum*, and matter is not necessarily in all places, it may be also allowed that God is able to create particles of matter of several sizes and figures, and in several proportions to space, and perhaps of different densities and forces, and thereby to vary the laws of nature, and make worlds of several sorts in several parts of the universe. At least, I see nothing of contradiction in all this.

As in mathematics, so in natural philosophy, the investigation of difficult things by the method of analysis, ought ever to precede the

---

[9] See n. 6 above.

method of composition. This analysis consists in making experiments and observations, and in drawing general conclusions from them by induction, and admitting of no objections against the conclusions, but such as are taken from experiments, or other certain truths. For hypotheses are not to be regarded in experimental philosophy. And although the arguing from experiments and observations by induction be no demonstration of general conclusions; yet it is the best way of arguing which the nature of things admits of, and may be looked upon as so much the stronger, by how much the induction is more general. And if no exception occurs from phenomena, the conclusion may be pronounced generally. But if at any time afterwards any exception shall occur from experiments, it may then begin to be pronounced with such exceptions as occur. By this way of analysis we may proceed from compounds to ingredients, and from motions to the forces producing them; and in general, from effects to their causes, and from particular causes to more general ones, till the argument end in the most general. This is the method of analysis, and the synthesis consists in assuming the causes discovered, and established as principles, and by them explaining the phenomena proceeding from them, and proving the explanations.

In the two first books of these *Opticks*, I proceeded by this analysis to discover and prove the original differences of the rays of light in respect of refrangibility, reflexibility, and colour, and their alternate *fits of easy reflection* and *easy transmission*, and the properties of bodies, both opaque and pellucid [transparent], on which their reflections and colours depend. And these discoveries being proved, [they] may be assumed in the method of composition for explaining the phenomena arising from them: an instance of which method I gave in the end of the first book. In this third book I have only begun the analysis of what remains to be discovered about light and its effects upon the frame of nature, hinting several things about it, and leaving the hints to be examined and improved by the farther experiments and observations of such as are inquisitive. And if natural philosophy in all its parts, by pursuing this method, shall at length be perfected, the bounds of moral philosophy will be also enlarged. For so far as we can know by natural philosophy what is the first cause, what power he has over us, and what benefits we receive from him, so far our duty towards him, as well as that towards one another, will appear to us by the light of nature. And no doubt, if the worship of false gods had not blinded the heathen, their moral philosophy would have gone farther than to the four cardinal virtues; and instead of teaching the transmigration of souls, and to worship the sun and moon, and dead heroes, they would have taught us to worship our true author and benefactor, as their ancestors did under the government of Noah and his sons before they corrupted themselves.

Finis.

Index

Index

Densmore, Dana, xl
Descartes, ix, xiii, xv, xviii–xx, xxii, xxix–xxxi, xxxvi, 29–30, 32–35, 39, 47, 49–50, 52, 71, 86, 148, 155, 160, 167
  extension, 35, 38, 45, 48
  Geometry, 119
  Meditations, x, xi, 35
  motion, xxxiii–xxxiv, 28–35, 39
  Newton's relation to, ix, xviii–xix
  Principles of Philosophy, ix, xvii, xix, xxxi, 28, 77
  substance, xvii
dioptrics, 141
DiSalle, Robert, xxxi
divisibility, 125
Dobbs, Betty Jo Teeter, xix
Domski, Mary, vi, viii
Donahue, William, xl
Ducheyne, Steffen, viii, xxviii, xl
dynamics, x, xxii, xxxv

elasticity, 183
electricity, 179
ellipse, xxi, 122, 141
endeavor, ix, 18, 31–32, 51, 74, 80, 82, 86, 88–89, 91, 107. *See also* Conatus
energy, 126, 129
England, xxii, xxviii, xxxv, 141, 150, 163
Epicurus, 52, 136
equilibrium, 26, 53, 55, 57–58, 64, 74, 94, 104, 124–25, 132, 134, 147
essence, 35, 48, 86
eternity, 48, 111, 136
Euclid, xv, 27, 119
evidence, 42, 89, 157, 175, 180
  experimental, xv–xvii, 108, 167
  observational, xv
existence, xxiv, 38, 40–41, 43, 45, 70, 85, 175
experience, xii, xv, xxvi, 3, 16, 24, 63–64, 85, 88, 99–100, 103, 108, 176, 180
experiment, viii–ix, xvi, xviii, xxiv–xxv, 3, 6, 10, 12–13, 26, 62, 69, 75, 77, 99, 101–3, 108–9, 114, 151, 161–62, 165, 167, 171, 173, 187
  crucial, 4
  pendulum, 64, 66, 79, 100, 173
  prism, xvi
  with light, xv, xv
experimental philosophy. *See* philosophy, experimental
explanation, xv, 41, 60, 72, 90, 141, 144. *See* philosophy, experimental
  mechanical, 70, 175
  of gravity, xviii

extension, xxv–xxvii, xxix–xxx, 35–36, 38–39, 41, 43, 45–46, 48, 50–52, 69–70, 103, 108, 133, 151, 163. *See also* body, distinction from extension
  definition, 35
  emanative effect of God, 36
  generic, 35

faculty, xxviii, 38, 42, 44, 48–49, 76, 136
Flamsteed, John, 123
fluid, xxiv, xxxiii, 49, 53–58, 60, 73–76, 145, 148, 171, 173–74, 178, 180–82. *See also* matter, fluid. *See also* medium, fluid
  Cartesian, 32, 34
  celestial, 72, 75
  corporeal, 49
  non-elastic, 54
  occult, 62
force, vii, xxi–xxiii, xxvi, xxviii, 32, 35, 40, 49, 51, 53, 60–61, 63–70, 72, 74–76, 79–83, 88–89, 91–94, 99, 103–8, 114, 118, 125, 136–37, 145, 148, 155–56, 159, 161–62, 165–66, 170–71, 174, 177, 179–83, 185–87
  absolute, 64, 82
  absolute quantity of centripetal, 82
  accelerative, 82–83, 99, 106, 155
  as causal principle of motion and rest, 50
  as quantity, xxiii, 107
  attractive, xxi, 60, 64, 68, 125, 156, 176, 181
  centrifugal, 74
  centripetal, xxiii, xxvii, 65–67, 80–81, 106, 155–56
  continually acting, 64, 66
  direct, 93
  elastic, 60, 101, 103, 169–70
  impressed, xxii, xxvi, xxvii, xxxii, xxxiv, 32, 53, 64, 80, 87–88, 90–92, 98–99, 105, 182
  impulsive, 60
  infinite, 125, 171
  inherent, 79, 104, 109
  magnetic, 80, 82–83, 132
  mathematical treatment of, 68, 83, 107, 124, 166
  motive, 82–83, 91
  motive quantity of centripetal, 82
  oblique, 93
  physical causes, 83, 166
  physical proportion, 107
  physical treatment of, 166
  quantity, 82
form, 43–44, 46, 76
  of body, 43–44, 62
  specific, 166, 185
  substantial, 43, 46, 59

191

Index

inertia, xxvi, xxxi–xxxii, 28, 50–52, 72, 75–76, 79, 172–73, 182
 force of, xxvi, 51, 75, 80, 104, 108–9, 151, 172
 vis inertiae, 151–52, 172, 174, 185
infinity, 37–39, 87, 111
inherence, xxviii, 41, 43, 47, 131, 136

Jacobs, Margaret, xl
Johnson, Christian, xlii
Journal des Sçavans, 149

Kant, Immanuel, x–xi
 Critique of Pure Reason, xi
 Metaphysical Foundations of Natural Science, x
Keill, John, xi, xxxiv
Kepler, Johannes, xv, xxi, xxxiii, 130, 141
Kochiras, Hylarie, xxx
Korsgaard, Christine, xii
Koyré, Alexandre, xix, xxiv, xxxix, xli, 162, 175

Lami, Francois, 149
laws, vii, xxiii, xxv, xxvii, xxxii, xxxiv, 13, 42, 45, 61, 63, 66–67, 69, 71, 74, 77, 91–92, 95, 98–100, 107, 110, 113, 136, 141, 143–44, 147, 150–52, 156, 158–59, 165–67, 179, 183, 185
 Cartesian, xxxi–xxxii
 mathematical, 59
 mechanical, 62
 of motion, vii, xxv, xxxii–xxxiii, 43, 90–99, 103–4, 106, 110, 157–61, 185
 of nature, ix, xxxi, 28, 64, 77, 146, 150–51, 155, 159–60, 168, 185–86
 of refraction, 1
Leibniz, Gottfried Wilhelm, vii, xiii–xiv, xviii, xx, xxii, xxiv–xxv, xxvii, xxix, xxxii, xxxiii–xxxiv, xxxvi–xxxvii, xl, 141, 146, 150–54, 161, 172
 calculus controversy with Newton, xxxiv–xxxv, xliv
 correspondence with Clarke, x, xiv, xxxiv, xxxvii
 correspondence with Hartsoeker, xxxiv, xliii, 70, 144, 149, 157
 correspondence with Huygens, xviii
 correspondence with Newton, xiii, xxxiii–xxxv, xxxvii, xliii, 72, 140, 142–43, 150, 157, 160, 167
 Essay on the Cause of Celestial Motions [Tentamen], xxxvii
 letter to *Memoirs of Literature*, xxxiv
Leibnizians, xi, xx, xxx
Lennon, Thomas, xxx

light, xiv–xv, xvii, xxxvi, 1–5, 9–11, 13, 16, 42, 142, 157, 170–72, 175, 177–79, 187.
 See also Color, as quality of light. *See also* body, rays of light. *See also* prism. *See also* theory, of light and color
 as body, xvi
 as corpuscle, xvi
 as particle, xvi–xvii, 1, 9, 11, 170, 178
 as quality, xvi–xvii, 11
 as substance, xvii
 as wave, xvi–xvii
 cause of, 141
 corporeal nature of, xviii
 emission, 114, 178, 181
 explanation of, 141
 feature of, xv
 inflection, 114
 motion of, vii
 nature of, xxii, 170
 qualifications of, 7
 rays of, xvi–xvii, xxiv, 3, 6–7, 9, 11, 170–71, 176–81, 187
 reflection, 114
 refraction, 114
 speed of, 170
Locke, John, xiii–xiv, xxvi, xxxvii, 27
 Essay Concerning Human Understanding, xxxvii
London, xxxvi–xxxvii, 5, 15, 40, 150, 157

machine, 71, 95, 104, 106, 149, 152
MacLaurin, Colin, xi
magnetism, 132, 141, 178–79. *See also* force, magnetic
manual arts, 59–60
Mariotte, Edme, 100
mass, xxiii, xxvi–xxvii, 19, 52, 79, 120, 124, 129, 131, 133–34, 137, 148, 184
mathematical treatment of force. *See* force, mathematical treatment of
mathematics, xxxv, 65, 89, 109, 117, 140–41, 161, 186
 relation to natural philosophy, 59
matter, xxiii, xxviii–xxx, 28, 33, 39, 41, 43, 48, 54, 64, 70, 72–76, 79, 120, 122, 124, 126–29, 131, 133–34, 136–37, 144, 146, 148, 150, 163, 167, 172–75, 180–81, 184, 186
 aetherial, 32, 132, 134
 as homogenous, 62
 attracting, 64
 dense, 175
 fine, 143
 fluid, 34, 75–76, 148, 184

Cambridge Texts in the History of Philosophy

Titles published in the series thus far

Aquinas *Disputed Questions on the Virtues* (edited by E. M. Atkins and Thomas Williams)

Aquinas *Summa Theologiae, Questions on God* (edited by Brian Davies and Brian Leftow)

Aristotle *Eudemian Ethics* (edited by Brad Inwood and Raphael Woolf)

Aristotle *Nicomachean Ethics* (edited by Roger Crisp)

Arnauld and Nicole *Logic or the Art of Thinking* (edited by Jill Vance Buroker)

Augustine *On the Free Choice of the Will, On Grace and Free Choice, and Other Writings* (edited by Peter King)

Augustine *On the Trinity* (edited by Gareth Matthews)

Bacon *The New Organon* (edited by Lisa Jardine and Michael Silverthorne)

Berkeley, *Philosophical Writings* (edited by Desmond M. Clarke)

Boyle *A Free Enquiry into the Vulgarly Received Notion of Nature* (edited by Edward B. Davis and Michael Hunter)

Bruno *Cause, Principle and Unity* and *Essays on Magic* (edited by Richard Blackwell and Robert de Lucca with an introduction by Alfonso Ingegno)

Cavendish *Observations upon Experimental Philosophy* (edited by Eileen O'Neill)

Cicero *On Moral Ends* (edited by Julia Annas, translated by Raphael Woolf)

Clarke *A Demonstration of the Being and Attributes of God and Other Writings* (edited by Ezio Vailati)

Classic and Romantic German Aesthetics (edited by J. M. Bernstein)

Condillac *Essay on the Origin of Human Knowledge* (edited by Hans Aarsleff)

Conway *The Principles of the Most Ancient and Modern Philosophy* (edited by Allison P. Coudert and Taylor Corse)

Cudworth *A Treatise Concerning Eternal and Immutable Morality* with *A Treatise of Freewill* (edited by Sarah Hutton)

Descartes *Meditations on First Philosophy,* with *Selections from the Objections and Replies* (edited by John Cottingham)

Descartes *The World and Other Writings* (edited by Stephen Gaukroger)

Fichte *Attempt at a Critique of All Revelation* (edited by Allen Wood, translated by Garrett Green)

Fichte *Foundations of Natural Right* (edited by Frederick Neuhouser, translated by Michael Baur)

Fichte *The System of Ethics* (edited by Daniel Breazeale and Günter Zöller)

Greek and Roman Aesthetics (edited by Oleg V. Bychkov and Anne Sheppard)

Hamann *Philosophical Writings* (edited by Kenneth Haynes)

Mendelssohn *Philosophical Writings* (edited by Daniel O. Dahlstrom)
Newton *Philosophical Writings* Revised Edition (edited by Andrew Janiak)
Nietzsche *The Antichrist, Ecce Homo, Twilight of the Idols and Other Writings* (edited by Aaron Ridley and Judith Norman)
Nietzsche *Beyond Good and Evil* (edited by Rolf-Peter Horstmann and Judith Norman)
Nietzsche *The Birth of Tragedy and Other Writings* (edited by Raymond Geuss and Ronald Speirs)
Nietzsche *Daybreak* (edited by Maudemarie Clark and Brian Leiter, translated by R. J. Hollingdale)
Nietzsche *The Gay Science* (edited by Bernard Williams, translated by Josefine Nauckhoff)
Nietzsche *Human, All Too Human* (translated by R. J. Hollingdale with an introduction by Richard Schacht)
Nietzsche *Thus Spoke Zarathustra* (edited by Adrian Del Caro and Robert B. Pippin)
Nietzsche *Untimely Meditations* (edited by Daniel Breazeale, translated by R. J. Hollingdale)
Nietzsche *Writings from the Early Notebooks* (edited by Raymond Geuss and Alexander Nehamas, translated by Ladislaus Löb)
Nietzsche *Writings from the Late Notebooks* (edited by Rüdiger Bittner, translated by Kate Sturge)
Novalis *Fichte Studies* (edited by Jane Kneller)
Plato *Meno, Phaedo* (edited by David Sedley and Alex Long)
Plato *The Symposium* (edited by M.C. Howatson and Frisbee C. C. Sheffield)
Reinhold *Letters on the Kantian Philosophy* (edited by Karl Ameriks, translated by James Hebbeler)
Schleiermacher *Hermeneutics and Criticism* (edited by Andrew Bowie)
Schleiermacher *Lectures on Philosophical Ethics* (edited by Robert Louden, translated by Louise Adey Huish)
Schleiermacher *On Religion: Speeches to its Cultured Despisers* (edited by Richard Crouter)
Schopenhauer *Prize Essay on the Freedom of the Will* (edited by Günter Zöller)
Sextus Empiricus *Against the Logicians* (edited by Richard Bett)
Sextus Empiricus *Outlines of Scepticism* (edited by Julia Annas and Jonathan Barnes)
Shaftesbury *Characteristics of Men, Manners, Opinions, Times* (edited by Lawrence Klein)
Smith *The Theory of Moral Sentiments* (edited by Knud Haakonssen)
Spinoza *Theological-Political Treatise* (edited by Jonathan Israel, translated by Michael Silverthorne and Jonathan Israel)
Voltaire *Treatise on Tolerance and Other Writings* (edited by Simon Harvey)

Printed in the USA
CPSIA information can be obtained
at www.ICGtesting.com
LVHW061224200823
755743LV00001B/36